CROCE•ARNOLD•GOETHE• STENDHAL•FREU

BEETHOVEN•LEONARDO DA VINCI•COLERIDG

VICO•BROWNING•FRANC

ELL•POE•LAFCADIO

THENAEUM•SAINTSBURY• NOVALIS•ALBRECHT DÜ

LARIST•PROGRESS•THE   ACADEMY•THE NATIONA

ARWIN•LEOPARDI•VIRGIL •DARWIN•LEOPARDI•VIRG

JS•CLEANTHES•PLATO• ST. AUGUSTINE•CATO•ECCL

MILTON•TENNYSON• BLAKE•PASCAL•SHELLEY•LU

ARNOLD•GOETHE• STENDHAL•FREUD•DE QUINC

EN•LEONARDO DA VINCI•COLERIDGE•WILLIAM JA

NING•FRANCESCO DE SANCTIS•THOMAS CARLYLE•

FCADIO HEARN• SCHOPENHAUER•GIOVANNI GEN

SAINTSBURY• HAZLITT• ALBRECHT DÜRER•CHARL

OGRESS•THE   ACADEMY•THE NATIONA

ARDI•VIRGIL •DA

HENRY PAOLUCCI

JAMES THOMSON'S

THE CITY OF
DREADFUL NIGHT

A STUDY OF THE CULTURAL RESOURCES
OF ITS AUTHOR AND A REAPPRAISAL OF THE POEM

WITH A PREFACE TO THE 2000 EDITION BY ANNE PAOLUCCI

THE BAGEHOT COUNCIL
1401 Pennsylvania Avenue
Wilmington DE 19806

Library of Congress Cataloging - in - Publication Data

Paolucci, Henry.
    James Thomson's The city of dreadful night : a study of the
cultural resources of its author and a reappraisal of the poem /
Henry Paolucci ; with an introduction to the new edition by Anne
Paolucci.- - 2nd ed.
        p. cm.
    Includes bibliographical references.
    ISBN 0-918680-87-5 (cloth)
    1. Thomson, James, 1834-1882. City of dreadful night. 2.
Pessimism in literature. 3. Despair in literature. I. Title.

    PR5657.C63 P35 2000
    821'.8 - - dc21
                                                    00-058654

———————————

Published for
THE BAGEHOT COUNCIL
by Griffon House Publications
1401 Pennsylvania Ave., Suite 105
Wilmington, DE 19806

CONTENTS

PREFACE TO 2000 EDITION, by Anne Paolucci   5

AUTHOR'S PREFACE   7

I.   INTRODUCING THE CITY AND ITS INTERPRETERS   11
      A. Original Reception
      B. Literary Character of the Work
      C. Unresolved Problems of Criticism
      D. Purpose of this Study

II.   RELIGIOUS AND MORAL PREPARATION   32
      A. Early Religious Crisis
      B. The "Doom of a City"
      C. Religious and Social Satire
      D. Indolence

III. LITERARY EDUCATION   64
      A. Reputation as a Critic
      B. English Literature
      C. Foreign Literature
      D. Theory of Art

IV.   PHILOSOPHICAL PESSIMISM   106
      A. The Limitations of Philosophy
      B. The Ethics of Schopenhauer
      C. Stoicism
      D. Pascal and Leopardi
      E. Liebestod

V.   THE CITY OF DREADFUL NIGHT   145
      A. Subject Matter
      B. Structure, Characters, Thoughts and Sentiments
         and Language
      C. Analysis: Proem

BIBLIOGRAPHY   192

ABOUT THE AUTHOR   197

HENRY PAOLUCCI

By the time he completed this study on James Thomson, Henry Paolucci had known the eminent Dantist, Dino Bigongiari, for over fifteen years and had become a close friend of his mentor and former teacher. After taking Bigongiari's "Dante and Medieval Culture" as part of his Ph.D. course requirements at Columbia University, Paolucci continued to attend the class as an unofficial guest. For several semesters, and with Bigongiari's permission, he took down, verbatim, his teacher's lectures, with a view toward helping Bigongiari prepare a book on Dante. (Several separate and distinct sets of those lecture notes still wait to be sorted out.) When his health forced him to take a year off, Bigongiari told the University administration that his former student, Henry Paolucci, was the only person he knew who was prepared — in his easy grasp of Greek and Latin texts, the Church Fathers, and modern philosophy, and in his extensive reading of modern texts — to take over his Dante class for the year. Nicholas Murray Butler, President of Columbia at the time, made sure Bigongiari's request was granted.

But long before meeting Bigongiari and continuing his appreciative study of Dante under that legendary teacher and scholar, Paolucci had read and re-read *The City of Dreadful Night* as Thomson himself meant it to be read: as a Dantesque journey into a hell without hope of redemption. His concentrated reading in Dante served him well in his analysis of the *City*; his familiarity with ancient and modern authors enabled him to appreciate the literary buttressing of the poem. He saw reflected in the *City* a deep-rooted atheism and agnosticism which he fully understood; but eventually, all his preparation came to focus on the Augustinian burden of the poem, which he saw as a modern version of the city of Man, built "even in contempt of God" — the antithesis of the City of God, a Dantesque Hell without the possibility of reprieve. Clearly, he was culturally and emotionally prepared to do justice to Thomson's *City of Dreadful Night*.

And because he knew he was writing about a poem which had for the most part been ignored by students and critics as simply the ravings of a raw undisciplined talent, a poem which discouraged readers because of its profound and unrelieved pessimism, he approached his task with an impressive scholarly apparatus which established in no uncertain terms Thomson's access to ancient and modern authors and prepared the reader for a detailed *explication de texte*. Ultimately, he let the poem speak for itself, quoting passages at length (indeed, he knew most of the lines by heart), with an appreciative understanding that translates into an easy yet memorable recitation.

With this edition, his careful analysis of Thomson's *City* is made accessible to a wide readership, here and abroad. For those of us who knew Henry Paolucci, the book will recall those qualities that endeared him to so many colleagues and friends: an incredible memory, a flair for "translating" difficult subjects into terms his listeners would understand; his willingness to answer questions, his wit and humor, his dramatic flair in and out of the classroom. In his written words we hear that same compelling voice encouraging us into the intellectual life he knew so well, a life which — he never tired of saying — is its own reward.

ANNE PAOLUCCI
New York City
July 31, 2000

James Thomson's *The City of Dreadful Night* is generally acknowledged by its readers to be one of the most impressive utterances of despair in western literature. As Professor Hoxie N. Fairchild recently asserted in his *Religious Trends in English Poetry*, it is "one of the most powerful poems produced within the nineteenth century . . . . Its ideas and feelings are far from unique in this period, but nowhere else are they set forth with such uncompromising intensity of despair."[1] The current *Encyclopedia Americana* represents the poem, in an article by Professor James H. Hanford, as "the most remarkable example in English literature of the unrestrained expression of an intense and overpowering gloom."[2] Paul Elmer More, many decades ago, judged it to be an expression of "pessimism, which stands quite alone in English literature, and which has, I believe, no precise equivalent in any language."[3] And William James, in his essay "Is Life Worth Living"?, cited its verses as the most powerful statement he could find of the profoundest arguments against sanguine optimism regarding the value of human existence.[4]

Yet even among readers who acknowledge the gloomy impressiveness of the poem, questions have been raised, doubts have been expressed, as to its intellectual and literary significance. Against staunch admirers who find a "rounded philosophy" in it, who urge that it "be read as *Ecclesiastes* or Aeschylus should be read,"[5] and who sometimes go so far as to suggest that its vision of godlessness can withstand comparison as an imaginative construction with Dante's heavenly vision, there have been not a few critics contending that the poem is "in reality devoid of philosophic significance,"[6] that it expresses only a narrowly private abnormal experience of frustrated egoism, that it is monotonous, redundant, rhetorical, labored in its versification, betraying again and again, to the practiced ear, the defective literary and cultural preparations of its author.

The aim of this study is to encourage close study and reappraisal of the significance of Thomson's poem in the light of the variety of questions raised by its readers. The work begins with a brief description of the poem, indicating its imaginative dependence on the *Divine Comedy* and on the pessimistic thought and poetry of Giacomo Leopardi, and a review of the unresolved problems of literary criticism, underlying all of which is the question of the poet's cultural resources. This is followed by a series of chapters examining evidences of the cultural sources and resources of the poet — his moral, religious, literary, and philosophic preparation — as found in his own writings. The last chapter presents a commentary on *The City of Dreadful Night*, using the examined evidences of the poet's preparation to facilitate critical analysis of the content and form of the poem. Biographical materials enter into the study only incidentally, and for the basic details the source is Henry S. Salt's *Life of James Thomson*.[7]

Of the resources he was able to draw upon in writing the *City*, Thomson has left an extensive record consisting of moral, critical, and philosophic essays, religious and social satires, translations, metrical imitations and experiments, most of them originally published in little-read secularist and trade journals. That record is examined here not on the assumption that acquaintance with it is a prerequisite for appreciation of the poetic and intellectual significance of the poem, but rather in order to dispel some of the prevalent misconceptions about the poet's preparation — misconceptions that have made adequate appreciation difficult.

In his youth, Thomson wrote a long narrative poem, "The Doom of a City," which is obviously a preliminary draft of *The City of Dreadful Night*. Dissatisfied with his early treatment of the theme, he determined to perfect himself as a poet, refining his literary art, informing his intellect, purging his will, until, in his thirty-sixth year, he at last felt competent to write of his City of *Melencolia* with sufficient "knowledge and power to deal with the theme in its epic integrity." The course of this moral, literary, and philosophic self-discipline is traced in the second, third, and fourth chapters.

In Chapter V, after close examination of the text, the conclusion is drawn that the poem, as a finished work of art, reflects less what the author thought and felt in writing it than what the reader thinks and feels and brings to bear in reading it. If words can stir him, he will be struck by the force of Thomson's lines. He will not fail to "see" imaginatively that the poem represents the effects of a great loss of some kind. If he reads with a purely biographical interest, he will think that he sees evidences of poverty, insomnia, and alcoholism on every page. If he comes to it with a mind full of concern for nineteenth-century social and religious problems, he will trace in its stanzas the effects of the new geological, biological, and social sciences that call all things in doubt. If he takes Professor Gerould's advice and reads it "as *Ecclesiastes* or Aeschylus should be read . . . for purification through pity and fear," he will certainly get more out of it. Whatever his intellectual or moral disposition, he will find that the poem manages to expand in meaning as his interests expand.

According to Thomson's intention, however, there is — this study suggests finally — a minimal requirement: the least one should bring to bear in attempting to read the poem intelligently is a fair acquaintance with the poetic world of Dante. For it is the loss or exhaustion of all the good things of that world — not a personal but an historical loss that is represented in *The City of Dreadful Night*.

NOTES

1. Hoxie N. Fairchild, *Religious Trends in English Poetry*, Vol. IV: 1830-1880 (New York, 1957), p. 469.

2. James H. Hanford, "The City of Dreadful Night," *The Encyclopedia Americana*, VI, 717-18.

3. Paul Elmer More, *Shelbourne Essays*, V (New York, 1900), 188.

4. William James, *The Will to Believe and Other Essays* (New York, 1917), pp. 34-35.

5. Gordon Hall Gerould, editor, *Poems of James Thomson* (New York, 1927), p. xviii.

6. T. P. Cross, C. T. Goode, editors, *Heath Readings in the Literature of England* (Boston, 1927), p. 1364.

7. Henry S. Salt, *The Life of James Thomson* ("B.V."), revised edition (London, 1914).

I. INTRODUCTION: THE CITY AND ITS INTERPRETERS

A. ORIGINAL RECEPTION

When James Thomson's *The City of Dreadful Night* first appeared in print, anonymously, in the columns of Charles Bradlaugh's *National Reformer*, some subscribers protested vigorously that a secularist periodical was hardly the place for publication of so gloomy a view of the spiritual lot of virtuous atheists.[1] Nevertheless, the four issues in which portions of the poem appeared (March 22, April 12 and 26, May 17, 1874) were quickly bought up, and the work was widely circulated, provoking favorable comment from a number of prominent authors, including George Eliot, George Meredith, Philip Bourke Marston, and William M. Rossetti.[2]

Literary attention had been directed to the poem by a review in the *Academy*, which had treated it with distinguished respect, comparing its unknown author with the renowned Italian poet of pessimism, Giacomo Leopardi.[3] Gratified by the unexpected notice, Thomson wrote a letter of thanks to the editor of the *Academy*, remarking that he considered it a "brave act, on the part of a respectable English periodical, to spontaneously call attention to an atheistical writing (less remote than, say, Lucretius), treating it simply and fairly on its literary merits, without obloquy or protesting cant."[4] In 1880, when the poem reappeared in a volume bearing the author's name, it reportedly "made a sensation in the London world of letters only to be compared to the issue of Swinburne's *Atlanta in Calydon*."[5] Most of the leading literary periodicals reviewed the volume, and critical appraisal was, on the whole, favorable. The publication actually proved to be a financial success, selling especially well at Cambridge and Oxford — Thomson was pleased to note — at a time when all publishers were "firm that no volume of verses, however good, can now pay its expenses, unless bearing one of three or four famous or popular names."[6]

Thus twice in less than a decade publication of the *City* excited considerable literary interest. Yet it was clear from the outset that the kind of interest the poem excited would bring notoriety rather than fame to its author, for despite the exceptional notice in the *Academy*, the praise it received was almost invariably tempered with moral strictures regarding its theme. George Saintsbury, for instance, in his review of the 1880 volume, tactfully advised Thomson against "a concentration of his ideas upon certain riddles which the wise indifference of the wise is apt to leave unattempted." The poem it-self he hailed as a masterpiece of its kind, a work of "extreme beauty," "singularly melodious in expression, dignified and full of meaning." Yet he could not help wishing, Saintsbury concluded, "that Mr. Thomson had read Shakespeare more and Leopardi less. Byronism was bad enough but Leopardism would be something to shudder at."[7]

It is to be noted, however, that while Thomson lived, no critic presumed to interpret his *City* biographically as an utterance of personal despair. Theodore Watts-Dutton was perhaps alone in his persuasion that Thomson had "simply written 'dreadful' poetry because just now it is the fashion to be dreadful";[8] but that the poem's inspiration was rather literary than personal must have seemed fairly obvious to all who had only the evidence of the text to inform and guide their judgments. No critic could then have imagined that such a poem, dedicated with obvious literary flourish to "the younger brother of Dante, Giacomo Leopardi," bearing three captions of verse in Italian and inlaid from beginning to end with a mosaic pattern of literary allusion and literal quotations from Shakespeare, Milton, the Bible, Spenser, Shelley, and Blake, as well as from Leopardi, Lucretius and Dante, would one day be so overshadowed by a pair of apologetic biographies that subsequent generations of critics would be ill-disposed to interpret it otherwise than biographically.

Rare is the reader today who comes to the *City* with a mind devoid of preconceptions about the life and character of its author. First acquaintance is apt to come through school anthologies or histories of English literature which, more often than not, introduce the poet as an ill-begotten, poorly schooled, weak-willed, love-lorn congenital drunkard, doomed to wander deliriously through the night streets of London, piping his gloomy masterpiece in uncontrollable fits of passion — if not *per intervalle insaniae*, as St. Jerome said of Lucretius. The editor of one popular anthology writes: "No other Victorian perhaps had such a wretched childhood as did James Thomson."[9] Another adds: "His whole philosophical and moral existence was determined by the death of a young and beautiful girl."[10] Another: "Opium, alcohol, and insomnia played their sorry parts in it."[11] Another: "Penury, despair, insomnia and drink brought him to his grave at forty-eight. These things must be kept in mind in judging of his poetry."[12] And the first of the literary guides cited concludes his sketch with the words: "From such an existence as is depicted in these poems, his death could have come only as a welcome relief."[13]

The picture thus sketched in lurid details has a certain fascination, of course. Thomson's poem would undoubtedly lose much of its appeal, for some readers, if it could not be interpreted as the "utterance of a poet ... whose vigor has been sapped by folly and misfortune, who with shattered nerves and strengthless hands tries vainly to grasp some good that has durability and three dimensions."[14] Needless to say, once such a picture has imprinted itself in the imagination it is difficult to shake loose. Yet there is little support to be found for it in the text which, when closely studied, appears rather to be a literary tour de force, a display of literary power by a poet anxious to put his talent on trial, asking only that his effort be judged simply — as he wrote to the editor of the *Academy* — on its literary merits, "without obloquy or protesting cant."

B. LITERARY CHARACTER OF THE WORK

Thomson evidently expected his readers to come to his *City* not with vaguely informed curiosity about his personal life, but with the sound of poetry in their ears. He must have hoped, surely, that some of them would notice the disciplined artistic symmetry of his work: the careful arrangement of the twenty-one numbered cantos according to length, with the first and last, second and penultimate, third and antepenultimate corresponding exactly; the "winged" disposition of the various stanzaic forces employed, with the same rhyme scheme recurring regularly in the odd-numbered cantos, and with a balanced pattern of varied rhyme schemes in the even-numbered, marked decisively at the midpoint of the poem by the appearance of blank verse. He must have expected also that readers of literary cultivation would notice, upon reconsideration if not at first, that many lines from the Bible, Shakespeare, Milton and other poets — touchstones of literary excellence — had been woven almost imperceptibly into his poetic fabric. Indeed, many of the most moving passages of the *City* — passages in which the expression of grief has seemed to some critics to be too intense and personal for enjoyment as poetry — are found, upon close inspection, to contain unmistakable evidences of literary inspiration and of very conscious artistic purpose. A reader who comes to the poem persuaded that Thomson drew his inspiration "from life, not books,"[15] is apt to imagine that he hears in its opening lines —

Lo, thus, as prostrate, "In the dust I write

My heart's deep languor and my soul's sad tears"[16]
— an irrepressible cry wrenched from the poet's own agonized heart,
despite the fact that they contain literally quoted the words of
Shakespeare's Titus Andronicus, begging for the lives of his sons.[17]
Again, a reader familiar with details of Thomson's personal life may
imagine that the poet has candidly represented himself in the figure
of a young man wan and worn kneeling beside his dead bride, murmuring:

> But I renounce all choice of life or death,
> For either shall be ever at thy side,
> And thus in bliss or woe be ever well.[18]

Yet an obvious literary source is indicated by that *bliss or woe* and the
renunciation of choice between life and death. Milton's Adam cries
to his fallen Eve:

> . . . from thy state
> Mine never shall be parted, bliss or woe.
> . . . I wish thee have fixed my lot,
> Certain to undergo like doom, if Death
> Consort with thee, Death is to me as Life.[19]

Thomson's "Oh, dark, dark, dark, withdrawn from joy or light,"[20]
surely owes less to a tormented heart than to Milton's "O dark, dark,
dark, amid the blaze of noon," in *Samson Agonistes*.[21] And his "the
oracles are dumb or cheat," coming at the climax of the poem's vision of despair, obviously derives from Milton's nativity "Hymn":

> The oracles are dumb,
> No voice or hideous hum
> Runs through the arched roof in words deceiving.[22]

Thomson makes similar use of many other poetic touchstones.
But it is not simply in such verbal particulars that the distinctly literary inspiration of his poem reveals itself. Its dedication to Giacomo
Leopardi and the untranslated captions from Dante and Leopardi
were evidently intended to indicate a literal and imaginative dependence on the *Divine Comedy* and on the pessimistic thought and poetry of Leopardi. Read in the light of that dependence, Thomson's
poem may readily be recognized for what he obviously intended it
to be: a revision, for modern readers, of the desolate worldly approaches to the hell of Dante's poetic universe. The first of the captions is in fact the familiar warning from Dante, *Per me si va nella città
dolente*[23] — obviously appropriate for a revision of the approaches to
hell. The second and third captions, from Leopardi's *Canto Notturno*[24]
and *Coro de' Morti*,[25] indicate the kind of change that the reader may

expect in this poetic revision. The point of view is to be not that of
Dante on his way through a purposeful universe to a glorious vision
of a just and merciful God; but that of a Leopardi confined to a
world where all things happen of necessity but in vain, and where
death alone is the comforter of men.

Following the pilgrim narrator of Thomson's poem, an attentive
reader finds himself once again on the edge of hell, within sight of
the "portal common spirits fear," with

> . . . words above it dark yet clear,
> "Leave hope behind, all ye who enter here."[26]

The place of Thomson's *City* in Dante's universe is indicated
by one of its inhabitants who complains:

> Our destiny is fell;
> For in this Limbo we must ever dwell,
> Shut out alike from Heaven and Earth and Hell.[27]

In the fourth canto of the *Inferno*, as Dante approaches the
nobil castello, his guide, Virgil, asks

> Tu non dimandi
> Che spiriti son questi che tu vedi?[28]

and proceeds to explain that the inhabitants of the noble castle are
not sinners (*non peccaro*), that they knew and practiced all the cardinal virtues, and that they are condemned thus to live in desire without hope, on the edge of hell, simply for want of Christian baptism.
In the *City* the pilgrim narrator asks: "What men are they who haunt
these fatal glooms . . . wherein expire the lamps of hope and faith?" —
and his answer echoes Virgil's explanation:

> They have much wisdom yet they are not wise
>   They have much goodness yet they do not well,
> (The fools we know have their own paradise
>   The wicked also have their proper hell)
> They have much strength but still their doom is stronger,
> Much patience but their time endureth longer,
> Much valour . . . .[29]

They have all the cardinal and related virtues; but as Virgil explains, *s'elli hanno mercedi, non basta.* Moral virtues are of no avail
when "faith and hope and love are dead."[30]

But having noted these similarities, a student of Dante reading
Thomson's poem will at once also mark certain important differences. Dante's noble castle, like most medieval castles, has been reduced to ruins, and the limbo now is dominated by a mighty phan-

tom city, in which the old residents of the place — heroes, poets and sages of the Greco-Roman and Islamic worlds — have become an aged minority, the majority being constituted by the mass of neo-pagans born into the world since Dante's time. The most important difference to be noted, however, is that the Godless night of limbo is now no longer relieved, as it was in Dante's representation, by a gracious hemisphere of light.[31] Its night has become — to use Thomson's word — dreadful, as it ought to have been for the Christian poet yet obviously was not. Dante tells his readers that the spirits suspended in limbo are wracked with hopeless desire; he tells them that Virgil's aspect became deadly pale upon approaching the place where he is destined to spend all eternity shut out from the light and love of God; and yet it has been observed that Dante somehow fails to make his readers feel the truth of what he says. And the obvious explanation is, according to the critics, that he himself found it not *dreadful* but *good* to be there; *in me stesso n'esalto*[32] are his very words, and that inner exaltation is the feeling he conveys to most readers.

But, of course, Dante was professedly a hurried traveler on the edge of hell. His high purpose permitted him to linger only long enough to exchange a few words with the illustrious poets there, and to glance in passing at the assembled sages and heroes. The pilgrim narrator of Thomson's poem, on the contrary, is not pressed for time. Where Dante's poetic journey begins, his journey ends. He can say with Virgil: *di questi cotai* — of these spirits in Limbo — *son io medesmo*.[33] He has ample time, therefore, to search out details, to probe a situation left almost altogether unprobed, as Benedetto Croce remarked,[34] by Dante. And in so doing he comes at last to know far more intimately than Dante was able to imagine what it is really like to live in hopeless desire.

Approaching his Limbo, Dante noted the *sospiri che l'aera eterna facean tremare*; he noted the *turbe . . . d'infanti e di femmine e di viri*, who had brought to the edge of hell all sorts of frustrate longings. *Parlavan rado*, he says;[35] and the narrator of the *City* agrees: "they speak to one another seldom." But a more intimate knowledge of the place permits Thomson's pilgrim to specify that the people one meets with there are

> Mature men chiefly, few in age or youth,
> A woman rarely, now and then a child.

And, as for the sighs that make the atmosphere tremble: "All the air," he says, is charged with human feelings, human thought," charged with "joys and sorrows," "unspoken passion, wordless meditation," breathed into it by the spirits exiled there, each of whom adds

> . . . poison to the poisoned air;
> Infections of unutterable sadness . . .
> Infections of incurable despair.[36]

Regardless of literary success or failure, Thomson's imaginative purpose is clear. From his Leopardian point of view, it is as if all the fears and hopes of mortal existence which in Dante pass on to fruition in the sorrows of everlasting hell and in the joys of Heaven had been sealed up in the narrow space described in the fourth canto of the *Inferno*. Or rather, it is as if Dante had concentrated as much impassioned thought in delineating the spiritual lot of his virtuous pagans as he did in representing the glories of the *civitas dei*.[37]

Thomson has, in fact, filled his poem with unmistakable indications that he intended his *City* to represent, as Dante himself might have represented it, a modern earthly antithesis of the city of God. As the poem develops, antithetical echoes become more and more numerous; and Thomson evidently expects his readers to recognize them. Just as Dante must demonstrate his knowledge and possession of the spiritual virtues before he can be admitted to the final beatific vision, so Thomson's pilgrim must be found wanting in Christian faith, hope, and love he can be admitted to the final vision of Godless despair. When Thomson writes, "But as if blacker night could dawn on night,"[38] he is obviously echoing, antithetically, Dante's *parve giorno a giorno / essere aggiunto*.[39] And when, in the concluding stanzas of the poem he characterizes the spirit of Godlessness as the "'Melencolia' that transcends all wit,"[40] he expects the attentive reader to remember Dante's sublime *letizia che trascende ogni dolzore*,[41] as well as the Biblical "peace of God which passeth all understanding."[42]

But detailed study of the literal dependence of Thomson's *City* on the *Divine Comedy* and on Leopardi is reserved for the concluding chapter of this book. Here our purpose has been merely to refresh the reader's acquaintance with the work and to remind him of its literary character, before proceeding to review briefly the problems of critical interpretation that literary scholarship has already confronted, as well as those that still require investigation.

C. Unresolved Problems of Criticism

Three interrelated yet distinguishable questions have consistently occupied the attention of critics of Thomson's *City*. There is, first, the question of the suitability of its subject matter for poetic representation. Growing out of this is the question of the biographical significance of the poem. And, underlying both, or rather, partially concealed by them, is the problem of the poet's cultural resources — least explored of the three, yet most worthy of investigation.

Samuel C. Chew, writing in 1948, emphasized with particular clarity the relevance of the first of these problems. "The impact of [Thomson's] poem upon a sensitive reader," he wrote, "is so soul shaking that there is danger lest it be appraised too highly." For guidance to a sounder judgment, he reminded his readers of "Arnold's remark . . . that there is one kind of situation unsuitable for poetry . . . namely a situation 'in which a continuous state of mental distress is prolonged, unrelieved by incident, hope, or resistance, in which there is everything to be endured, nothing to be done'"[43] — a remark which, it must be granted, describes the condition of the God-forsaken citizens of Thomson's *City* even more accurately than it describes the situation in Arnold's own *Empedocles*. And it must be granted, also, that on some of its readers, at any rate, the poem has indeed produced an impression that perhaps exceeds the limits reserved for purely literary experience. It was, for instance, the considered judgment of William James that it was "less well-known than it should be, for its literary beauty, simply because men are afraid to quote its words — they are so gloomy and at the same time so sincere."[44] A few years earlier a critic in a leading periodical had written: "that man would have small poetic sensitiveness who should read *The City of Dreadful Night* precisely for pleasure . . . . One reader, at least, was plunged into more than his native gloom after looking at life through the smoked glass of this poet."[45] And later, Hugh Walker wrote that, while it was impossible to withhold from the poem the "tribute of deep admiration for the masterly execution," yet "the thought forces itself upon the reader that it is *not* good to be there. If Thomson's philosophy were true, even truth itself would be dear bought at the price of belief in it; for it must result in present misery and sooner or later must paralyze action."[46]

But the question is of long standing. George Eliot had raised it with extraordinary candor as early as 1874, in a letter addressed to the unknown poet shortly after the poem's original appearance in the *National Reformer*. "Dear Poet," she had written, "I cannot rest satisfied without telling you that my mind responds with admiration to the distinct vision and the grand utterance of the poem." But then abruptly, in terms reminiscent of Arnold's moralistic argument in the Preface of 1853, she added: "I trust that an intellect formed by so much passionate energy as yours will soon give us more heroic strains with a wider embrace of human fellowship in them . . . . To accept life and write much fine poetry is to draw with it necessarily some recognition, affectionate and even joyful, of the manifold willing labours which have made such a lot possible.[47] Indeed, while Thomson lived, many of his militant secularist friends and admirers "trusted" that he would eventually resolve the moral dilemma of his poem, that he would turn, at last, from considering that men despair and think things impossible, to speak concerning Hope. But the expected turn never came. In 1882, just two years after the publication of his first volume of poetry, Thomson died, suddenly, as carelessly as he had lived, leaving for sentimental admirers the burden of apologizing for a poetic utterance of unrelieved pessimism which (to repeat the words of Paul Elmer More) "stands quite alone in English literature, and which has, I believe, no precise equivalent in any language."[48]

Apology for the poem might have taken a variety of forms. By stressing comparison with Lucretius or Leopardi, apologists might have prepared a way for more general acceptance of the criterion suggested subsequently by Oliver Elton, who urged Englishmen to take pride in Thomson's *City* on the grounds that "without at least one poem expressing the extreme spirit of negation with grandeur and sincerity, no literature can be called complete."[49] Or they could have ignored the moralistic criticism, anticipating that subsequent generations of critics would be less willing than their own was to accept the standard of literary utility proposed by Arnold in the preface of 1853.[50]

Unfortunately, the first apologists to emerge pursued neither of these alternatives. They were Bertram Dobell, better known to students of English literature for having recovered some of the writings of Thomas Traherne, and Henry S. Salt, humanitarian and man of letters, later an intimate friend of George Bernard Shaw. Though they had not known Thomson intimately in life, these two men were devoted admirers, laboring assiduously to attract a wider audience for his writings. Dobell wrote a number of short memoirs, introductions to posthumous editions of the poet's works, and also published a little volume entitled *The Laureate of Pessimism*.[51] Salt, at the request of Dobell, who put at his disposal the journals and letters of the poet, wrote the standard *Life of James Thomson*, published in

1889.[52] Bent on apologizing for the gloomy view of life represented in the *City*, these two men proceeded to interpret the work biographically, and to stress in their representation of Thomson's life the importance of factors operating beyond the control of his will. They explained that he had suffered much, that he had inherited a family curse of some sort, that his poetic vision of the world, great as it was, was not always the product of a sound mind; and as a last resort, they suggested that he might have been kept from going astray, perhaps, had the world shown him some kindness in the critical years.

The writings of Dobell and Salt immediately aroused intimate friends of Thomson to protest against what appeared to be a distinctly false impression. The secularist publisher, G.W. Foote, an old friend of the poet, complained especially of the "apologetic tone, which is very regrettable," in Dobell's memoirs. "Mr. Dobell," he wrote, "I am quite sure, did not intend this; but it is there nevertheless. It is not conspicuous in particular sentences but it runs with persistent sadness in every page. No greater mistake could be made."[53] Shortly after the appearance of Salt's biography, another friend, Walter Lewin, wrote: "Mr. Salt . . . is, if possible, a worse offender even than his predecessor . . . . In [one] place he says, 'The sense of Doom' (capital D) — 'mysterious, incalculable, immitigable — broods darkly over his genius almost from the first.' This is the prevailing tone of the book." The truth, Mr. Lewin insisted, was quite the contrary; Thomson "was not a grumbler at fortune or fate . . . he was not a pessimist by nature. So far from this, his temperament seems to have been if serious, yet serene and cheerful . . . . He was a self-contained man who did not talk about his sorrow."[54]

Despite such protests from friends, the impression created by Dobell and Salt prevailed. But the effect on subsequent criticism was surely not what the apologetic biographers had hoped it would be. They had hoped to establish the importance of James Thomson as a poet; instead he soon became an object of pity, and his poem, as a direct consequence of their labors, came to be regarded as one of the curiosities of English literature.

What adverse effect the apologies were to have on admirers of the *City* was soon revealed in a response of George Meredith to a request from Salt that he write a preface for a new collection of Thomson's poems. Meredith had been an outspoken admirer of Thomson's poetry, and of his literary criticism also, which he had read as it appeared in the *National Reformer* and other secularist journals. Of the "City of Melencolia," as he called it, he had written:

"There is a massive impressiveness in it that goes beyond Dürer, and takes it into the upper regions where poetry is the sublimation of the mind of man, the voice of our highest."[55] In his last years Thomson had twice visited Meredith, and there are entries in his diaries noting the delight he took in long hours of stimulating conversation with the novelist.[56] After reading Salt's biography, Meredith recalled with bewilderment those pleasant visits Thomson had paid him "when I was unaware of the extent of the tragic affliction over-clouding him." [57] What personal visits could not make him aware of, Meredith learned only too easily from Salt's biography. Thomson, he was thereafter convinced, had done himself immeasurable harm in writing the *City*, for his very life seemed to have been poured out in its composition. The massive impressiveness of the poem's imagery seemed to Meredith, thereafter, to have been copied by Thomson "directly from the impressions carved in him by his desolate experience of life. Nothing is feigned, all is positive. No Inferno could be darker." The voice of our highest suddenly became for him "a litany of the vaults below."[58]

But how should a sensitive critic treat such poetry in presenting it to new readers? Thomson had thanked his earliest critic for treating it "simply and fairly on its literary merits." And Meredith, surely, would hardly have been tempted to treat it otherwise had he not been swayed by the apologetic fervor of Salt's biography. But the harm was done. "The task of a preface," Meredith wrote to Salt, "would be to show [Thomson] pursued and precipitated by his malady in the blood to do this poetic offense of dark monotonousness, which the clear soul of the man would have been far from committing had he not been so driven — as the beautiful Om-el-Bonain may witness. Bright achievement has been plucked out of the most tragic life in our literature." But having thus defined the task, Meredith wisely declined to attempt it. With pathetic frankness he excused himself:

> I am in fact jaded and broken. I have gone through James Thomson's works to spur myself. He was a man of big heart . . . . Still I find that to expound rightly, doing justice to him, with satisfaction to his admirers — to show how the noble qualities of the man, harried, though never more than physically conquered at times by the Fury he inherited, affected his verse, making it record the gloomy imagery absolutely conceived by him — this is more than I can undertake . . . . Now and then I have had in me . . . an endeavor to hit the delicate balance that would give the just portrait of a brave good man and true poet, hapless in his birth, fighting his best, and, as the book would prove, not failing, though baffled. I cannot. Hold me excused as well

as you can.[59]

The biographical incubus created by the apologists had overwhelmed the novelist. Salt himself, not recognizing his own handiwork, was dismayed by Meredith's new attitude. "No greater mistake," one of Thomson's friends had insisted, could have been made; and Meredith's response proves the point.

But where Meredith hesitated to tread, others, unfortunately, have rushed in, too often attracted by precisely what ought to have repelled them. There have since appeared two full-length biographies of Thomson in English, both by American authors wholly dependent on the works of Dobell and Salt for details, each vying to surpass his predecessors only in intensity of apologetic compassion. In the first of these, published in 1917, the author, J. Edward Meeker, admitted to "having made free" with the works of Dobell and Salt. The "over-curious" reader, he confided, might find many passages in the book where he "despaired of improving on the phrase of his predecessors, but has forgotten always to designate them by scrupulous quotation marks."[60] Of the second American biography — Imogene B. Walker's *James Thomson (B.V.), A Critical Study*, published in 1950[61] — Professor Graham Hough has written: "Miss Imogene Walker described her book as a critical study inspired by disappointment at previous treatments of Thomson's life and work. It is difficult to see what she supposes herself to have added." Earlier in his review Professor Hough noted: "She is only faintly aware of the rest of nineteenth century poetry, and is under the impression that Leopardi was a philosopher. She therefore does little to clear up Thomson's literary affiliations. And her gesture toward psychological interpretation is so slight that it were almost better left unmade."[62]

Professor Hough has here touched upon the third kind of critical problem we have distinguished: the problem of Thomson's cultural resources and literary affiliations. Various facets of this question have in fact been explored, in short studies, by a number of competent critics, including Louis Cazamian, Henri Peyre, Jeannette Marks, Paul Chauvet, Edmund Blunden, Gordon Hall Gerould, Lyman A. Cotton, George M. Harper, Benjamin M. Woodbridge and Hoxie N. Fairchild.[63] But, excepting only Edmund Blunden, they have all been more or less encumbered, if not overwhelmed as Meredith was, by the biographical incubus. And even Blunden's work is not altogether free of the burden, for it is part of a small edition of Thomson's chief poems on the flyleaf of which the publisher has pictured a haggard face, allegedly a sketch of the poet, in a drunken stupor, juxtaposed upon a drawing of Albrecht Dürer's "Melencolia."

"Probably the best general consideration of Thomson," Lionel Stevenson has written in his excellent though brief bibliographical survey for *The Victorian Poets* (1956),[64] is Jeannette Marks' "Disaster and Poetry" — a chapter in her volume entitled *Genius and Disaster*.[65] Professor Marks' study deserves particular attention because it brings into sharp focus the interrelatedness of the problems of interpretation we have been considering. Though her primary concern is evidently psychological, and even medical, she devoted many interesting pages to exploring Thomson's literary affiliations and to appraising the cultural significance of his *City*. "There can be no question," she writes, "but that *The City of Dreadful Night* has the quality of greatness."[66] The picture of Thomson bequeathed by Dobell and Salt may not have influenced Professor Marks to shape that judgment, but surely just such a picture, and not the test of the poem, prompted her to believe that Thomson "paid his very life for what he produced,"[67] and to ask pathetically in her final appraisal: "Who is that Shylock who would knowingly and willingly purchase a great poem at the price of such disaster to a fellow human being?"[68] How heavily the "tragic life" weighed upon her judgment she herself very candidly revealed, admitting that in the "very instance of his most impressive poem" she seemed to "detect the quality of one who sees life as an intellectually gifted and tragically condemned member of the Salvation Army might see it."[69]

Exploring Thomson's literary affiliations, Professor Marks resisted the temptation to regard him as an "intuitive" poet, unaffected by "fashions in poetry."[70] Listening with an ear no doubt sharply tuned to the cadences of English verse, she found that even in his "greatest poem — the sole creation we could hope to call wholly and adequately his own — there is too close analogy between intellectual inquiry and outward form to leave us any choice, but still to place Thomson among the imitative." Thomson, she was convinced, had learned his poet's trade, not by intuition but by reading and conscious imitation. He had had a literary master, and one very close at hand. Correspondence between certain portions of the *City* and Tennyson's *Two Voices*, Professor Marks concluded, "is not merely that of *terza rima* [needless to say, Tennyson's poem is not in *terza rima*], of a similar subject, of figures much alike. The correspondence goes deeper than that: it is dependence — the dependence of James Thomson on Alfred Tennyson."[71]

Of course, Professor Marks could hardly have been unaware that the verse form, subject matter, and figures of Tennyson's *Two Voices* were not without precedent. Perhaps had she known Italian poetry as well as Thomson knew it, or as well as she knew English, she might have been reminded instead, as Piero Rébora and René Lalou were, of the subject matter of Leopardi and the verse form and figures of Dante. "It is certain," wrote Rébora in 1920, "that Thomson more than any other English writer enters into the thought of Leopardi with abandon, sensibility and conviction."[72] René Lalou wrote of the *City* in 1924: "Cette allégorie évoque forcément le souvenir de Dante: elle supporte sans en être écrasée la redoutable comparison."[73] Louis Cazamian found in Thomson's *City* "le décor terrible et grandiose que Dante avait cherché, pour les damnés, dans les cercles de son enfer."[74] And more recently, the English poet and critic, J.H. Heath-Stubbs, whose translations of Leopardi reflect a competent knowledge of Italian prosody, has remarked that Thomson's poem "does really approach nearer, as regards atmosphere, to the Inferno of Dante, than does any other English poem."[75] Despite the dedication and captions of the poem, not once in Professor Marks' study of the literary and cultural influences discernible in it, does the name of Dante or Leopardi occur. For the literary cultivation of her "tragically condemned" Salvation Army poet, Tennyson's *Two Voices* evidently sufficed.

Hoxie N. Fairchild's study of Thomson in the fourth volume of his *Religious Trends in English Poetry* illustrates how adversely the biographical legacy of Dobell and Salt can affect critical judgment. After introducing Thomson's *City* as "one of the most powerful poems produced within the nineteenth century,"[75] Professor Fairchild tells his readers that, in organizing his materials, he had been strongly tempted to give the poem special prominence. To conclude his discussion of the Victorian poets with a study of Thomson's *City*, he writes, "would greatly enhance the rhetorical effectiveness of my thesis. The device would show us romantic pride soaring to its climax in 'Glory to man in the highest!' and descending to the inevitable catastrophe in *The City of Dreadful Night*, the final outcome of the tradition of Blake and Shelley." Professor Fairchild resisted the temptation, finally, not because of any inconvenience in the text of the poem itself, but because of the general impression derived from the apologists that Thomson was a desperately "sick" man whose case, "though precious," was "too exceptional to reflect the normal situation."[77]

Would critics be bolder in their appraisals of Thomson's poem if they could be persuaded to dismiss from consideration the pathetic portrait that overshadows it? There is good reason to believe that they would. Cazamian, for instance, despite his impression that Thomson was an uncultured man, did not hesitate to suggest that the *City* deserved to be regarded as an historically important literary monument, marking the end of a great era of poetry. "*La Cité de la Nuit Tragique*," he wrote, "est la conclusion singulièrement romantique d'un âge positif et rationnel. C'est une preuve éloquente de la meurtrissure profonde, incurable, des sensibilités, que de comparer cette obsession désespérée à la philosophie tranquille du premier âge classique, au 'tout ce qui est, est bien' du Pope dans *L'Essai sur L'Homme*."[78] It was Paul Elmer More's considered judgment that the pessimism in Thomson's *City* "was the pessimism that lurks unawakened or stunned by multifarious noise, in the background of our present eager civilization."[79] Edmund Blunden was persuaded that the "generation which has honored Mr. T. S. Eliot for his allegorical interpretations of its spiritual troubles . . . will comprehend the actualities of B.V.'s 'desert,' and, in the main, will value the many kinds of direct and metaphorical, of bare and ornamental expression, through which the Victorian poem has shaped out his gloomy judgment of life."[80] T. S. Eliot himself has not written of any direct influence of Thomson's *City* on his poetry; but, in the light of his own role as a poet and apologist for what some unfriendly critics have called a Christianity of little faith, less hope, and no charity, the passing reference to Thomson in his essay on Tennyson suggests that he may have been conscious of a relationship between his own wasteland poems and Thomson's *City*. Eliot has written: "*In Memoriam* is a poem of despair, but of despair of a religious kind. And to qualify its despair with the adjective 'religious' is to elevate it above most of its derivatives. For *The City of Dreadful Night*, and *A Shropshire Lad*, and the poems of Thomas Hardy, are small work in comparison with *In Memoriam*. It is greater than they and comprehends them."[81] Basil Willey has challenged Eliot's main point, holding on the contrary that *In Memoriam* cannot be considered a religious poem in the traditional sense of the word;[82] and we, in the course of the following pages, will have occasion to note how much more religious significance there is in the despair of the city of "Melencolia" — where faith and hope and love are dead — than Eliot imagines. But perhaps Eliot, too, has read the *City* as the work of a poorly educated man, reflecting only lower class acquirements and experiences; perhaps his impression of the poet accords with that of Allan Tate,

who, writing of Thomas Hardy, has said: "Had he been 'better educated' he might have been like Browning or Swinburne — both men
his inferiors: had he been worse educated, it is not inconceivable
that he should have been even more like James Thomson than he
was."[83]

Edmund Blunden, in his essay on Thomson cited earlier, attempted to confound this generally accepted notion that Thomson
was poorly educated. It is unfortunate, perhaps, that in doing so he
isolated for criticism some phrases of Lafcadio Hearn, who was by
no means the worst offender. Nevertheless Blunden's words are to
the point. Hearn, a great admirer of Thomson, had written: "Only
one of his compositions can be termed great; but it is very great, the
greatest thing of the kind in English verse . . . and the surprise of the
work is that a man who never had any real literary training could
have composed it."[84] With this and other similar statements in mind,
Blunden replied with partisan ardor: ". . . when [Hearn] alleges that
Thomson was 'uneducated, or almost uneducated,' and lacked 'literary training,' the City of wonderful fineness of phrase asks him a
question which he could not have answered. There, intense agony of
spirit has fought out the battle for general and minute flawlessness
of diction and allusion, and all that remains is moonlight symmetry
and tracery, accomplished and unimprovable; but this result did not
come from imperfect resources."[85]

D. Purpose of this Study

Of the kinds of resources he was able to draw upon in writing
the *City,* James Thomson has left an extensive record consisting of
moral, critical, and philosophic essays, religious and social satires,
translations, metrical imitations and experiments, most of them originally published in secularist and trade journals, some few re-issued
in the two volumes of poetry and one of prose published in his lifetime, and many, though by no means all of the others collected and
published posthumously together with manuscript materials. Much
of this extensive record will be examined in the following chapters,
not on the assumption that acquaintance with it is necessary for an
adequate appreciation of the poetic and intellectual significance of
Thomson's *City,* but rather in order to dispel some of the prevalent
misconceptions regarding the cultural preparation of the poet — misconceptions that have in fact made adequate appreciation difficult.

Ultimately it is not what Thomson may have known and felt, but what the reader himself knows and feels and is willing to bring to bear that will determine what he gets from reading the poem. A serious literary work, Thomson himself once wrote, reviewing with only seeming satiric intent the difficulties of critical interpretation, is a mirror "which reflects more or less clearly our own features and surroundings, a Spanish country inn where merely that is served up to us dressed which we carry with us crude, a bank which will not suffer us to overdraw our little account though it may hold much larger sums on account of others. Thus the small Dobbs turned loose in Shakespeare cannot gather a single thought beyond what is veritably Dobbish, as a cup cannot hold more than a cupful whether dipped in can or ocean."[86] Thomson would not have agreed with Edmund Blunden's assertion that his *City* is able to ask unanswerable questions of critics who underestimate it. He knew only too well that, as Socrates says in the *Phaedrus*, when words "have been once written down they are tumbled about anywhere among those who may or may not understand them, and know not to whom they should reply, to whom not; and, if they are maltreated or abused, they have no parent to protect them; and they cannot protect or defend themselves."[87] Socrates, on that account, refused to commit any of his thoughts to writing. Those who have been less prudent must suffer the consequences. They can attempt to ward off readers whom they consider "Dobbish," as Dante does at the beginning of *Paradiso*:

> O voi, che siete in piccioletta barca . . .
> tornate a rivader li vostri liti:
> non vi mettete in pelago . . . .[88]

— or, as Thomson attempts to do even more emphatically in the "Proem" to his *City*:

> Surely I write not for the hopeful young,
>   Or those who deem their happiness of worth,
> Or such as pasture and grow fat among
>   The shows of life . . .
> Or pious spirits with a God above them,
> To sanctify and glorify and love them,
>   Or sages who foresee a heaven on earth.
>
> For none of these I write, and none of these
>   Could read the writing if they deigned to try.[89]

But such warnings are utterly vain. Printed words cannot discriminate: they must take their readers as they come. And where a Blunden finds "minute flawlessness . . . accomplished and unimprovable," a

Cornelius Weygandt, though "eager to sympathize with the rejected of the world," is apt to find only "second-rateness long drawn out, the essence of mediocrity."[90]

Perhaps the best an adoptive parent can hope to do for words that have been abused is to tumble them about further where they are apt to be taken up by readers better disposed to treat them well. Though he may not succeed in discouraging "Dobbish" interpreters from their labors, he can at least remind serious readers that, while more may and no doubt should be read into a poem than its author puts into it, there can be no justification for reading less into it, as some critics have done with *The City of Dreadful Night*, on the false assumption that its author was deficient in cultural preparation.

NOTES

1. Salt, *Life*, p. 85.

2. *Ibid.*, p. 81.

3. Quoted in James Thomson's *Vane's Story, Weddah and Om-el-Bonain, and other Poems* (London, 1881), appendix, p. 4.

4. Salt, *Life*, p. 86.

5. "Paris Letter," *Liverpool Daily Courier*, cited in James Thomson, *Essays and Phantasies* (London, 1881), appendix, p. 8.

6. From Thomson's diary, January 7, 1881, cited by Imogene B. Walker, *James Thomson (B.V.)* (Ithaca, 1950), p. 137.

7. George Saintsbury, "The City of Dreadful Night," *The Academy*, XVII (1880), 432.

8. Theodore Watts-Dutton, "The City of Dreadful Night and Other Poems," *The Athenaeum* (1880), pp. 561-62.

9. George B. Woods, etc., editors, *The Literature of England* (Chicago, 1941), pp. 818-19.

10. W. Lewis Jones, "Matthew Arnold, Arthur Hugh Clough, James Thomson," in *Cambridge History of English Literature*, XIII, 120.

11. Edward Mortimer Chapman, *English Literature in Account with Religion* (Boston, 1910), p. 174.

12. Sir Herbert J. C. Grierson, J. C. Smith, *A Critical History of English Poetry* (New York, 1946), pp. 498-99.

13. See note 9 above.

14. John Matthews Manly, *English Poetry (1177-1892)* (New York, 1907), pp. xxvii-xxviii.

15. Grierson and Smith, *History of English Poetry*, pp. 499-500.

16. James Thomson, *The Poetical Works of James Thomson*, edited by Bertram Dobell (London, 1894), I, 122.   Since this edition is not generally available, and since most of the lines of Thomson's *City of Dreadful Night* will be cited in the course of this work, it will be convenient merely to indicate the relevant section, or canto of the poem.   The lines quoted in the text here are from the introductory "Proem."

17. Shakespeare's *Titus Andronicus*, Act III, Scene I, ll. 12-13.

18. Thomson's *City*, X.

19. John Milton's *Paradise Lost*, Book IX, ll. 15-16 and ll. 954-54.

20. *City*, XIV.

21. John Milton, *Complete Poetry and Selected Prose* (New York, n.d.), p. 459.

22. *Ibid.*, p. 15.

23. *Inferno*, III, 1. 1.   Quotations from Dante Alighieri are, unless otherwise indicated, from *Tutte le Opere di Dante Alighieri* (Firenze, 1926).

24. Giacomo Leopardi, *Tutte le Opere di Giacomo Leopardi*, edited by Francesco Flora (Milan, 1945), I, 82.

25. *Ibid.*, p. 922.

26. *City*, VI.

27. *Ibid.*, VI.

28. *Inferno*, IV, 11.   31-32.

29. *City*, XI.

30. *Ibid.*, II.

31. *Inferno*, IV, 11.   68-69:   "un foco / Ch'emisperio di tenebre vincia."

32. *Ibid.*, 1.   120.

33. *Ibid.*, 1.   39.

34. Benedetto Croce, *The Poetry of Dante* (New York, 1922), p. 17.

35. *Inferno*, IV, 11.   29-30, and 1. 114.

36. *City*, XV.

37. *Paradiso*, XXX, 1.   130.

38. *City*, XXI.

39. *Paradiso*, I, 11.   61-62.

40. *City*, XXI.

41. *Paradiso*, XXX, 1.   42.

42. *Philippians*, 4, 7.

43. Samuel C. Chew, in *A Literary History of England*, edited by Albert C. Baugh (New York, 1948), p. 1420.

44. William James, *Will to Believe*, p. 34.

45. "Academy Portraits: James Thomson," *The Academy*, LV (1898), p. 383.

46. Hugh Walker, *The Literature of the Victorian Era* (Cambridge, 1910), p. 590.

47. Salt, *Life*, p. 81.

48. P. E. More, *Shelbourne Essays*, V, 188.

49. Oliver Elton, *A Survey of English Literature, 1830-1880*, II (London, 1920), 124.

50. Lionel Trilling, in *Matthew Arnold* (New York, 1939), writes: "the human mind . . . finds its literary therapy in more ways than Arnold admits" (p. 140).

51. Bertram Dobell, *The Laureate of Pessimism* (London, 1910).

52. Henry S. Salt, *The Life of James Thomson ("B.V.")*, first edition (London, 1889). Most references in this work are to the revised edition (London, 1914).

53. G. W. Foote, "James Thomson," *Progress*, III-IV (1884), 250.

54. Walter Lewin, editor, *Selections from Original Contributions by James Thomson to Cope's Tobacco Plant* (Liverpool, 1889), pp. 12-13.

55. George Meredith, letter dated April 27, 1880, quoted in Salt, *Life*, pp. 114-115.

56. Salt, *Life*, p. 116.

57. *Ibid.*, p. 136.

58. George Meredith, *Letters*, edited by W. W. Meredith, II (New York, 1912), 436.

59. *Ibid.*, p. 434.

60. J. Edward Meeker, *The Life and Poetry of James Thomson (B.V.)* (New Haven, 1917), pp. ix-x.

61. Imogene B. Walker, *James Thomson (B.V.)* (Ithaca, 1950).

62. James Hough, review of "Imogene B. Walker's *James Thomson*," *Modern Language Notes*, LXVI (1951), 283.

63. References to most of these works occur later in the chapter. Lionel Stevenson's bibliographic chapter on Thomson in *The Victorian Poets*, edited by Frederic E. Faverty (Cambridge, 1956), provides a good critical review.

64. In Faverty, *The Victorian Poets*, p. 237.

65. Jeannette Marks, *Genius and Disaster* (New York, 1926).

66. *Ibid.*, p. 121.

67. *Ibid.*, p. 105.

68. *Ibid.*, p. 126.

69. *Ibid.*, p. 106.

70. Grierson and Smith, *History of English Poetry*, p. 499.

71. Marks, *Genius and Disaster*, p. 115.

72. Piero Rébora, "Traduttori e Critici Inglesi di Leopardi," *Nuova Antologia di Letture, Scienze ed Arti* (1920), p. 271.

73. René Lalou, *Panorama de la Littérature Anglaise Contemporaine* (Paris,

1924), pp. 106-107.

74. Louis Cazamian, *Etudes de Psychologie Littéraire* (Paris, 1913), p. 226.

75. John Heath-Stubbs, *The Darkling Plain* (London, 1950), p. 115.

76. Fairchild, *Religious Trends*, IV, 469.

77. *Ibid.*, p. 473.

78. Louis Cazamian, *L'Evolution Psychologique et la Littérature en Angleterre*, 1860-1924 (Paaris, 1920), p. 240.

79. P. E. More, *Shelbourne Essays*, V, 189.

80. Edmund Blunden, editor, *The City of Dreadful Night* (London, 1932), pp. 6-7.

81. T. S. Eliot, *Essays Ancient and Modern* (London, 1936), p. 294.

82. Basil Willey, *More Nineteenth Century Studies* (New York, 1956), p. 81.

83. Allen Tate, *On the Limits of Poetry* (New York, 1948), p. 196.

84. Lafcadio Hearn, *A History of English Literature* (Tokyo, 1941), p. 630.

85. Blunden, *The City of Dreadful Night*, p. 10.

86. James Thomson, *Poems, Essays, and Fragments*, edited by John M. Robertson (London, 1903), p. 237.

87. Irwin Edman, editor, *The Works of Plato* (New York, 1928), p. 324.

88. *Paradiso*, II, 11. 1-5.

89. *City*, Proem.

90. Cornelius Weygandt, *The Time of Tennyson* (New York, 1936), p. 306.

II. RELIGIOUS AND MORAL PREPARATION

On November 4th, 1869, a few months before he began to write the *City*. Thomson spent a long afternoon burning all his "old papers, manuscripts, and letters, save the book MSS. which have been already in great part printed." For five hours he kept the fire burning, scarcely looking into any of the old papers — letters, diaries, youthful poems and essays — many of which he had treasured for ten and even twenty years. "I felt," Thomson wrote in a literary notebook he had only then begun to keep, "like one who, having climbed half-way up a long rope (35 on the 23rd inst.) cuts off all beneath his feet; he must climb on, and can never touch the old earth again without a fatal fall."[1]

In that ceremonial fire marking the "middle of the journey" of his life, Thomson brought to completion a process of depersonalization, or "extinction of personality" (to use T. S. Eliot's phrase),[2] upon which he had entered many years earlier, when he first felt the need to prepare himself as a poetic medium. By his thirty-fifth year he had liberated himself intellectually from religious and moral self-concern, from willful bondage to the personal hopes and dreams of his youth; but to cleanse his sentimental heart he had literally to "consume the past." The success of his effort to do so is amply attested by his biographers. Bertram Dobell laments over the "wholesale sacrifice" of that holocaust.[3] Imogene Walker acknowledges that, because of the fire, "little factual material is available" concerning Thomson's parents and his youth, beyond what is contained in "a letter of autobiography to his sister-in-law in the last year of his life."[4] And Dobell and Salt agree that for the nine years from 1861 through 1870 "there is little actual record of Thomson's doings," although, "in a literary point of view, these years were perhaps his best and most productive period."[5]

Among the papers that Thomson spared from that fire were the manuscripts of two youthful poems which, taken together, may be read as a first draft of the *City*. The older of the two, one of Thomson's earliest extant poems, is dated July, 1855, and carries the notation "Suggested by Matthew Arnold's 'Stanzas from the Grande Chartreuse.'" The second, dated 1857, is a long narrative entitled "The Doom of a City." Although the poems were not intended to be read together, and were never deemed worthy of publication by Thomson, they are of considerable value for students of the *City* because of the light they throw on its genesis.

A. Early Religious Crisis

Dobell and Salt in their biographies devote many pages to a discussion of what they call the religious crisis of Thomson's youth. It
may well be that, as they insist, the circumstances of Thomson's childhood, the religion of his mother, the mental failure of his father,
and also the death of a young girl whom he loved, greatly influenced
the course of Thomson's religious experience. But, if we confine
ourselves to the evidence of his own writings, as we mean to do in
this study, the earliest and only explicit indication of any religious
crisis he may have undergone is to be found in Thomson's elegiac
poem of 1855, written in response to the "brooding quietness" of
Arnold's "dirge for a mighty creed outworn"[6] which had just been
published. In the first of three parts, the poet joins Arnold in grieving over the death of Christianity; in the second, he comes to realize
that only the external form, only the body can die, not the spirit; in
the third he anticipates a new incarnation, a new revelation of divinity about to dawn upon the benighted world, promising to "flood us
with His summer noon!"[7] But it is vain, the poet insists, to pretend
that Christianity, the latest embodiment of divinity, still lives — for
grim honest men are always at hand to crush a dream that lies. With
Arnold, the poet sees the banners of modern thought unfurled, and
hears the resounding bugle summoning recluses to the duties of
industrious life. But he is even less willing than Arnold to leave the
living tomb of silent mourners, to turn away "from mighty death to
petty life":

> Say not that it is weak to grieve;
> Duty does *not*, *now*, urge us on:
> In vain *ye* urge . . . .
>
> When God keeps still can *ye* not rest?
> When He sends night so dark and deep,
> Why shrink from renovating sleep?[8]

Rejecting absolutely the enlightenment of man-made lamps, the
poet vows, finally, to wait in darkness beside the silent form of the
dead body of Christ, till death's veil shall have fallen from his face.

In later years Thomson directed some very pointed satires against
the maturer Arnold, who turned from poetry to social criticism; but
he never forgot the powerful impression the "Stanzas" had made on
him in 1855. Allusions and quotations are encountered again and
again in Thomson's prose writings and minor poems; but his most
significant tribute to Arnold the poet is to be read in cantos XII-XVI

of the *City*, in the dialogue of the great "cathedral scene" where the lesson of his response to the "Grande Chartreuse" is stripped of its immediate personal significance and rendered timeless.

B. THE "DOOM OF A CITY"

As is often the case in youthful religious crises, Thomson's loss of faith was accompanied by a quickening of the moral sense. If it is true that Christianity is dead, what are we to make — he asks — of this mighty England of ours with its concubinage of Church and State? What are we to make of the deceived deceivers who, either in ignorance or hypocrisy, fill our youthful minds with lies? How ugly is the reality that suddenly comes to view when once the veil of youthful piety is rent. In the "Doom of a City," second of the important poems that survived the fire of 1869, Thomson poured out all his youthful moral resentment against the chief institutions and personalities of his age whom he charged with perpetrating the greatest of injustices. "The Doom of a City," with its variety of meters and stanzaic forms, is obviously a first sketch of *The City of Dreadful Night*. In the first of four parts the narrator sails forth from London on a fantastic journey that carries him to a far-off land dominated by a golden-domed metropolis. In the second part he enters the city only to learn to his dismay that its "passionate, heaving, restless, sounding life" has been "arrested in full tumult" —

> Frozen into a nightmare's ghastly death,
> Struck silent from its laughter and its moan;
> The vigorous heart and brain and blood and breath
> Stark, strangled, coffined in eternal stone.[9]

As in the later *City*, the narrator here explores the silent metropolis, describing all that he sees and hears in its precincts vast. He encounters and describes in detail men, women, and children of every rank and station, "grouped as in social converse or alone," all petrified in their characteristic acts, and attempts to read in the fixed forms their fixed destinies. In the later *City* each of the inhabitants will have a distinctive poetic voice of his own, and will himself reveal his fixed lot in anguished discourse. Here, on the contrary, the inhabitants are but stony forms that cannot speak for themselves. The narrator alone has a voice, and the only feelings expressed in the poem are his own. After a while, even he begins to feel a creeping petrification possessing his members, blending his "mad discordant life . . . / With all this realm's unsuffering death of stone."[10]

Suddenly there is an earthquaking thunder that restores the narrator's faculties in time to enable him to fulfill the mission of his journey. In the third part the entire community is subjected before his sight to a series of cosmic judgments: the false, the evil, the proud, the lustful among its inhabitants are called to life for an instant only to be consumed in an "ever-burning, unrelenting, irresistible flame;"[11] while the "strong and wise and pure and true"[12] among them find themselves suddenly swept aloft into a "noonday Heaven of Bliss," pervaded with the "Divine eternal breathing / Of Life and Light and Love."[13]

Exhausted by the vision of judgment, the narrator returns to the sea whence he came and is carried in dreamful ease back to the city on the Thames. He is so weary upon his arrival that death, which has touched his brow, disdains to "lay its plenary pressure" on so feeble a heart. Suddenly, however, he feels himself uplifted like a "passive instrument," seized and shaken by that "Spirit which will never be withstood." Through his lips, with irresistible might, the spirit that had guided him on his journey pours forth its message of warning to mighty England and her people:

Haughty and wealthy and great, mighty, magnificent, free
Empress in thine own right of the earth surrounding sea . . .
Thy merchants are palaced princes, thy nobles scorn great kings,
Thy meanest children swell with pride beneath thy shadowy
                                                                        wings.[14]

The various classes of English society are called to account: the pampered rich who "dribble bland alms" to the poor, never dreaming that "all their life is one huge embezzlement"; the brute-like poor, "who feel but their bread distress"; rulers who live with scarcely one noble aim, "deaf to the holy voice of the Conscience of the World"; the exploiting priesthood of a Church that has "long been becoming the Fossil of a Faith"; poets who sing only of their own lusts; sages who hide from stern truth, leading themselves and others astray; and prophets who "smile Peace, Peace, and it is a sword." Each of these classes is condemned to pay its share of the debt of guilt when mighty England shall have been brought at last under the just judgment of

                                                   that fire
Which hath tested so sternly the glitter of Venice and Carthage
                                                   and Tyre;
For no wealth can bribe away the doom of the living God,
No haughtiest strength confront the sway of his chastening rod.[15]

Although it is scarcely known, this early draft of the *City* has won some significant critical praise, notably from Gordon Hall Gerould. "This magnificent if not wholly achieved and sometimes incoherent poem," Professor Gerould wrote, "is a work of youth, but it could have been written only by a youth of genius . . . . Like *Alcastor* and *Endymion* the *Doom of a City* is a precious and beautiful work of the human imagination, which no lover of poetry can afford to ignore."[16] In mood, it differs fundamentally from the later *City*; and its thoughts and sentiments are of a kind with which the average reader can more readily sympathize. Like Shelley's *Prometheus Unbound*, which it imitates in many sections, it is charged with humanitarian indignation against the mighty of the world, and full of that desperate romantic hope which "creates / From its own wreck the thing it contemplates."[17]

In a note appended to a copy of the poem, which he had allowed a friend to read, Thomson himself assessed its intellectual and literary defects. "I can it a Fantasia," he wrote, "because (lacking the knowledge and power to deal with the theme in its epic integrity) I have made it but an episode in a human life, instead of a chapter in the history of Fate. Thus it is throughout alloyed with the feelings and thoughts, the fantasies of the supposed narrator; and the verse has all the variableness and abrupt transitions of a man's moods, instead of the solemn uniformity of the laws of Fate.[18] Thomson was aware that the vision he had received of a mighty Babylon under judgment for its worldliness transcended his powers of artistic expression. He knew that he had not yet attained sufficient detachment from his personal feelings to be an adequate poetic medium. The vision had seized his imagination, as the narrator of the poem says; and then it had passed, leaving him to struggle under the burden of that "double transcendence" precisely described by Dante in the closing paragraphs of the *Vita Nuova*,[19] which is the boast as well as the complaint of inspired poets. Like the young Dante, Thomson could neither remember accurately what he had seen nor represent adequately what little he remembered. But the experience taught him what his life's task must be. Gradually perfecting himself as a poetic medium — refining his literary art, informing his intellect, purging his will — he returned to the theme of his vision again and again in the course of his life, treating aspects of it and occasionally reviewing the whole in prose and poetry of varying moods. He paced the streets of London through long hours of many nights and days, familiarizing himself with its scenes. His writings of those years

abound with descriptions of streets and squares, churches and palaces, rivers and bridges, beggars, workers, merchants, soldiers, statesmen. He read the social reformers, the preachers, journalists and
sages. He steeped himself in the poetry of France, Germany, and
Italy, as well as England, translating the thoughts and feelings of
others so as to render his own language more universal and pliant as
a poetic medium. But primarily he struggled with himself to crush
the assertive movements of his will, rendering himself "impotent in
the Latin sense"[20] — as Saintsbury later diagnosed his condition — so
that he might heighten his sensitivity to even the slightest manifestations of will in others. Leopardi and Schopenhauer were his intellectual guides in this struggle; but, as we shall have occasion to show, he
eventually surpassed his masters. It was a struggle of long duration.
Not until he had burned the last traces of his personal life in that
ceremonial fire of his thirty-fifth year did he consider himself prepared to write of his City of *Melencolia* with sufficient "knowledge
and power to deal with the theme in its epic integrity." In subsequent chapters, the evidences of his literary and philosophic preparation will be considered in detail; but first we must examine the
evidences of his religious and moral preparation, begun when he
pledged himself, after reading Arnold's "Stanzas" of 1855, to wait in
darkness and silence beside the dead figure of Christ.

C. Religious and Social Satire

Had it been within his power, young Thomson might have willingly isolated himself, like an Eastern hermit, from the banner-wav-
ing world of Victorian England. And in fact, fate did seem for a time
to be securing for him a niche apart, far removed from the pressures
of worldly existence. In 1855, when he read Arnold's "Stanzas," he
was already serving as an army schoolmaster — a socially humble
position, yet one that offered him the prospect of a life of leisure to
study and write, with little care required for the procurement of
material necessities. In military isolation he might have nourished in
himself a lower-class equivalent of that nostalgia for a departed faith
which Arnold nourished throughout his poetic life, after having heard
its "last enchantments" whispered from the moonlit tower of an old
school.

But while still an apprentice teacher, Thomson met a hero of
self-reliance of the sort idealized by Emerson. The man was Charles
Bradlaugh, then an enlisted soldier, but later to become the most

notorious atheist of Victorian England. The meeting was important, for it resulted in a friendship that largely determined the course of Thomson's literary career. Like Thomson, Bradlaugh was of humble birth. Under twenty when he entered the army, he had already dedicated his life to "free thought" and republicanism. After three years of service he bought his release and soon established a periodical called the *London Investigator,* in which he editorialized under the name "Iconoclast." But it was only with the establishment of the *National Reformer* in 1860 that he began to attract national attention. Through a series of journalistic campaigns and court actions, he forced recognition of an atheist's testimony in court, vindicated his conception of a free press, and finally induced Gladstone to introduce legislation admitting non-believers and Jews to Parliament.[21] It is said that he was "hard, arrogant and dogmatic" — a man of enormous physical proportions, with a real gift for popular oratory; "a natural leader in causes with society against them," whose "sincerity was as unquestionable as his combativeness."[22]

Of such character was the man destined to be Thomson's first friend and benefactor. After Bradlaugh gained his discharge, Thomson remained in military service many years, betraying not the slightest inclination to follow his friend into the great world of political and social strife. Knowing himself to be a poet, he seemed to appreciate the fact that his military assignment allowed him to enjoy some of the advantages of a man of leisure that he might not otherwise have known. Already he had begun to seek publication for his poems, and not without some success.

But Bradlaugh soon called upon his talented friend to contribute with his pen to the success of his radical enterprises. In a spirit of fellowship Thomson responded with a few poems and critical essays for which he received no compensation. But in none of his early contributions did he so much as pretend to take up Bradlaugh's cause. In fact, one of his first prose writings, an essay on Burns published in the *London Investigator* in 1859, reaffirms the argument of the unpublished poem of 1855 suggested by Arnold's "Stanzas." Attempting to draw a moral lesson from the life of Burns, young Thomson writes: "Trust not . . . in warm-hearted joviality with honest comrades; nor in wit and intellect and fulgent bursts of genius." The modern world is, for men of sensibility like Burns, an impassive sphinx looming in a desert wasteland; "the rigid lips will not wreath into smiles for all your abounding humor; the stark blind eyes will not moisten with tears for all your lamentable dirges; the stony heart will never throb responsive to your yearning, your passion, your enthusiasm."[23] But, Thomson concludes, life was not always thus:

> Once it was very different — the men of old had a God; but we, like Burns, are shut out from his presence. They who dwelt at home with their father, happy and loving and beloved, might indulge freely their moods and impulses; we here in prison with the deaf and dumb jailer must guard ourselves as sternly as he guards us. Patience, fortitude; our father may in time recall these terrible *lettres de cachet* which have sealed our doom, and let us see his face again in glad liberty. In the meanwhile, to love our fellow prisoners, helping and serving them as we can, is the sanctitude and piety of our miserable existence. And it is also the happiness, such happiness as the dungeon admits; for though a broad love and sympathy is a broad target for the arrows of Beelzebub, the poison of the shaft which wounds us through another does not rankle in our heart.[24]

It is not difficult to recognize in the phrases here quoted anticipations of the language and imagery of the concluding cantos of the *City*, where sphinx and heroic man again confront one another and the *Melancolia* of indomitable will is characterized. Had he been permitted to remain in the army, Thomson might have sustained unbroken the nostalgic mood of these lines. But chance took an unexpected turn that abruptly cut him loose from the security of military life. A minor incident of insubordination led to his sudden discharge. It is reported that he refused to give the name of a soldier companion who had been seen swimming, on a dare, in an off-limits lake.[25] As a consequence he was thrust out upon the busy world, into the welcoming arms of his notorious friend, Charles Bradlaugh. Bradlaugh at first sought other forms of employment for the twenty-eight year old Thomson, but eventually drew him into active participation in the work of the *National Reformer*.

After his discharge, Thomson lived for a number of years in Bradlaugh's household, where atheism — not the kind which the fool whispers in his heart, but the kind to be published from the housetops as a new gospel — was the élan vital. There he suffered an almost incurable enchantment. To the company of atheists who frequented that household, and gradually to their personal trials and struggles, though never to their ultimate aims, Thomson opened his heart. Their kindness, their courage, the exemplary lives many of them led, constituted an irresistible claim on his allegiance, a claim as irresistible for him as was that of the "voice speaking so clearly in my conscience" for John Henry Newman. Yet he could not share their faith in the utility of atheism. Atheism was for Bradlaugh a

positive creed which he hoped to institutionalize on a national scale
so that it might be in fact what men like Arnold were saying the
Church of England was: a "great national society for the promotion
of what is commonly called goodness."[26] For Thomson, on the contrary, atheism was essentially negative, like darkness — a bare ground
on which "wrinkled truth" is stripped of its beguiling vestures.

The literary temper of the *National Reformer* had been established
before Thomson was invited to contribute to it. Its object, according
to the dedication of the first issue, was to promote the general wel-
fare of mankind. In practice, however, its efforts were confined to
attacking what secularists considered to be the foremost obstacles
to public well-being and enlightenment: the functionless throne with
its attendant aristocracy and the parasitic Established Church. The
leading article was often a comparative study of Biblical texts, probably to dazzle the eyes of working-class readers. In addition, there
were always "liberal" articles on history, economics, science, current
affairs, and literature. Thomson supplied only literary essays and
poems at first, refusing to write on controversial subjects. But, by
giving him leave to write as he pleased, for or against the secularist
cause, his friend eventually cajoled him into it, and he abandoned
himself to the task. Week after week over various pseudonyms and
initials, he poured out his thoughts in essays and satires on the Established Church, the Dissenters, Roman Catholicism, muscular
Christianity, the Bible, natural science, "culture," Darwinism, the
utilitarians, the middle class, the figurehead monarchy, the functionless aristocracy, economic imperialism, jingoism, journalism,
reform bills, and, of course, the aspirations of the restless lower
classes.

Many of these polemical writings were collected and published
posthumously by G. W. Foote in a volume entitled *Satires and Profanities*.[27] The titles of some sufficiently indicate their contents: "The
Devil in the Church of England," "The Story of a Famous Old Jewish
Firm," "A Word on Blasphemy," "Religion in the Rocky Mountains,"
"Heine on an Illustrious Exile," "Jesus as God; as a Man," "The
Swinburne Controversy," "A Bible Lesson on Monarchy," "Principal Tulloch on Personal Immortality." For readers of the journals in
which they originally appeared, these hastily written pieces probably provided a vicarious outlet for pent-up resentments, although
very frequently the satire was turned on the secularists themselves.
For Thomson they were an emotional drastic. To identify the spirit
that moved him in writing many of them, Thomson quoted Goethe's

lines:

> Ich hab' mein Sach' of niches gestellt,
>   Juccha!
> Drum ist's so wohl mir in der Welt,
>   Juccha!

— lines that had already provided Max Stirner with the motto for his masterpiece of intellectual anarchism, *Der Einzige und sein Eigentum*, almost forgotten now, but once powerfully influential throughout Europe as a sustained cry of individual emancipation. Having literally committed himself to nothing that society could grant or deny him, Thomson thoroughly enjoyed the opportunity to indulge in print a venting of his spleen, flaying about him against all things on the Victorian scene that presumed to lay claim on his allegiance or respect.

In a satire entitled "Great Christ is Dead!", Thomson has indicated how he reconciled in his own mind his blasphemous utterances and the tender religious sentiments he was capable of expressing in serious poetry and prose. Thomson recounts the story, from Plutarch, of the proclamation of the death of the great god Pan in the reign of Tiberius Caesar — a story so touching that it brought tears as large as ostrich eggs rolling from the eyes of Rabelais' Pantagruel, who mistakenly referred it to "our Lord and Savior, Jesus Christ, 'ignominiously put to death by the envy and iniquity of the pontiffs, doctors, presbyters, and monks of the Mosaic dispensation.'"[28] Thomson then reminds his readers that the passing of the pagan gods, the revolution that saw nature annulled and supernature enthroned, has been a favorite theme of the great poets who, according to their religion, fantasy, and mood, have variously celebrated it in song. Milton in his hymn on the Nativity shouts harsh puritanical scorn on the "oracles striken dumb and the deities overthrown." Shelley in "Hellas" does not contest the justice of their doom, but predicts the same doom for their conqueror in his turn. Swinburne has bewailed the vanquished immortals, "with nothing but aversion and contempt for the pale Galilean." Leopardi in an early poem, "beautiful but not one of his deepest," regrets the loss of the ancient divinities, and appeals "to Nature to restore to his spirit its first fire, if indeed she lives." Schiller passionately laments them in his "Gods of Greece," and Mrs. Browning has no less passionately answered him. Novalis also laments the unsouling of Nature, but "goes on to celebrate the resurrection of humanity in Christ." But Thomson's favorite on this theme is Heine. He recalls Heine's wild picture of

the Olympians "holding high revelry, with nectar and ambrosia, with
Apollonian music and inextinguishable laughter." Suddenly there is
an unexpected commotion: "a wretched Jew staggers in, his brow
bleeding from a crown of thorns, trailing on his shoulder a heavy
cross, which he heaves upon the banquet table; and forthwith the
revel is no more, the divine feast disappears, the everburning lights
are quenched, the triumphant gods and goddesses vanish terror-
stricken, dethroned for ever and ever."[29] And now it is time, writes
Thomson, coming to the point of his essay, "to proclaim the death
of the great god Christ." Scientific enlightenment has extinguished
him and his entire Hebrew dynasty of gods. His priesthood and
Churches still hold Europe, America, and Australia, even as the
"priesthood and shrines of the Olympians held possession of the
Roman Empire centuries after the crucifixion of Jesus." But it is
plain to see that the noblest hearts and most vigorous intellects have
abandoned the creed. The knell of its doom has run and its burial is
only a matter of time. "At the risk of being thought bigoted or preju-
diced," the satirist concludes seriously,

> I must avow that to my mind the decomposition of Christianity is so
> offensively manifest and advanced, that, with the exception of a very
> few persons whose transcendent genius could throw a glamour of
> glory over any creed however crude and mean, and whom I recognize
> as far above my judgment, I can no longer give my esteem to any
> educated man who has investigated and still professes this religion,
> without grave deduction at the expense of his heart, his intellect, or
> his conscience, if not all three. Miraculous voices are not heard in
> these days; but everywhere myriads of natural voices are continually
> announcing to us, and enjoining us to announce to others, Great
> Christ is dead![30]

Thomson's conclusion here is, from the point of view of our
study, on several counts remarkable. For one, substitute "Catholicism" for "Christianity" in the penultimate sentence, and it might be
a statement of Kingsley against Newman. More remarkable is
Thomson's reservation exempting a few persons of transcendent
genius from his judgment. But most notable, perhaps, is Thomson's
easy command of the great poetry inspired by the theme. Of itself
this hastily written piece should suffice to dispel the notion that
Thomson drew primarily on "poverty, loneliness and bad health"[31]
in writing his *City*. The verses of Milton, Shelley, Leopardi, Schiller,
Novalis and Heine on the subject provide a much better gloss for
the religious argument of many parts of the *City* than the conjec-
tural insights of Dobell and Salt regarding the religious atmosphere

of Thomson's parental household.

In some of his merriest religious satires, Thomson indulges him-self with Heine, Rabelais, and Boccaccio in the pleasant expectation that gloomy, institutionalized Christianity may someday be banished from the face of the earth by hearty laughter. Boccaccio, who in some of his works presented Christianity as a spiritual plague more infectious and destructive than the merely physical plague from which his story-tellers fled, dreamt in his *Ninfale Fiesolano* of a world re-stored to pristine pagan innocence. If priests and monks and nuns would but say the word of truth that is in their hearts, the thick cloud of gloom would at once be lifted; bright laughter would once again envelop this marvelous earth. The Italian renaissance, Thomson reminds his readers, almost brought such a transformation to pass. Even the Reformation, despite its religious core, was a blessing in this regard, for it rent the entrenched ecclesiastical institution into hundreds of fragments thereby greatly diminishing its hold on the hearts and minds of men. Of the free-spirited men of the sixteenth century, Thomson writes:

> What an age was theirs! The Bible newly set free from its monastic prison house, and the veil of the temple rent in twain from the top to the bottom by the earthquakes of the Reformation; the languages and literatures of Greece and Rome just become universal scholarship. Physical science just beginning to awake from its long swoon, and a New World of marvels, half-discovered in the West. The thirst and the capacity of these men were equal to the most profuse outpourings from these fountains . . . . They received all and believed all; devoured all and digested all . . . . Whatever their religious faith, they, in thought and action, refused to be bound by its narrow limitations, and were forever bursting through their own creeds and systems, as Samson through the ropes and the withes with which he let himself be bound. A creed or system is a straight-waistcoat for Nature; and if you will persist in trying to force it upon Her, you will soon experience that the great Titaness not only flings it off with wrathful disdain, but makes yourself fit for a strait-waistcoat in recompense for your trouble.[32]

Yet, while praising the Reformation, as well as the Renaissance, for having liberated men's minds, Thomson does not confound the results of the religious upheaval with the intentions of the reform-ers, "who were just as bigoted and dogmatical" in their own way as "any of the most narrow-minded doctors of the Church." Indeed, many of the sectarian churches that emerged from the upheaval proved in the end, Thomson asserts, to be a more pernicious influence than the institution they had overcome. The medieval Church had fought the emerging monarchic states; the new churches, on the contrary, had willingly become their merest concubines. And of these concubines the most despicable surely, Thomson rants satirically, is England's Established Church, British branch office, as he calls it in one of his bitterest attacks, of a famous old Jewish firm — bastard offspring of "what is called the English Reformation, the most ignoble in Europe; which, as Macaulay remarks, merely transferred the full cup from the hand of the Pope to the hand of the King, spilling as little as possible by the way."[33]

Thomson's attacks against the Anglican Establishment simply carry to their logical conclusion a number of the arguments of the Catholics, Modernists, Dissenters, and pious agnostics of his day, all of whom in their various ways were dissatisfied with the Church of the via media, "Romish in its liturgy, Protestant in its articles, Erastian in its government, and committed to an untenable Bibliolatry."[34] But for his sharpest cuts of satire Thomson preferred to draw on the prudence of those adherents and friends of the Church who were laboring assiduously to get it to live religiously on what Lionel Trilling has called "a somewhat reduced budget."[35] One cannot help admiring, Thomson says, their Anglo-Saxon business sense. In "The Story of an Old Jewish Firm," published in 1865, Thomson traces the history of the *business* of the Judaic Christian religion from its foundation by ancient Jah, who did business exclusively with the Jews, through the long course of its world-wide expansion under the management of Mary and Jesus, to the current operations of the British branch office, whose broad-minded clerks openly acknowledge that its operation does not depend for its continuance on the actual existence of its founding Father, Son, and Holy Spirit, that it, in fact, "merely uses the names and would be precisely the same business if these names covered no personages."[36] The long satire is remarkably well-informed from a historical point of view, and is, in effect, a working out in unambiguous language of what Carlyle meant by his Hebrew old clothes and what Arnold was to suggest a few years later with his image of the "three Lords Shaftesbury." The piece has had its enthusiastic admirers. For W. K. Clifford, the eminent mathematical physicist, it was a "piece of exquisite mordant satire worthy of Swift."[37] And for Professor B. I. Evans, also, it was a work of "assaulting power," of the sort "Swift might have produced had he been an atheist and not a Christian."[38] Yet, on some modern readers, the satire is apt to leave a very different kind of impression.

Scholars who have followed the steady retreat of rationalistic "higher criticism" in recent decades are apt to feel a second edge cutting in Thomson's satire; for it is simultaneously a burlesque of ecclesiastical history and *a reductio ad absurdum* of the arguments and methods of rationalistic historiography.

In *The City of Dreadful Night* Thomson will represent an "established church" reduced to an absolutely minimal budget — Christless, Godless, attempting to make a religion of humanity's self-love. The actual Church, he felt, was already essentially emptied of true believers. In "The Established Church," one of his less boisterous satires, he distinguishes five classes of professed Christians usually numbered among the adherents of the Church who are really not members of it in a religious sense and who therefore constitute rather its weakness than its strength. The first class consists of the great mass of cowards and hypocrites who "simply cling to what appears the dominant party, and who would therefore call themselves atheists were atheism in the ascendant."[39] Thomson contemptuously rules them out of consideration with Dante's phrase: *non ragionam di lor*. The second class consists of those who are incapable of sane affection, though they may easily be frenzied by an *in*sane fanaticism, "in which state they can die as devotedly as they can murder atrociously." The third group consists of eminent practical men-soldiers, sailors, lawyers, engineers, statesmen — who acquiesce in whatever creed is prevalent because their real church is the world; and they "no more add to the strength of their nominal church than did the *savants* to that of Napoleon's army in Egypt — those *savants* whom the wise Napoleon always ordered (with the donkeys) to the center whenever an attack was expected."[40]

To these three groups, whose connection with the Church is more or less accidental, Thomson adds two others whose adherence is deliberate. The first consists of the supersubtle: laymen and divines of first rate talent, who enjoy exercising their intellects and who "instinctively feel that it is much harder to champion any existing institution than to attack it, and naturally (like all unconquerable knights errant) prefer the most difficult *devoir*." Thomson recalls Macaulay's remark that Halifax, the Trimmer, always joined the losing side as a matter of honor. Thus the adhesion of such men to the Church, Thomson argues, "though seeming to strengthen it, really proclaims its weakness."[41] The fifth and final class consists of the supremely reverential, "men whose lofty reason is drowned in a yet deeper faith, as mountain peaks high as the highest in the air are said to be sub-

merged in the abysses of the Atlantic." We noted earlier that
Thomson in "Great Christ is Dead!" exempted a few men and women
of transcendent genius from his judgment against educated persons
who profess to be Christians. Here he attempts to characterize them
more fully in words that recall the "Grande Chartreuse" and anticipate some of the inverted religious images of the *City*. These supremely reverential spirits, he explains, do not conceal from themselves the defects of their Church.

> They even realize the danger of its total fall; but they cannot tear
> themselves away from the venerable building wherein all their fore-
> fathers were buried in hopes of a happy resurrection; whose chants
> were the rapturous music and whose windows were the heavenly
> glories of their pure childhood; whose prayers they repeated night
> after night and morning after morning at their mother's knee. Can
> they leave this, with all its treasured holiness of antiquity for some
> new bold glaring erection, wherein men certainly congregate to talk
> about God, but which might just as well be used as a warehouse or a
> manufactury? No; rather than leave it they will believe, they will force
> themselves to believe that some miraculous renovation is at hand.

The members of this fifth group keep the Church from falling
into insignificance, but they are not essentially hers. They "do not
derive their religiousness from, but really bestow it upon the Church
in which they pray." She is the dead stone animated by their
pygmalion artistry. And they are indeed idolaters, writes Thomson,
"for they worship a creation of their own souls." Poignantly he concludes: "When one thinks of certain noble men and women — as
Maurice and Kingsley, Ruskin and the Brownings — devoting themselves in spite of themselves to an effete faith, one is sadly reminded
of poor Abishag the Shunamite wasting and withering her healthful
youth to cherish worn out David, 'who knew her not,' who could fill
her with no new life, and who was, despite her cherishing, so certainly near death."[42]

But while Thomson can be tender with those who persist in hoping that the lifeless state of the Established Church is but a swoon
from which it may yet awaken, he is mercilessly harsh in his treatment of those who live off the pretended vitality of the mummy.
Shall we keep that mummy from its sepulchre? he asks. Shall we
"continue to allot immense revenues to her army of servitors who
have no service to render?" In a satire entitled "The Primate on the
Church and the World," Thomson examines the Archbishop of
Canterbury's claim that "no other body" in England "can claim that
commanding influence over the thought of the age, which by God's

blessing" has been assigned to the ecclesiastical hierarchy. In the present age, with "uneasy thought seething throughout the nation," it is fortunate, the Archbishop had said, that the arrangements of cathedral bodies provide places for study where men of "serious and earnest learning" may prepare themselves to guide an anxious age. Thomson replies: "Is it not as notorious as it is disgraceful . . . that, with few exceptions, the canons and other dignitaries make scarcely any contribution to the thought or scholarship or science of the age, in return for the large leisure and ample stipends with which they are endowed?"[43] The thought of the age is embodied not in stalled, ruminating canons of the Church, but in "such persons as Spencer and Darwin, Huxley and Tyndall, Carlyle and Browning, George Eliot and George Meredith; and what a commanding influence the State Church has over these!"[44] As for its national influence, everyone knows, Thomson concludes, that "a large portion of the educated classes, and the great bulk of the artisans, are either skeptical or indifferent, and that more than a half of the shopkeepers are Nonconformists bent on Disestablishment and Disendowment."[45]

The ruminating dignitaries of the Church are easily satirized. But what of the young, healthy-minded new element popularly known as muscular Christianity? It is generally taken for granted, Thomson writes in a satire entitled "Kingsley's Convertites," that the new muscular Christianity offers a cheerful improvement over the old Christianity; that it is a "liberal cultus which does not sacrifice body to soul any more than soul to body."[46] And yet if one troubles himself to read Kingsley's novels (Thomson asserts that he has duly "read and enjoyed" all that have appeared), one finds that the doctrine illustrated in them is altogether at variance with the popular impression. Each of Kingsley's novels portrays at least one important figure who is "more or less naturally good but decidedly Godless at the beginning," and who undergoes a conversion that makes him "Godfearing and saintly at the end." Thomson proposes to run through the stories of these conversions, holding with Shakespeare's Jaques that "Out of these convertites / There is much matter to be heard and learned."[47] In a series of lively summaries Thomson shows that in every case the conversion is effected through misfortune. The characters become religious not when healthy but when diseased. Such a view of religion, Thomson remarks, may be correct or incorrect, wise or foolish; but surely it is strangely at variance with the one commonly ascribed to Kingsley's group and "strangely identical with that which Doctor Newman explicitly avows in the most

eloquent pages of his 'Apologia'."[48] Thomson says that he had followed with pleasure the recent quarrel between Kingsley and
Newman "in which the latter got the former 'into chancery' and
punished him so pitilessly"; and that he had been particularly amused,
as the fight continued, to realize how thorough was the "agreement
at the bottom of the two who were struggling so fiercely at the top."[49]
Squirm though they may, the Kingsleys and the Maurices remain
inextricably caught in an impossible dilemma. Attempting to be both
worldly and Christian they succeed in being neither. To glorify the
power and grace of God they must show men plagued with misfortune, in utter need and unable to help themselves. Yet in their efforts to call men to a more active muscular Christian life, they must
show their God in need, unable, without the help of zealous men, to
realize His plans for the world. It is the ancient dilemma of pious
Pelagianism — and there is, Thomson agrees with Newman, no *via
media*. Of the God of these muscular Christians, Thomson writes:
"Of all the rulers we hear of — the ex-King of Naples, the King of
Prussia, the Elector of Hesse-Cassel, Abraham Lincoln and the Pope
included — the poor God of Maurice is most to be pitied: a God
whose world is in so deplorable a state that the good man who owns
Him lives in a perpetual fever of anxiety and misery in endeavoring
to improve it for Him."[50] And of the manhood and womanhood of
Kingsley's romances, he concludes: "If the Church of the future is to
be composed of creatures like Kingsley's convertites, Westminster
Abbey must be turned into a Grand Chartreuse, and St. Paul's into
an Hospital for Incurables, and the metropolitan Cathedral of England must be bedlam."[51]

But the most interesting of Thomson's essays on the English
Church, from the point of view of this study, are those in which he
focuses his satire on Arnold's unorthodox defense of it. We have
already touched upon the relation of Thomson's poetry to Arnold's —
a relation that has not altogether escaped the notice of critics. In a
recent study of the language of nineteenth century poetry, *The Romantic Assertion*, R. A. Foakes has attempted to show in detail that
the "disintegration of the romantic vision" which forms the substance
of the best poetry of Arnold is brought to completion in that "most
remarkable sequel to Arnold's poetry . . . James Thomson's *The City
of Dreadful Night*."[52] Half a century earlier, Bertram Dobell had remarked that "Matthew Arnold . . . in Thomson's place might very
well have written 'The City of Dreadful Night," while Thomson,
brought up as Arnold was, might conceivably have been the author

of 'Literature and Dogma.'"[53] That Arnold's poetry expressed the "main movement of mind" of the Victorian era, Thomson would readily have admitted. But for Arnold's religious and social "criticism" he had far less regard. The rigorous teachers of Arnold's youth whose voices seemed to chide him for weeping over his lost faith in the Grande Chartreuse, had not been rigorous enough, apparently, to prevent him from becoming, later in his career, an amateur of Christianity. Addressing himself primarily to a class of people who still cherished the religion in which he could no longer believe, Arnold sometimes permitted himself to fall back, as Lionel Trilling phrases it, "on a juggling both with facts and with terminology — and into unreality."[54] Thomson, guarded against such lapses by the continued scrutiny of militant atheists, judged him severely on that account, but tempered his severity with a touch of good-humored satire.

Arnold, Thomson seems to have believed, was urging the Church of England to resolve the dilemma that troubled the Maurices and Kingsleys by minimizing its supernatural character and by emphasizing a social concern. Fearful of the social disorders that secularist reforms invariably foment, Arnold was anxious to channel the aspirations of the lower classes through a Church reconstituted to serve as a great national society for the promotion of goodness. Replying to Arnold's public assertion that the Church "may yet recover its hold upon the non-religious working-classes," Thomson writes: "To me, studying signs of the times as well as I can, and perhaps knowing more of the non-religious working-classes than Mr. Arnold has had the opportunity of learning, it appears manifest that these are ever growing more and more alienated from not only the State Church but from all revealed religion, and that their numbers are continually increasing."[55] What are the grounds, Thomson asks, for Arnold's confidence in the Church as a vehicle of social reform? With all his willingness to juggle words Arnold could not pretend that the Church in its present condition inspired confidence. He therefore looked to its past, arguing eloquently that every Church is to be judged by its great men whose utterances survive as authoritative, who "strike the note to be finally taken by the Church." There is truth in this, Thomson admits; but truth for the future. Just as a man's prime gives the true measure of his career when it is over, so the great men of the Church will provide the measure of its worth when it has passed into history. But what of the present? When we must deal with a senile and distracted old man in his senility, the accomplishments of his prime are hardly relevant. "It is just so," Thomson argues, "with the verdict we must pass on the Church of England in its present condition. It had great men in it of old, because of old men could be great in it; it has great men in it no longer, because men can no longer be great in it, in being great they are too large for it, in growing great they outgrow its limitations."[56]

Yet, Thomson cannot readily forget that Arnold, the Church apologist, is also the author of the "Stanzas from the Grande Chartreuse." He finds it pathetic as well as comical to see that fine poet at work "trimming" arguments in his anxiety to keep the old Church going. "Mr. Arnold's proper fields," Thomson writes, "are poetry and artistic literary criticism; there he can cultivate his serene temper, his large views, and his fine distinctions to the utmost advantage of himself and his readers." But when he enters upon the "brawling controversies of the day" he makes one think, Thomson says, of a "mild and soft-speaking gentleman who should saunter about gracefully among the vehicles during the hubbub of the crush in Fleet-street or Cheapside, addressing words of sweet soothing and calm admonition to the exasperated and abjurgating drivers." Lionel Trilling in his biography reminds us that when Whitman saw Arnold as the "perfect Philistine" he was seeing "something that had to be seen."[57] Thomson saw that "something" and, despite his sympathy for the poet, could not resist the temptation to portray candidly what he saw:

> If it may be written without disrespect, I will venture to hint that on these occasions he rather reminds us of that lord, neat and trimly dressed, who came to Harry Hotspur after Holmedon fight . . . . And it must be confessed that his very serene bearing and very superior cool and gentle talk makes most of us sympathize with Hot Harry:
>
>   . . . he made me mad
> To see him shine so brisk and smell so sweet
> And talk so like a waiting gentlewoman
> Of guns and drums and wounds . . . .
>   . . . that it was great pity, so it was,
> This villainous salt-petre should be digg'd
> Out of the bowels of the harmless earth,
> Which many a good tall fellow had destroy'd
> So cowardly; and but for these vile guns,
> He would himself have been a soldier.[58]

Yet Thomson, too, had a sentimental regard for Christianity that occasionally broke through his satire. Though he never mitigated his severe judgment against the many who seemed to make a comfortable living by religious pretense, he felt himself occasionally "smitten with shame and remorse" by the realization that his blasphemous writings may have offended persons of true faith. On such occasions, he says, he seems to see "faces worn with suffering and fasting and self-renunciation" looking reproachfully at him from the gloom of the past. And on every face he reads the sad question: "Did I, O my dear friend, live and die thus and thus that you should laugh and fleer?"[59] It is the question Luther had to confront, as he tells us in his great treatise on the servile will (*De Serveo Arbitric*), the question that seared his heart when he determined to put Christian charity aside and to judge all things by the rule of faith alone. According to the rule of Christian charity, which is kind, loves its enemies, returns good for evil, and gains in being deceived, Thomson, like Luther, admits that he has been a through transgressor. But he has pledged himself to truth, and truth does not suffer itself to be deceived, even for love's sake. In words reminiscent of Luther's eloquent reply to the reproofs of Erasmus, Thomson addresses himself apologetically to the truly religious:

> Beloved and pure and beautiful souls, these whom I was mocking are not of you, though indeed they assume your name; they are of the fraternities of those who in your lifetimes mocked and hated and persecuted and killed you; they have caught up your solemn passwords because these are now passwords to wealth and worldly honour, which for you were passwords to the prison and the scaffold and the stake . . . . They desecrate your holy mysteries, they stereotype your rapturous prayers into jargon and cant; for your eucharistic wine they have publicans' gin-and-water, and your eucharistic bread they butter on both sides and flavour with slander at tea. Even I, poor heathen and cynic, am nearer to you, ye holy ones, than are ninety-nine in a hundred of these.[60]

One might indeed make a case for Thomson on this last point, but the task would be difficult and the result, at best, bathetic. It is simpler to treat him as a disreputable rebel, and, as one turns from his account with religion to his view of Victorian society and politics, not only simpler but more accurate. Thomson committed himself emphatically on the subject very early in his journalistic career. In the essay on Burns from which we quoted earlier, he wrote: "Alas for the times when honesty and valour must turn rebels! Not the least harm done by shallow and hypocritical respectability is its disgusting sincere men into disrespectability."[61]

By the time Thomson was writing his political and social satires, rebellion against the conventions of English middle class society was itself fast becoming a socially acceptable convention. After Carlyle, Thackaray, Ruskin, and Arnold, Gigadibs too was ready to cry "Philistine!" with the expectation that he might even earn a living at it, like the court jesters of old who used now and then to rally their royal masters. But in Thomson's mode of satire there is something that guards against its adoption by Leslie Stephen's "prigs." Herman Melville remarked its distinctive character in a letter to an English friend who had sent him a volume of Thomson's prose writings. "It is a long time," Melville wrote,

> . . . since I have been so interested in a volume as in that of the "Essays and Phantasies" — "Bumble," "Indolence," "The Poet," etc. Each is so admirably honest and original . . . that it would have been wonderful indeed had they hit the popular taste. They would have to be painstakingly diluted for that — diluted with that prudential worldly element wherewith Mr. Arnold has conciliated the conventionalists, while at the same time showing the absurdity of Bumble. But for [Thomson] this would be too much like trimming . . . . The motions of his mind in the best of these essays are utterly untrammelled and independent and yet falling naturally into grace and beauty. It is good for me to think of such a mind — to know that such a brave intelligence has been."[62]

Like Arnold, Thomson directed his political and social criticism primarily against the middle class — heirs in spite of themselves to the power formerly wielded by absolute monarchs, landed aristocrats, and merchant adventurers. But he did not in the least pretend that his writings were designed to improve the lot of the lower classes, much less to awaken a sense of responsibility in those whom he satirizes. His criticism is sheerest satire, indulged in for its own sake, providing an emotional catharsis for the writer and a vicarious equivalent for sympathetic readers.

In an essay entitled "Bumble, Bumbledom, Bumbleism," written in 1865 in response to Arnold's essay on Heinrich Heine in the *Cornhill Magazine*, Thomson argues against the adoption of the German term *Philistinism* to designate the monotonous routine of English middle-class existence. He agrees with Arnold that the English term *respectable*, as scornfully used by Carlyle, and the French term *épicier*, are less apt and expressive than the German *Philistine*. But he objects to the German term because, he says, it misrepresents the English situation. The so-called Philistines of the continent are indeed, like the English middle class, "slaves to routine, enemies of light, stupid and oppressive"; but they operate very differently. They uphold the despotism of absolute governments and, by their "stupid and cowardly passivity" or active connivance, empower the agents of tyranny to oppress the children of light by brute force and the more merciless machinery of bureaucracy and *espionage*. Ranged against the Philistines are the continental "men of ideas," who resort to conspiracies, assassinations, and revolutions in their desperate struggles for "liberty of speech, liberty of press, and civil freedom, with imprisonment or exile or death as the forfeit if they lose."[63] In England the social warfare is of an entirely different order; and therefore, Thomson argues, the contenders ought to have different names. Thomson recommends as the English equivalent for the continental Philistine the term Bumble — which is not only heavy, obese, rotund, a "genuine John Bull mouthful of awkwardness," but also happily associated in sound with many other fine English words such as grumble, stumble, mumble, jumble, fumble, rumble, crumble, tumble, "all heads of families of the very choicest middle-class blood in the language."[64]

Arnold, Thomson continues, flatters both the oppressors and the oppressed with his designations. By suggesting that a Goliath oppresses them, he encourages the children of light in England to imagine that they are heroic Davids. There had once been an English Goliath but he was thoroughly overcome in the seventeenth century, his spear broken and his armor shattered. Englishmen now are no longer deprived of the extreme necessaries, but merely of some of the comforts and many of the luxuries of intellectual and moral freedom. They have liberty of speech and press and civic independence. All that oppresses the children of light in their midst is the inertial weight of Bumble, "who is by no means terrible, except as a 'terrible bore.'" The men of ideas in England advance against their oppressors not with swords but with Reform Bills, or a repeal of the Corn Laws. When they undertake to rouse the people, they do not think of barricades; they write to and for journals, have public dinners, meetings, and debates, get up petitions, and frame bills for presentation in Parliament. Good society may reject them, but they are not threatened by fortress, bullet, or scaffold; and society's contempt does not really hurt them, for "their own particular society, the people among whom they live day and night are full of admiration and enthusiasm."[65]

Thomson was well aware of the course of political expediency that had led historically from a regime of absolute monarchy to the predominance of the middle class in England. He acknowledged the great services rendered by the royal houses of old in securing economic power and political unity for the country during the era of emerging national states. Glorious in his eyes were the "great men who fronted Charles I with the sword, and at last beheaded him with the axe"; and admirable also were the lesser men "who got William of Orange to shoulder James II out of his palace and then finessed his flight into abdication." Those were the last "really desperate and dangerous national battles with Philistinism" fought and won in England; and then it was that Goliath was reduced to a figurehead, maintained in complete subordination to Parliament merely as a guard against tyranny or a further devolution of political power.[66] Since that time social conflicts in England, according to Thomson's view, have taken on a character anything but heroic. Throne, nobility, and clergy, now constitute a facade government sustained by laissez faire capitalism as a system of protection against foreign aggressors and the awakening appetites of the traditionally docile working classes. The political future of England will depend, Thomson was predicting in the sixties, not on revolutions, but on a well-timed extension of suffrage, and eventually on the capacity of an elite of wealth or intellectual cunning to sway the votes of the enfranchised masses.

But it was already clear in Thomson's day that popular vote could be swayed in England only by raising the popular standard of living. And it was equally clear that the gains of the lower classes could be realized without loss to the upper classes only by intensifying English economic imperialism. Thomson was by no means a doctrinaire anti-imperialist. In fact, he held the old imperialism, built up after the defeat of the Spanish Armada, and sustained through the Napoleonic wars by official daring and popular restraint, in high esteem as an heroic institution. But the new imperialism instituted to satiate the great lord of many stomachs and pockets — the masses — was of an entirely different kind. It fought "brutally iniquitous battue-wars against tribes of ill-armed savages," and popular writers added to the ignominy by celebrating the miserable skirmishes in Asia and Africa as though they were new Waterloos. Thomson saw signs of a total degradation of national character in the fact that "the Court, the Senate, Pall-Malldom, the majority of the nobles and clergy and middle classes," were vying "with the slums, the music halls, the hirelings of the Press, and the cosmopolitan gamblers of the Exchange" in glorifying that "vilest Blatant Beast, Jingoism."[67] But in any event, with the institution of this new imperialism, it is absurd to pretend that there are any serious class struggles going on in England. The lower classes are receiving their reward, with the backward regions of the world supplying the margin of gain. Talk of oppressors and oppressed in Victorian England, therefore, readily lends itself to satire.

The wealth of Bumble, Thomson elaborates, rules the minds of men in England primarily by its control of press and publication. Journalists, who are always boasting of their independence of mind, deny that they are controlled. But how many of them, Thomson is fond of asking, really dare to speak their thoughts honestly? In a short piece entitled "The Swinburne Controversy," Thomson vented his spleen on the subject, defending *Poems and Ballads* (which he had not read) on principle against the critics of the *Saturday Review* and the *Athenaeum* who had been shocked by it. Replying to a charge that his verses were hardly fit to be read aloud to young ladies in a drawing room, Swinburne had asserted that he wrote for grown men; to which one of his critics responded that men had read the book and had condemned it. Thomson comments with a snarl:

> . . . as if our present brood of periodical critics were men. At home in private life some of them probably are: but in their critical capacity, that is to say, incapacity, how many of them have any virility? . . . These men who know well what they are doing are the accomplices of Bumble who does not know what he is doing, who fondly thinks that he is doing something very different, in starving on thin diet and stupifying with narcotic drugs the intellect of our nation once so robust and active; and assuredly if the process goes on much longer we shall come to rank mentally as a third rate power in Europe.[68]

The press is constantly proclaiming itself the liberator of popular intelligence; and Bumble is constantly seconding the claim by accusing it of leading the "poor ignorant people astray . . . to perish in the Wilderness of Sin and New Ideas!" It is a good joke between them, Thomson writes; and "we poor stupid people," resolved to emigrate from Bumbledom, are thereby easily induced to follow these self-proclaimed leaders of public opinion round and round and round, until, weary and disheartened, we come to rest where we started, "discontentedly contented for another period."[69]

But the poets and literary men themselves, on the whole, are hardly less subservient than their journalistic critics. Of the English writers able to earn a living with their pen, there are not more than half-a-dozen, Thomson asserts, "who have ever attempted since they were mature to publish their thoughts and feelings on subjects interdicted by Bumble." He cites the example of Thackeray who, after having proposed to supply, in *Pendennis*, a full and faithful portrait of a man such as no English novelist since Fielding had attempted, quietly abandoned his scheme when the circulation of the journal in which the novel was appearing serially began to fall off. When such is Thackeray, Thomson asks, "what must be Gigadibs."[70]

Thomson does not, however, wholly spare himself on this score. He too, as a journalist, is in his own way determined by circumstances, and he therefore concludes by turning his satire upon himself:

> . . . one little confession. Were I a well known author, flourishing on authorship, and writing for a respectable periodical, I should never dream of exposing, even so slightly as I have exposed, the solemn mysteries of Bumbleism. Luckily I am an author thoroughly unknown, and writing for a periodical of the deepest disrepute. One is very free, with no name to lose; and one is freer still, with such a name that it cannot possibly be lost for a worse; and, between us, we possess both these happy freedoms . . . . There are always two or three really great writers living who fling assured wealth and reputation to the winds, and dash their heads against Bumbledom. But these exceptions are so rare . . . that, though very important in themselves, they are hardly worth reckoning as a limitation to the broad rule that he who attacks Bumbledom is he who has not the power to thrive in the world as it is.[71]

D. INDOLENCE

Had he been willing to support the "working-class ideals," Thomson might easily have made a career for himself as a journalistic and literary champion of a better and happier democratic society. Bradlaugh, the Holyoakes — indeed, all the leaders and publicists of the radical reform movement — held him in the highest esteem, despite his unwillingness to identify himself positively with their cause; and they would no doubt have welcomed him as a chief literary spokesman for their position had he been willing to assume the charge. But Thomson could no more pretend to believe in "the people" than he could pretend to be a Christian. In fact, his longest essay in social criticism, "Proposals for the Speedy Extinction of Evil and Misery," contains a devastating attack on the "popular ideal." Writing of the Electoral Reform Bill of 1867, shortly after its passage, and addressing himself to readers of a journal dedicated to the establishment of a radical democracy, Thomson thus pointedly appraises its political significance:

> The problem is: Given a vast number of timbers, nearly all more or

less rotten, it is required to build a sea-worthy ship. To which our Reform Bill answers in triumph: Let us use the whole lot indiscriminately! Or in other terms: Given a foul and deformed body politic, full of all manner of diseases, required to make it pure, handsome and healthy. To which our Reform Bill answers cheerfully: Let us clothe it in fine new constitutional garments, with splints, bandages, padding, a good wig, a glass eye, a few false teeth, and so forth, and a complete cure will doubtless be effected![72]

The long satire is valuable as an index to Thomson's thought because it reviews almost all the proposals advanced in Victorian England for the improvement of man's lot on earth. In the twelfth canto of *The City of Dreadful Night*, inhabitants of the City, entering its great cathedral, will confess their former adherence to equivalents of many of these Victorian schemes in response to a cowled preacher's challenge: "Whence come you in the world of Life and Light / To this our City of Tremendous Night?" In "Proposals for the Speedy Extinction of Evil and Misery," the list of optimistic creeds is spun out to include the various Christian reform groups, National Secularists, Atheists, Theists, Deists, Pantheists, Necessitarians, Utilitarians, Positivists, "the International League of Peace and Liberty, together with all other Peace Societies and Liberal Associations, Socialists, Communists, Internationalists,"[73] Temperance Societies, Vegetarians, political radicals, republicans, conservatives, royalists, ritualists, spiritualists, ultramontanes, and faithful worshippers of Mumbo Jumbo. The satirist calls upon all these to support his own modest proposal as the surest way of gaining the sublime ends they have been striving to attain. His scheme calls for a radical attack upon the two-fold ultimate cause of all evil and misery: the misconduct of men and the misconduct of nature. Once men are made perfect instead of imperfect, and once the universe of Nature is "made altogether and exactly such as the perfect men shall require," surely the "pilgrimage of man from hell on earth to heaven on earth will be completed . . . evil and misery, both as suffering and vice, will be extinct beyond resurrection . . . everybody will be good and happy everywhere evermore."[74] To those who object that the radical reform of man will not be easy to effect, Thomson replies that it must be easier than any of the partial reforms heretofore proposed, which have, for the most part, attempted to get "plentiful fruit from a barren tree, and clean water from a foul stream." Moreover, nearly every reformer, "whether social or political, moral or religious," has hitherto attempted to make large numbers of people, all fundamentally different in character, temperament, minds, bodies and circum-

stances, act together as if they were not different. This modest proposal, on the contrary, strikes at the root of the difficulty, attempting to eliminate at once all the inequalities, differences, imperfec-
tions that move men to treat one another unequally, differently,
imperfectly[75] — including distinctions of sex. Is it possible, the satirist asks, that "when all social, political, religious, moral, intellectual,
and other distinctions have been done away with . . . these perfect
human beings will allow nature to violate decency and thorough
equality by perpetuating the gross distinctions of sex?" But perhaps
the perfecting process itself will either unsex or androgynise its subjects, "so that all alike shall be regenerated either neutral or epicene."[76]

With men rendered absolutely equal in perfection, the next task
will be the reformation of the universe of Nature. That task too is
much simpler than people have heretofore realized, says the satirist.
Man is, after all, the "very crown and head of Nature," the sole rational being, as all secularists and Darwinians are well aware, that Nature can boast of. It ought to be clear, therefore, that, "since man is
the head of Nature, to cut off him would be to decapitate her." In
the past Nature has had other heads, and, if given time, she will
probably manage to replace her present head with a better or at
least stronger one. But what if man were to threaten Nature with
sudden decapitation, depriving her of time to develop a replace-
ment? Nature loves life too passionately (self-preservation is her first
law) to defy a threat that would mean her certain destruction if carried through. From this inexpugnable proposition, the satirist draws
the fateful practical corollary, "that the human race, so long as no
other is ready to supersede it, can compel Nature to do what it pleases,
by resolving on instant universal suicide in case of her refusal."[77]
With all due modesty, and without disrespect for the scientists of
the past, Thomson continues, it must be acknowledged that this is
the "most important law of nature discoverable by man," for it gives
him the "simplest and easiest of formulas for working instantaneously
the perfection of the universe." The idea of cowing nature by such a
threat should commend itself especially to working-class leaders, for
it is merely "the forcible plan of 'strikes' by labour against capital,
applied in its utmost extension by man against nature." You already
have mere trades' unions, the satirist argues pointedly; you have
only to organize a "universal Man-union, and threaten, if all your
demands are not immediately granted to 'strike' living, to 'turn out'
of human existence, and you will at once bring the everlasting em-
ployer to reason."[78]

But what of the past? Will perfect men be so callous in their feelings, the satirist asks, as to ignore all the past sufferings of men, all the past disorders of nature? Hardly. They will know that time — past, present, and future — is essentially one, and that "to thoroughly reform the present and the future, we must thoroughly reform the past." In a paragraph that anticipates many images of the *City*, Thomson writes:

> This great river of human Time (rivers were expressly created to feed metaphors, allegories, and navigable canals) which comes flowing down thick with filth and blood from the immemorial past, surely cannot be thoroughly cleansed by any purifying process applied to it here in the present; for the pollution, if not in its very source (supposing it has a source), or deriving from unimaginable remotenesses of eternity indefinitely beyond its source, at any rate interfused with it countless ages back, and is perennial as the river itself. This immense poison-tree of Life, with its leaves of illusion, blossoms of delirium, apples of destruction, surely cannot be made wholesome and sweet by anything we may do to the branchlets and twigs on which, poor insects, we find ourselves crawling, or to the leaves and fruit on which we must fain feed; for the venom is drawn up in the sap by the tap roots plunged in abysmal depths of the past.[79]

But the past can be reformed as thoroughly as the future, the satirist urges, through the instantaneous plenipotentiality of the dual-perfecting process proposed by him. To the ordinary imperfect intelligence this may seem paradoxical. And yet to anyone who has pondered the mysteries that underlie simple arithmetic, geometry, algebra, and the higher mathematics, to anyone who has worked "with negative signs, surds, imaginary roots, with infinite series and infinitesimals, which metaphysically baffle human comprehension," paradox will be no hindrance. As in the infinitesimal calculus, so in the reformation of Man and Nature, "useful and practically trustworthy results are the real and sufficient justification of the paradox and mystery."[80]

Innate modesty, regard for the great modern rule of the division of labor, physical exhaustion brought on by the intense exertion of elaborating these proposals, commercial etiquette that requires the promoter of a venture to keep in the background, horror of the indignities that attend fame — all these, the author says, keep him from working the marvelous change he proposes in himself. He awaits but the initiative of another, and wonders, with Alfred de Musset, who will be the first among us to make himself divine — "*Qui de nous, qui de nous va devenir un Dieu?*"[81] But if, after all he has done, other men refuse to take the initiative, his conscience will be clear; the responsibility of the damnation of Man and Nature will not rest on him. With Stoic firmness he is prepared to stand alone, comforted by the thought that he has done his duty:

> And remaining thus in a sublime minority of one (as remaineth eternally the most dread Lord God of monotheism), I can administer unto myself the consolation of that blessed truth which Cacciaguida in Paradise administered to Dante (to Dante Durante, the long-enduring Giver), the supreme stoical truth for the honest and independent thinker: Well shall it be for thee, to have made thyself a party by thyself:
>
> Sì ch'a te fia bello
Averti fatta parte per te stesso.[82]

Thomson, in fact, thought of himself as an exile among the secularist reformers even as Dante had been an exile among the Bianchi and Ghibellines of Florence. He shared the secularists' hostility toward the established order of society, but none of their hopes for national reform. All the while he lived in their noisy company, he was attempting to make good his youthful vow to wait in silence and darkness beside the dead body of Christ. A few years after completing the *City*, Thomson severed entirely his connections with Bradlaugh, even to the extent of accusing his old friend publicly of having betrayed his original forthright purposes in order to advance himself by any means as a popular leader.[83] But much earlier, in a pair of satires written shortly before the ceremonial fire of his thirty-fifth year, Thomson had humorously confessed his isolation. The first, entitled, "Indolence: A Moral Essay," begins with a protest against Carlyle and his disciples, with their continual cry of work! work! work!, which is "simply the Imperative mood of a doctrine which, couched in the quiet Indicative, reads, 'Mankind is a damned rascal.'"[84] Thomson then proceeds, in praise of indolence, to distinguish seven classes of idlers, ranging from the common *lazzarone* type up to those who are idlers by Faith. The idlers by Faith, among whom he numbers himself, are of two kinds — the pious with their Almighty Father above them, and the fatalists with their universe of inexorable laws. "The spiritual root is the same in both," Thomson concludes, "though the one bears blossoms of mystical ravishment under the heaven of Providence, and the other dark leaves of oracular Stoicism under the iron vault of Destiny. Extremes meet; always, extremes meet."[85]

In the second essay, "A National Reformer in the Dog-Days," the satirist complains that lack of energy has compelled him to abandon his efforts to keep pace with the world's reformers. All he can do is sit quietly and look on glumly as the long column of valiant men and women in the army of progress marches by and gradually disappears down the edge of the horizon. But then suddenly he is reconciled with his lot. For it occurs to him that, if the reformers continue their progress, and if the world is truly round, they must inevitably reappear at the opposite edge of the horizon and eventually pass again the very place where he left them. And so the author resolves to recline comfortably on the ground where he finds himself and await the inevitable return of the reformers, using the interval of rest to write hymns of praise to their valor and fortitude; "panegyrics and high paeans which [he] had not the leisure to compose, or the voice to sing," while he himself was marching and fighting with them.[86]

Thomson was a skillful idler. Alcohol and tobacco set him physically in a dull comfortable stupor, he used to say; music overwhelmed his emotions; and in literature he found an idler's substitute for living.

NOTES

1. Salt, *Life*, p. 46.

2. T. S. Eliot, *Selected Essays* (New York, 1932), p. 7.

3. Bertram Dobell, ed., *The Poetical Works of James Thomson* (London, 1895), I, liii.

4. Walker, *James Thomson (B.V.)*, p. 2.

5. Salt, *Life*, p. 45: Bertram Dobell, ed., *A Voice from the Nile*, by James Thomson (London, 1884), p. xxvii.

6. *Poetical Works*, II, 368.

7. *Ibid.*, II, p. 380.

8. *Ibid.*, II, p. 378.

9. *Ibid.*, II, p. 132.

10. *Ibid.*, II, p. 147.

11. *Ibid.*, II, p. 190.

12. *Ibid.*, II, p. 163.

13. *Ibid.*, II, p. 166.

14. *Ibid.*, II, p. 182.

15. *Ibid.*, II, p. 183-89.

16. Gerould, *Poems of James Thomson*, p. viii.

17. *The Complete Poetical Works of Percy Bysshe Shelley*, Thomas Hutchinson, ed. (New York, 1933), p. 264.

18. *Poetical Works*, II, 442-43.

19. Dante Alighieri, *Opere*, p. 261.

20. George Saintsbury, *A History of Criticism and Literary Taste* (London, 1922), III, 553.

21. Hypatia Bradlaugh Bonner's *Charles Bradlaugh* (London, 1908) is the chief source for our account of Bradlaugh's life.

22. *Encyclopedia Britannica*, III, 1008.

23. *Poems, Essays & Fragments*, p. 93.

24. *Ibid.*, p. 94.

25. See Salt, *Life*, pp. 34-35.

26. Matthew Arnold, *St. Paul and Protestantism* (New York, 1924), p. 312.

27. Thomson, *Satires and Profanities*, ed. G. W. Foote (London, 1884).

28. *Ibid.*, p. 106.

29. *Ibid.*, pp. 106-107.

30. *Ibid.*, pp. 108-109.

31. R. A. Foakes, *The Romantic Assertion* (New Haven, 1958), p. 169.

32. Thomson, *Essays and Phantasies*, (London, 1881), pp. 186-189.

33. *Satires and Profanities*, p. 39.

34. Willey, *More Nineteenth Century Studies*, p. 12.

35. Lionel Trilling, *Matthew Arnold* (New York, 1955), p.192.

36. *Satires and Profanities*, p. 45.

37. Quoted in *Satires and Profanities*, Introduction.

38. Benjamin I. Evans, *English Poetry of the Later Nineteenth Century* (London, 1933), p. 195.

39. *Satires and Profanities*, p. 187.

40. *Ibid.*, pp. 188-89.

41. *Ibid.*, p. 189.

42. *Ibid.*, pp. 190-91.

43. *Ibid.*, pp. 158-59.

44. *Ibid.*, p. 158.

45. *Ibid.*, p. 159.

46. *Ibid.*, p. 155.

47. *Ibid.*, p. 147.

48. *Ibid.*, p. 155.

49. *Ibid.*, p. 146.

50. *Ibid.*, p. 4.

51. *Ibid.*, p. 156.

52. Foakes, *The Romantic Assertion*, p. 169.

53. Bertram Dobell, *The Laureate of Pessimism* (London, 1910), pp. 1-2.

54. Trilling, *Matthew Arnold*, p. 328.

55. *The Secularist*, Vol. I, No. 15, Saturday, April 8, 1876, p. 239.

56. *Ibid.*, p. 238.

57. Trilling, *Matthew Arnold*, p. 361.

58. *The Secularist*, Vol. I, No. 15, p. 238.

59. *Essays and Phantasies*, p. 202.

60. *Ibid*, pp. 202-203.

61. *Poems, Essays & Fragments*, p. 89.

62. James Billson, "Some Melville Letters," *The Nation and the Athenaeum*, XXIX (August, 1921), p. 712-13.

63. *Essays and Phantasies*, p. 106.

64. *Ibid.*, p. 105.

65. *Ibid.*, p. 107.

66. *Ibid.*, p. 107.

67. *Ibid.*, p. 200.

68. *Satires and Profanities*, pp. 99-103.

69. *Essays and Phantasies*, pp. 114-115.

70. *Satires and Profanities*, p. 104.

71. *Essays and Phantasies*, p. 123.

72. *Ibid.*, p. 58.

73. *Ibid.*, p. 78.

74. *Ibid.*, p. 55.

75. *Ibid.*, p. 56.

76. *Ibid.*, pp. 84-85.

77. *Ibid.*, p. 90.

78. *Ibid.*, p. 92.

79. *Ibid.*, pp. 91-92.

80. *Ibid.*, pp. 94-95.

81. *Ibid.*, p. 102.

82. *Ibid.*, pp. 102-103.

83. See Salt, *Life*, pp. 92-93.

84. *Essays and Phantasies*, p. 144.

85. *Ibid.*, p. 159.

86. *Ibid.*, p. 175.

III. LITERARY EDUCATION

Literary activity was the chief solace of Thomson's life — but he was never tempted, as so many of his contemporaries were, to mistake it for the supreme end of human existence. In 1865, when Matthew Arnold was just beginning "to proclaim the importance for the modern world, of the qualities of mind and spirit which literary culture can give,"[1] Thomson wrote a long polemic on the subject, anticipating and satirizing many of the ideas Arnold was later to expound in *Culture and Anarchy*. Entitled "Per Contra: The Poet, High Art, Genius," and obviously designed as a companion piece for "Bumble, Bumbledom, Bumbleism" written in the same year, the essay begins by asking: What suitable names have we in English for designating the extremest opponents of middle-class Philistinism with its low-mindedness, monotony, and stupidity? Even Mr. Arnold, Thomson is certain, would not suggest that we call them Jews, Hebrews, or Israelites. The terms chosen people, children of light, *ideologues* or idealists, are much too vague; high-flyers is too German; Bohemians is "too much associated with loose-living and poverty," and, as used by Balzac and Henri Mürger, extends beyond the artist-tribe to include types that hold art itself in contempt. No; the champions of the good and the true in England can be nothing less than a priesthood of divinely inspired poetic geniuses consecrated to the "loftiest Expression of the Beautiful" in high art.[2]

Men usually boast of the prerogatives of power, Thomson remarks, when their possession of it is least secure. James I, who was despised, Charles I, who was beheaded, Charles II, "angel" of the Restoration, and James II, who was kicked out of his palace — all had made "the divine right of Kings" the favorite theme of their reigns. And so it is today with the "divine right of Genius." Once upon a time a good writer was the *ingenious* or *talented* Mr. Blank, or *that great wit*. But today, if critics refer to anyone in such terms we immediately understand that he has "patented a new washing-machine or something of the kind," or that he is addicted to framing puns. Nothing but Genius will do now as an attribute of praise. Yet when we compare the most notable works produced in the midst of this "universal adoration of creative genius" with the notable works of ages that claimed less for art, can we dare, Thomson asks, to pretend that the advantage lies with the present? Artists of old aspired to *imitate* in their art the creative process of God, which is called *Nature*. Today, the pettiest of poets are disdainful of so lowly a role. Art, they say, is superior to nature, for nature is the product of mere chance, whereas art is the product of inspired human intelligence, the sole spark of genuine divinity in a universe shaped and sustained, as every child of science knows, by an accidental bumping together of atoms. Yet what have our "creative geniuses" actually produced? Can any of us sit down seriously "to read a new volume of poems, with the hope of finding therein some breath of a really divine afflatus"?[3] We have learned from experience, Thomson writes, to expect so little; "we condescend, and know that we condescend, to be amused." History teaches us, however, that there have been times when artists, without boasting of their creative power, were yet able to produce works that "in the fullest sense of the term inspired their students, and . . . wrought the hearers or spectators to ecstasy." Despite the boasting, we resort to art today for amusement, not earnestly, knowing that what the critics invest with epithets such as grand, noble, magnificent, consummate, will be in fact, at best, something pretty, graceful, clever, lively. In Thomson's opinion, the substitution of the novel, "padded out with easy and thoughtless pages of trite reflection, inventory description, and multitudinous insignificant detail," for the genuine drama of old, with its concentrated passion, intellectual and moral insight, energy and power, is at once a symptom and an effect of the general emasculation of contemporary literature. It is really astonishing, he remarks, to observe "what a large part of even a good modern book has been written without any exercise of the faculty of thought. Without going back to Shakespeare and Bacon, we may select works from a literary epoch upon which we affect to look down, works such as Pope's *Essay on Man* or Swift's *Tale of a Tub*, wherein nearly every sentence has required a distinct intellectual effort, and which thus, whatever their faults, shame by their powerful virility our effeminate modern books."[4]

Of course, the priesthood of beauty claims that creative activity is of inestimable worth in itself, like the agnostic pursuit of truth. What matters, the consecrated spirits say, is "self-expression," for man realizes his true purpose on earth only to the extent that he externalizes, manifests to the world his innermost being. Thomson concedes that "everything in the world consummates itself (*as the object of our knowledge*) in expression," and that "art is pre-eminently expression." One must not forget, however, that it is expression of a peculiar kind — slow, studied, mediate, complicated, laborious; while the best expression, we all instinctively know, is immediate, simple, unlaborious.[5] Not only Hindoo sages, but even some of the best western philosophers have taught that the "loftiest soul or essence of all things is supremely inexpressive"; that expression of the ultimately real in the universe of suns, planets, trees, and animals is a degeneration, and that regeneration is possible only through the "gradual extinction of all expression, the restoration to sole and infinite dominion of the primordial spiritual silence, perfect, immutable, eternal, self-involved, self-contemplating." Surely it is as a consequence of the fall of the evil angels, the satirist urges, that all things in the universe have been condemned to "wreak themselves into expression," and that "the whole creation groaneth and travaileth in pain until now, and not only it but ourselves also," striving to give perfect utterance to the unutterable. The book of *Genesis* admirably illustrates the point in its account of "God uttering himself in Creation." In response to the instinctive expression of jubilant power, "Let there be light," the sons of God shout for joy and the morning stars sing together. But after that fine beginning, the divine utterance grows daily more complex and elaborate, the rhetorical imagery of God becomes multitudinously profuse and ugly, "until on the sixth day, his figures of speech are cattle, and creeping things, and beasts of the earth, and finally, man and woman."[6]

Devotion to artistic self-expression in and for itself, Thomson asserts, is a symptom of weakness, of privation of power. The really great artistic geniuses have not regarded art as the highest good. It has been, historically, a profitable trade for some, notably the magnificent masters of the Italian Renaissance, who made the "most vigorous career possible of it, and . . . were universally felt to be greater in themselves than in their works." It has also been a consolation for men in dungeons, like Raleigh and Cervantes, who "dreamed grand dreams" only because "they could not live realities in the free air."[7] And have not the greatest poets in all ages worked at their art with a distinct awareness that it was an apology for better work they were prevented from doing by hostile circumstances? In a brilliant page Thomson catalogues the instances:

> Dante's work was heart and soul in "the petty and transitory interests" of his native town, until defeat and exile drove him into bitter immortality. Milton threw himself heart and soul into "the petty and transitory interests" of his age and country: his first poems were the refined amusements of youth, his last great poems the consolations of a defeated partisan, old and blind, and cut off from the active life to which the maturity of his powers had been passionately devoted. Shakespeare wrote no more when he could afford to live without

writing; and, in his Sonnets cx. and cxi., especially the latter, we may read how he condemned the art which has made him the crowning glory of our literature. Shelley yearned for the direct action of political life, and was disabled and outcast into the mere life of poetry. Novalis expresses himself with the utmost vigour: "Authorship is but a secondary thing; you judge me more justly by the chief thing, by practical life. I only write for self-education." Leopardi devoted himself in despair to scholarship and poetry, because physical infirmity excluded him from active life. Sir Thomas More, Raleigh, Bacon, Seldon, Vane, the two Sidneys, Bunyan, Swift, Defoe, Johnson, Scott, and, in fact, nearly all our greatest writers, ever held their authorship as thoroughly subservient to other ends of life.[8]

The true artist-nature, in its highest moments, in its spasms of strength, is conscious that its way is the way of weakness — a solitary way, "umsympathising with the world and unsympathised with by the world." The mass of petty artists, the swarms of poetlings "may glory in their isolation from the vulgar mass as an incontestable proof of superiority"; but the truly great poet starves in this dearth of sympathy. And as for the sense of personal superiority, he knows its true value; he knows that he is great only in comparison, and according to a trivial standard, "like the king of Liliput, almost a nail's breadth taller than any of his subjects, striking awe into the beholder."[9]

In other writings, of a theoretic turn, Thomson has attempted, as we shall show at the close of this chapter, to define philosophically the essence of aesthetic experience. In the essay we have examined he is concerned only with the alleged practical significance of art, combating the pretensions of those who claim that its professional cultivation is serious work of high moral and even religious purpose, serving the loftiest ethical and political interests of human society. For Thomson art, and literature in particular, had little if any practical significance because it involved him in no meaningful choice. He was a poet, but not as a matter of choice; he became a book reviewer, critic and translator, but only for want of something better to do.

A. REPUTATION AS A CRITIC

Thomson's lack of professional commitment to the life of letters is especially noticeable in his biographical and critical studies. Among the hundreds of pieces he wrote, ranging from brief book reviews to studies of Shelley's *Prometheus Unbound* and Ben Johnson's works

that extend to almost two hundred printed pages, there are very few
that exactly correspond to what students of literature in our time are
accustomed to expect from a professional critic. Even in his most
carefully written studies there is a latent cynicism that makes it un-
likely that he will ever be read as a model worthy of imitation.

Saintsbury, who is to be counted among the first admirers of
Thomson's poetry, was also quick to assess both his merits and defects as a critic. Writing of Thomson's critical production, he observed, in 1904, that it "ought to have been good; and sometimes
(especially under the unexpected and soothing shadow of *Cope's
Tobacco Plant*) was so." Unfortunately, however, because of the many
"tares of monstrous growth" in the circumstances of Thomson's life,
the full flowering of his critical talent was obstructed. The least of
these obstructions, Saintsbury amplifies, "should have been (but
perhaps was not) the necessity of working for a living," and "not the
necessity, but the provoked and accepted doom, of working for it
mostly in obscure and unprofitable, not to say disreputable places,
imposed upon a temperament radically nervous, 'impotent,' in the
Latin sense, and unresigned to facts. That temperament itself was a
more dangerous obstacle: and the recalcitrance to religion was one
more dangerous still." To these basic hindrances Saintsbury adds
the "ill effects of schoolmastering," which are hard to get rid of in
any case, and nearly impossible in the case of a "proud and rather
'ill-conditioned' man, who has not enjoyed full liberal education or
gentle breeding." But with all this, it remains true, Saintsbury asserts, that Thomson, having "much of the love, and some of the
knowledge required," was "in more ways than one, of the type of
those poets who have made some of the best critics, despite the alleged prodigiousness of the metamorphosis." He concludes by noting that, "on men like Shelley and Blake, of course, Thomson was
free from most of his 'Satans'; and he speaks well on them."[10]

Since Saintsbury's time no one has attempted a general appraisal
of Thomson's achievement as a literary critic, and it is not likely that
anyone will, so long as the majority of the essays remain scattered in
periodicals that are not readily accessible. It is noteworthy, however,
that literary scholars searching out materials on authors or subjects
Thomson wrote about have from time to time stumbled upon his
pages, and have occasionally been surprised by the quality of work
they have found there. Thomson's two essays on Walt Whitman, for
instance, cannot have been read by many students of the American
poet; and yet Professor Howard Blodgett, who encountered them in

the course of his research for his *Walt Whitman in England,* was moved to write emphatically: "Thomson's two articles are so vivid a report of Whitman's personality and writing that even today [1934] no better short introduction could be put into the hands of new readers of the poet."[11] Of Thomson's essay on Meredith's *Beauchamp's Career,* Siegfried Sassoon in his recent book on Meredith has written: "The most important review was one which must have passed almost unnoticed since it appeared in an obscure journal, *The Secularist.* It was signed 'B.V.' . . . The article was a defiant championship of Meredith's work as a whole. Nothing finer had hitherto been written about him in eulogy."[12] Francis C. Mason, in *A Study in Shelley Criticism,* covering the period from 1818 to 1860, concludes his long study with a detailed exposition of Thomson's essay on Shelley, declaring it to be "the most notable, suggestive and relevant appreciation of its subject which falls within the limits of our period." Mason adds that in Thomson's essay, "with climactic interest for our study," the new and true standards for a genuine appreciation of Shelley's art received their first formulation.[13] And, we may note in passing, in the third edition of *British Poetry and Prose,* edited by P. R. Lieder, R. M. Lovett, and R. K. Root, young students of William Blake's poetry are especially directed to Thomson's "penetrating and revealing essay on Blake's poetical method in *Biographical and Critical Studies.*"[14]

Blake, Shelley, Meredith, and Whitman were, of course, authors on whom Thomson was free, as Saintsbury says, from most of his "Satans." But to this list the names of Spenser, Jonson, Swift, Burns, James Hogg, Browning, Emerson, Christina Rossetti, Rabelais, Saint Amant, Stendhal, Flaubert, Goethe, Heine, and Leopardi must be added, for Thomson speaks well on all of these. Our concern here, however, in examining Thomson's writings, is primarily to trace in them the evidences of his literary education, stressing, especially, matters relevant to a reappraisal of the intellectual and literary significance of *The City of Dreadful Night.* For that reason we shall stress content rather than form, in most instances, and shall include in our survey other kinds of work, such as translations and imitations, that also bear witness to Thomson's literary preparation.

B. English Literature

The writings of Thomson that most show the "ill effects of schoolmastering," are his reviews of scholarly books on literary subjects — reviews that owe their existence, surely, only to the benevolence of Thomson's secularist publishers who permitted him to write whatever he wished for publication in their columns. Thomson could be warm in his praise for what seemed to him to be a job well done; but if he did not like a book he said so unambiguously. In either case, he scrupulously noted violations of syntax, redundancies, contradictions, and errors of fact, considering it a part of his duty as a reviewer to notice details of writing. Usually he listed "errata" in brackets at the close of a review, as a service to the author; but when it seemed to him that a book had been carelessly pieced together, he devoted most of his review to illustrations of that fact, as a service to the reader. The first of a series of five articles that Thomson wrote on Heine, for instance, begins with a review of William Stigand's *The Life, Work and Opinions of Heinrich Heine*. "Before speaking of Heine," Thomson writes, "it is my duty to speak of Mr. Stigand's book; and of this, unfortunately, it is my duty to speak in very strong dispraise." He cannot understand, he says, why such a man as Stigand, who is so out of sympathy with his subject that he feels constrained to apologize on every other page, should insist on writing a book on Heine. "If Mr. Stigand has so much reverence for the delicacy of the English readers," Thomson asks, "why could he not let our Heine alone? What constraint was there on him, the obscure Philistine, to undertake the interpretation of this splendid child of Light?" The blunders and defects, moreover, are so multitudinous that the reviewer has not the space to indicate more than a few score of them (which he proceeds to do); but, he adds, if Mr. Stigand wants to contest the assertion, and is willing to pay for their insertion as advertisements, he, in turn, will be willing to engage in the penal labor of supplying the editor with a column at a time for several weeks. Mr. Stigand, Thomson is convinced, employed some "poor devil of a foreigner as his hack to trudge through the longer prose translations included in the book, reserving his own blundering uncouthness for the shorter prose extracts" and the poems. Appraising the translations of poetry, he writes:

> Alas! dear Heine, your martyrdom did not end with the end of those long years on your "mattress-grave": twenty years have passed, and now you, who wrote a Summer-Night's Dream, even Atta Troll, such as no one but you since Shakespeare could have written; you who were once Puck and Oberon king of the fairies, must appear to us English even as Nick Bottom the weaver, crying "What do you see? You see an ass-head of your own, do you?" and we must respond with honest Peter Quince the carpenter, "Bless thee, Bottom, bless thee! thou art translated!" And to us you must declare, even you, of

the divine melodies, with this mask of Stigand upon you, "I have a reasonable good ear in music. Let's have the tongs and the bones" . . . . Bless thee Heine! bless thee! thou art translated."[15]

Thomson regularly reviewed the volumes in the "English Men of Letters" series, edited by John Morley, as they appeared in the course of his journalistic career. Some of the volumes he found to be so badly written that he wondered whether Morley actually read the books in his series or just gave his name. Dean Church's biography of Spenser seemed to him to be especially defective, in style and syntax as well as fact. In his review he supplies over fifty instances from the first part of the book to support his charge and concludes by offering to undergo several weeks' confinement with the hardest of hard labor in order to redact the book for the publishers, provided "these gentlemen 'come down' handsomely," for a service which they and their authors seem unable or unwilling to provide.[16] By contrast, Thomson's review of the very next volume in the series begins: "If we have had to complain of Mr. Morley's editorship, or rather, neglect of editorship, with regard to certain volumes of this series, we have little but praise for this, his first contribution to it."[17]

What is especially noteworthy in Thomson's book reviews is the evidence of habitual regard for the logic and syntax of meaningful expression. Thomson was an excellent linguist; he taught Latin grammar as a schoolmaster, knew some Greek, and soon acquired a competence in German, French, and Italian that enabled him to make translations which have earned him the highest kind of praise. Careful, analytical reading was for him the only sound foundation on which to elevate understanding. And the fact that he read even books he disliked with sufficient care to notice minutiae of composition is proof that his judgments, unfavorable as well as favorable, were not lightly arrived at.

Indeed, Thomson read his favorite authors with even greater care for minutiae than was his habit as a reviewer — as the series of studies on the structure of *Prometheus Unbound*, printed in 1881 in the September, October and November issues of the *Athenaeum* bear witness. In five long articles, the result of labors begun in 1860, Thomson notes the confusion of places and tenses, the anachronisms, the ambiguity of sexes, all the unessential contradictions, not to depreciate Shelley's masterpiece — for what are these inadvertences if not "instances of that 'brave neglect' which Pope here and there discovered in Homer?" — but as partial payment, he says, of an immense debt of gratitude. The study of minutiae, when moti-

vated by love, writes Thomson (agreeing with Swinburne's conten-
tion in "Notes on the Text of Shelley"), is the highest tribute that can
be paid a master-poet.[18]

It was Thomson's practice, once he had carefully studied a text,
to bring to bear on his subject the full extent of his learning, in order
to give a rounded interpretation of its intellectual and historical as
well as literary significance. Writing on a well-known author, his
method was generally analytic, attempting to display the integrated
substance of a work by considering its constituent elements sepa-
rately, according to the scheme of Aristotle's analysis of the elements
of drama in his *Poetics*. His method in writing on a new or neglected
author was, to use the corresponding word, synthetic, comparing
and contrasting the new or neglected writings with well-known works,
in order to identify the distinctive characteristics.

The earliest example of Thomson's use of the first of these two
methods is his essay on Shelley, originally published in 1860 — the
essay which, according to F. C. Mason, established for the first time
a valid standard for a just appreciation of Shelley's poetic achievement. Thomson begins by remarking that probably no man of the
nineteenth century has suffered more, in person and reputation,
from the "rash convictive bigotry" of professed Christians (who know
nothing of the mysteries of holy love) than Percy Bysshe Shelley.
"Florence to the living Dante," he writes, "was not more cruelly un-
just than England to the living Shelley." Nearly forty years have passed
since the poet's death, Thomson remarks, and only now do we begin to discern his merit. But even now, Thomson asks, by way of
introducing a brief review of recent criticism, what do our best living writers say of Shelley?

> Emerson is serenely throned above hearing him at all; Carlyle only
> hears him "shriek hysterically;" Mrs. Browning discovers him "blind
> with his white ideal;" Messrs. Ruskin and Kingsley treat him much as
> senior schoolboys treat the youngster who easily "walks over their
> heads" in class — with reluctant tribute of admiration copiously
> qualified with sneers, pinches, and kicks. Even Bulwer (who,
> intellectually worthless as he is, now and then serves well as a straw
> to show how the wind blows among the higher and more educated
> classes), even Bulwer can venture to look down upon him with pity,
> to pat him patronisingly on the back, to sneer at him — in "Ernest
> Maltravers" — with a sneer founded upon a maimed quotation.[19]

It is disappointing to find that men so noble as Kingsley and
Ruskin cannot surrender themselves to generous sympathy with a
spirit like Shelley's; yet one is consoled, Thomson writes, by the real-

ization that the great jury to be "impanelled by time from the selectest of many generations" does not yet sit in judgment.

Before entering upon his analysis of the elements of greatness in Shelley's poetry, Thomson reminds his readers of the distinction between the essence of poetry and the measure of its greatness. With a naiveté reminiscent of Dante's *De Vulgari Eloquentia*, he asserts that poetry is, essentially, "spontaneous musical utterance." A work may be enriched by great learning, profound thought, and keen moral insight, yet, if it lacks this "instinctive harmony" it will be no poem. Through absence of such instinctive musicality, he illustrates, "George Herbert is almost unread, and the 'Heaven and Hell' of Swedenborg is a dull map instead of a transcendent picture; through it — tainting both, but in a less degree — the works of the Brownings are less popular than those of Tennyson, though they in all other noble qualities are so far his superiors."[20] Tennyson's language is truly musical, but Shelley's, compared with that of Tennyson and most other poets, is as a river to a canal, a river "whose music is the sweet unpurposed result of its flowing." Thomson says he has often fancied, while reading Shelley, that the words were transparent, or that they throbbed with living lustres, their meaning firm and distinct, "but 'scarce visible through extreme loveliness.'" There is in his language a divine Apollonian strength, greater than that of Hercules, though it is ever veiled in the splendor of a "symmetry and beauty more Divine."

But, having ascertained that Shelley is truly a poet — what of the subject matter of his song? Is the incarnated thought and feeling worthy of the royal poetic form or is it intrinsically slavish? Thomson proposes four analytical inquiries: "(1) What are the favourite subjects of Shelley's song — great or small?   (2) Is his treatment of these great-minded?   (3) Is it great-hearted?   And, rising to the climax, (4) Is it such as to entitle him to the epithet inspired?"[21] It is not difficult to recognize the correspondence between these four questions and the once familiar "four senses" distinguished in antiquity by the Homeric critics and ancient interpreters of the *Old Testament*, which Dante defines and applies to the analysis of his own poetry in the *Convivio* and in his letter to Can Grande.[22]   The subject matter of an imaginative piece of writing is discovered in the literal sense; its intellectual content, the element of "mind" as distinguished from imagination, is discerned in the allegorical sense; its moral character, or "heart," appears in the tropological sense; and, of course, its inspiration, or final cause, is revealed in the anagogical sense. Young

Thomson introduces these questions casually here; but, as we shall notice when we consider his theory of artistic inspiration at the close of this chapter, he understood precisely their traditional significance as instruments of literary analysis.

Regarding the subject matter of Shelley's song, Thomson notes that, in addition to singing, as all great poets have done, the "beauty and harmony of the visible universe," Shelley is perpetually fascinated with "questions concerning the existence of God, the moral law of the universe, the immortality of the soul, the independent being of what is called the material world, the perfectibility of man," and kindred subjects. Thomson admits that more addictedness to great themes is no proof of poetic greatness; — "crude painters always daub 'high art;' adolescent journalists stoop to nothing below epics; nay, Macaulay long since told us that the very speculations of which we speak are distinctive of immaturity both in nations and in men. Nevertheless, believing that the essence of poetry and philosophy is communication with the Infinite and the Eternal, I venture to conclude that to be strongly inclined to such communication is to be fitted with the first requisite for a poet and a philosopher."[23]

But is the poet's treatment of his themes great-minded? Shelley, Thomson reminds his readers, upholds the old Manichean Doctrine, surely the most fascinating, though not the profoundest, conception of the nature of evil. According to that doctrine, the world, and the heart of each human being, is the battleground of a good and an evil spirit; evil has been and is still more powerful, but the good shall triumph. Many scoff at the Manichean view who are yet unable to account, intelligently, for the existence of evil in a universe created by an omnipotent all-holy God. But how magnificent, after all, is Shelley's conception of these hostile powers, "symbolized in the eagle and the serpent," in the opening of "The Revolt of Islam," and how sublime is their embodiment in the Jupiter and Prometheus of Shelley's great poetic drama. Some critics have scoffed also at Shelley's philosophic idealism, though the onus is on them to "expound by what possibility spirit and matter can influence each other without one attribute in common." Let them demonstrate, if they can, Thomson challenges, the existence of matter apart from our perception; or "let them show, if there be but one existing substance, that it is such as we should call matter rather than spirit." After laboring seriously with such epistemological difficulties they may find themselves better equipped to appreciate how gloriously Shelley expounds his idealism in the "Ode to Heaven" and the speeches of Ahasueras in "Hellas." Concerning Shelley's devotion to the doctrine of man's perfectibility, Thomson remarks: What matter that it offended orthodoxy and priestcraft? It is the role of orthodoxy to be offended by daring, whether noble or ignoble. Young Thomson fears that he must consider Shelley mistaken in his belief in the perfectibility of man, but, "perchance, were we more like him in goodness, we should be more like him in faith."[24]

The third inquiry, on the moral character of Shelley's treatment of his themes, has been partly considered already. Morally, Thomson asserts, the poet Shelley is a saint; "in what is understood by the present age as a truly Christian spirit" he bears comparison with the holiest of Christians. Emerson's fatal *per contra* at the close of his study of Shakespeare cannot be urged against him. Shelley did not submit his intelligence and heart to the visible world; indeed, who better than he perceived its symbolism? He rose to the beauty symbolized, and lost himself in it. He was "not 'master of the revels to mankind,' but prophet and preacher."[25]

Thus, Thomson continues, we come to the fourth and last inquiry: Is Shelley entitled, "in a high sense, to be called inspired?" And if so, what is it that distinguishes him from lesser poets and "exalts him to sit with Isaiah and Dante, as one of the small choir of chief singers who are called transcendent?" It is that in him with which his adverse critics have found most fault — his so-called "mysticism," which, it is alleged, makes him obscure. "I dare affirm," Thomson writes in reply,

> that no great writer is less obscure in manner, in expression than he: obscure in matter he is, and ever must be, to those in whom is not developed the faculty correlative to those ideas in whose expression he supremely delights. Were the most of us born deaf, we should reprobate as obscure and mystical those gifted men who dilated upon the ravishment of music. And to the ideal or spiritual harmonies, perfect and eternal, to whose rhythm and melody the universe is attuned, so that it is fitly named Cosmos — to these we *are*, most of us, deaf; and whoever, with reverence and love and rapture, is devoted to their celebration — be it Plato or Swedenborg, Emerson or Shelley — shall for ever to the great mass be as one who is speaking in an unknown tongue, or who is raving of fantasies which have no foundation in reality.[26]

Those who accuse Shelley of mysticism are but ignorantly affirming that he is in the sublimest sense a poet. Thomson quotes at length the passage on poetic madness from Shelley's translation of Plato's *Ion*, and restates the characteristics of inspired poetry as defined by

Plato and Sidney, and by Shelley himself in the *Defense of Poetry.* All
the distinctive marks of highest inspiration, he concludes, are dis-
played in the chief works of Shelley. As one must study Shakespeare
for knowledge of idealized human nature, "so will future men more
and more study Shelley for quintessential poetry." He is well named
the poet of poets.[27]

Thomson ends his essay with a characteristic expression of humility — a humility that might have been crowded out of his system,
together with the arrogant cynicism which was its counterpart, had
he been "better-conditioned" for his role as a literary critic. "If this
meagre essay attracts any worthy student to Shelley," he writes, "it
will fulfill the purpose of its publication, miserably as it fails to fulfill
my desire to render honourable tribute of love and gratitude to this
poet of poets and purest of men, whose works and life have been to
me, from my youth up, a perennial source of delight and inspiration."[28]

The second volume of Thomson's poetry published in his lifetime — *Vane's Story, Weddah and Om-El-Bonain,* and *Other Poems,* of
1881 — was "inscribed to the memory of the poet of poets and purest of men, Percy Bysshe Shelley, with the gratitude and love and
reverence of the author."[29] Young Thomson, as is well known, had
identified himself with Shelley, and with his German counterpart in
mystical longing for material death, Novalis, to the extent of adopt-
ing their names as his own; the initials "B. V." that he often used
stand for "Bysshe" and "Vanolis" — the latter an anagram of Novalis.
But what is of far greater significance is the fact that the poet of
extremest despair continued to feel "love and reverence" for the
humanitarian, Promethean-hearted mystic to the very end of his life.
It is an easy task to trace Shelley's influence in the early writings of
Thomson, in the humanitarianism of the "Doom of a City," in the
autobiographical "Vane's Story," in the beautiful mysticism of the
"Fadeless Bower"; and yet it is not in any of these but in *The City of
Dreadful Night* itself that Thomson has expressed his greatest debt to
Shelley. For the *City* is nothing less, in Thomson's judgment, than
the actuality of what absolute, Godless humanitarian love can build
and has built in the world, as contrasted with what it imagines it is
building. Young Thomson gloried in the "rhetoric and images of the
Romantic vision" of Shelley, but in the *City* he inverts them, as R. A.
Foakes has observed, and "applies" them to an assertion of despair,
the negation of that vision."[30] How conscious Thomson was of what
he was doing, and how well equipped he was culturally for doing it,

becomes obvious as one reads his critical writings on Shelley and other poets of the romantic tradition.

In his long essay on Blake, first published early in 1865, Thomson has provided a rapid review of one important aspect of the romantic tradition, tracing it from Blake's poems down to the writings of his own contemporaries. Just as his essay on Shelley exemplifies his analytical method of criticism in writing on a familiar subject, his essay on Blake exemplifies his critical approach to a new, or at any rate, unfamiliar subject. Thomson was among the first of the English poets to write on Blake. His essay appeared in print before Swinburne's, and not long after Dante Rossetti's in the Gilchrist edition of 1863. Before the appearance of that edition, Thomson says, he knew only one of Blake's poems, that on the Human Form, or Divine Image, quoted by John Garth Wilkinson in *The Human Body, and its Connection with Man*, published in 1851.[31] That little piece of itself, with its celestial simplicity, disposed him to love the author; but the selections edited by Rossetti in the second volume of the Gilchrist edition were to him a revelation far richer than his hopes. He found the selections not only beautiful, but also of "great national interest, as filling up a void in the cycle of our poetic literature." He had long felt that much of the poetry of his own time and of the preceding era "*must* have had an antecedent less remote in time than the Elizabethan works, and less remote in resemblance that the works of Cowper and Burns," though these two had been, since Macaulay's essay on Burns, continually named as heralds of the glorious poetic resurrection of the early nineteenth century. But surely Blake, though scarcely heard at all, was a third herald; and the fact must at length be recognized, Thomson declares, "that by him even more clearly than by them, was anticipated and announced both the event now already passed and the event still in process of evolution." It may be objected that because he was unknown, Blake could not have exerted much influence. The reply is, that influence is of little significance in literary history. The precursors of an age are like high peaks which first reflect the rays of dawn. The little people in the valleys below may not be able to see the soaring peaks; they may see a first glimmer of light only when it is cast down on them from the ridge of lesser peaks looming directly above the valley. But it is of little moment whether the people in the valley see the first glimmer of light or not; the high-noon must follow even if there are no mountains at all to announce its coming. Great literary movements do not result from the arbitrary activity of some individual here or there; on the contrary, individuals are caught up in them, as if swept along by an irresistible spirit of the times. Often the "illustrious prototypes of an age," he explains, "cast but a faint reflex upon those beneath them; and while pre-eminently interesting in biography, are of small account in history." Such personalities help us to read clearly the advance of time; but they do not cause the advance "any more than the gnomon of a sundial causes the procession of the hours which it indicates, or the tidal-rock the swelling of the seas whose oncoming is signaled in the white foam around it and in the shadowed water over it."[32]

The message of Cowper, neatly and honestly uttered, was heard, had its season, and is now passing out of mind; very little of it, Thomson judges, can be expected to survive the century. Burns, of course, will live as long as there is an English language:

> . . . but it must be remembered that his poetry is not blossom and promise; it is consummate fruition; it points to the past more than to the future; it is the genial life, the heroism, the history, the song of his whole people for ages, gathered up and sublimated in and by one supreme man. This King of Scotland happened to come in the guise of a herald to England, but none the less was he a king, the last and greatest of a glorious line; and no other majesty than his own was behind the messenger. Shakespeare made perfect the English drama, and there has arisen no English drama since; Burns made perfect Scottish song, and there has arisen no Scottish song since. When the genius of a nation has attained (human) perfection in any one form and mode, it leaves to ambitious mediocrity all future rivalry with that monumental perfection, itself seeking to become perfect in some new form or mode.[33]

Blake's poetry surely has roots deeply imbedded in the past, yet its flower is for the future. His first volume belonged to the past. When the *Poetical Sketches* were printed in 1783, the "spirit of the great Elizabethan Age was incarnate once more, speaking through the lips of a pure and modest youth." "My Silks and Fine Array" might have been written, Thomson says, by Sir Walter Raleigh or by Shakespeare himself; and he cites as an example a stanza (from the "Mad Song") which Edgar might have sung in the storm by the hovel on the heath:

> Like a fiend in a cloud,
>   With howling woe
> After night I do crowd,
>   And with night will go;
> I turn my back to the East
> Whence comforts have increased;

> For light doth seize my brain
>   With frantic pain.

"Mark," he observes, "the appalling power of the verb *crowd*, revealing, as by a lightning-flash, the ruins of sane personality, haunted and multitudinous, literally *beside itself*. Not one poet in twenty would have dared to use the word thus, and yet (although a careless reader might think it brought in merely for the sake of the rhyme) it was the very word to use."[34] One of the finest selections from the earliest volume, according to Thomson, is the Minstrel's song from Blake's fragment of an historical drama, "Edward the Third," a song which, he says, we should all, as Englishmen, come to know by heart and cherish "with the speeches of Henry at Agincourt and the 'Scots wha hae' of Burns, with Campbell's 'Mariners of England,' and Robert Browning's 'Home Thoughts from the Sea.'"[35]

When we turn from this early volume to the "Songs of Innocence," we learn the "strange fact that he who was mature in his childhood and youth became in his manhood a little child." Where in English, he asks, or any other literature is there an equivalent of "Infant Joy"? A "sudden throb of maternal rapture which one should have thought inarticulate — expressible only by kisses and caresses and wordless cradle-crooning — is caught up and rendered into song."[36] Blake did not act the infantine, he *was* infantine in the songs, by means of a regeneration as real, while as mysterious as ever a saint experienced. In the *City*, Thomson will devote an entire canto to a "dreadful-night" equivalent of this mysterious process of romantic regeneration, but here he is concerned with Blake's mystical expression of it. Blake, he writes, in terms anticipating a simile elaborated in the first numbered canto the *City*, is a true mystic:

> Like Swedenborg, he always relates things heard and seen; more purely a mystic than Swedenborg, he does not condescend to dialectics and scholastic divinity. Those who fancy that a dozen stony syllogisms seal up the perennial fountain of our deepest questionings, will affirm that Blake's belief was an illusion. But an illusion constant and self-consistent and harmonious with the world throughout the whole of a man's life, wherein does this differ from a reality? Metaphysically we are absolutely unable to prove any existence: we believe that those things really exist which we find pretty constant and consistent in their relations to us — a very sound practical but very unsound philosophical belief . . . . Supremely a mystic [Blake] was unlike common Christians as thoroughly as he was unlike common atheists; he lived in a sphere far removed from both. In the clash of the creeds, it is always a comfort to remember that sects

with their sectaries, orthodox and heterodox, could not intersect at all, if they were not in the same plane. Blake's esteem for argumentation may be read in one couplet: —

> "If the sun and moon should doubt
> They'd immediately go out."[37]

A critic in *Macmillan's Magazine* had objected to such couplets as the one just quoted on the ground that they expressed their little truths with such exaggerated emphasis as wholly to distort them and make them virtually untruths. Such an objection, Thomson comments, is the result of reading the author's intention precisely backwards. Blake was intent upon making great laws portable, not little events insupportable. His couplets are to be compared with those gems of the Bible: — "But the very hairs of your head are all numbered"; "But verily I say unto you, that every idle word that men shall speak, they shall give account thereof in the Day of Judgment." Blake has succeeded, says Thomson, in doing "what all profound poets and thinkers have ever most earnestly attempted — to seize a rude but striking image of some sovereign truth, and to stamp it with the roughest vigour on the commonest metal for universal circulation."[38]

On the longer poems, the so-called Prophetic Books, of which only fragments were published by Mr. Gilchrist, Thomson has only this to say: that the study of the whole of them, in order, would probably reveal that they are much less incoherent than even the sympathetic editor supposed. Men who live in seclusion, who develop an intense interior life, gradually come to give peculiar significance to certain words and symbols. The writings of such men are likely to appear obscure and even ludicrous to anyone reading them for the first time. But one ought not to be kept, by their apparent obscurity, from studying them, especially if one has found "in the easily comprehended vernacular writings of the same man (as in Blake's we certainly have found), sincerity and wisdom and beauty." Even the most mysterious of Blake's works would probably prove no more difficult to genuine lovers of poetry than many of the works of highest renown prove to nine-tenths of the reading public. Carlyle, Shelley, Robert Browning, and certainly Milton in "Samson Agonistes," are anything but easily understood. Yet, there are still in England men who understand them, men "who know Shakespeare in despite of the commentators, and understand Browning in contempt of the critics, and laugh quietly at the current censures and raptures of the Reviews: and these men would scarcely consider it a waste of time to search into the meaning of the darkest oracles of William Blake."[39]

But, having considered the selections in the Gilchrist volume, what may one seize upon as the distinctive element in Blake's poetry? The essential characteristic of this poetry, Thomson replies, "is mysticism, and the essence of this mysticism is simplicity," in the loftiest sense of that ambiguous word. It is a simplicity that is "continually rapturous with seeing everywhere correspondence, kindred, identity, not only in the things and creatures of earth, but in all things and creatures and beings of hell and earth and heaven, up to the one father (or interiorly to the one soul) of all." It pays little if any heed to the "countless complexities and distinctions of our modern civilization and science." It is religious, but by no means strict in its theology, for it can be "Swedenborgian in one man and Pantheistic in another, while in the East it has readily assimilated Buddhism and Brahminism and Mohammedanism. Its supreme tendency is to remain or to become again childlike, its supreme aspiration is not virtue, but innocence or guilelessness: so that we may say with truth of those whom it possesses, that the longer they live the younger they grow, as if 'passing out to God by the gate of birth, not death.'"[40]

With these partial hints serving as a point of departure, Thomson undertakes to trace, in a series of rapid comparisons and contrasts, some of the slender lines of relation between William Blake and the principal subsequent poets. Wordsworth, he begins, ever aspired toward the simplicity which was Blake's, but "the ponderous pedantry of his nature soon dragged him down again when he had managed to reach it." A conscientious, awkward pedagogue charmed by the charms of childhood, he "endeavored himself to play the child." But Thomson saw him mainly through Shelley's eyes, toiling up Parnassus with a heavy bundle of sermons and moral old clothes on his back, an old Sunday-school teacher who once, in his youth, had

> . . . touched the hem of Nature's shift —
> Grew faint — and never dared uplift
> The closest all-concealing tunic.[41]

Coleridge, of course, had much of Blake's simplicity: supremely in the "Ancient Mariner." It is there, but fading, in "Christabel," and quite gone after that. The lines in his great Ode "And haply by abstruse research to steal / From my own nature all the natural man," are a witness to his own consciousness of the loss.[42] Thomson never attempted a critical study of Coleridge's poetic achievement, but he frequently cited the opinions of the great romantic critic, and there are distinct echoes of the "Ancient Mariner" in the *City*.

Scott, according to Thomson, had little of Blake's mystical simplicity. Yet he had a simplicity of his own. "Expansive not intensive," a thoroughly objective genius, Scott developed no interior life, but diffused himself over the exterior life. He was a poet of action, not of thought; "a mighty and valiant soldier, whom we seek on the field of battle, not in the school of the prophets." In the essay on Shelley, examined earlier, Thomson had written: "As Scott was the poet of the past, and Goethe of the present, so was Shelley of the future . . . ." But as the years passed he came to prefer Scott's novels to the poetry.[43]

In Byron, Thomson finds no trace of this simplicity. Byron is exceedingly great; "but great as the expression of intense life, and of such thought only as is the mere tool and weapon of life, never great as the expression of thought above and beneath life commanding and sustaining it." His was a very earthy spirit, with "just ideality enough to shed a poetic glow upon powers and passions all essentially commonplace, but very uncommonly vigorous, overflowing with the energy of daemonic possession — an energy most mysterious, but in itself most impatient of mysticism."[44]

Shelley, needless to say, possessed, or rather was possessed by this Blakeian mysticism to the uttermost. But enough has been said of him. And Keats — who shall dare to judge? "I doubt not," Thomson writes, "that everything pure and beautiful would have had its season in him who, dying at twenty-four, wrote 'Hyperion' a few years after 'Endymion.'"[45] In a later essay Thomson contrasts the blank verse of "Hyperion" with that of *Paradise Lost*: "Keats avowed imitation of Milton in the structure of his rhythm. Similarity to the Council in Pandemonium there of course could not but be in the Council of the overthrown Titans; but the verse of Keats (if I have any ear and intelligence for verse) is as different from the verse of Milton as with the same language and the same metrical standard it possibly could be. It is in my judgment even more beautiful and more essentially powerful and sublime than Milton's."[46] But Keats and Shelley are still so far beyond the range of just criticism, Thomson concludes, "that they would not have been mentioned thus cursorily here had it been possible to omit them."[47]

Tennyson, almost to the same degree as Byron, lacks this mystical simplicity. He knows its value, however, and "woos it like a lover, in vain, as Byron wooed it in the latter parts of 'Childe Harold' and in 'Manfred.'" In a few short lyrics, and in one great exception among his longer poems, the *Lotus Eaters*, Tennyson is eminently successful. He has the singing voice for true poetry, but lacks the rich inner substance of it. He is "an exquisite carver of luxuries in ivory; but we must be content to admire the caskets, for there are no jewels inside."[48] In "Indolence: A Moral Essay," written a year earlier, Thomson had expressed a somewhat harsher judgment. *The Lotus Eaters*, he had then written, "is so decidedly the best work of our weak and exquisite Tennyson, that it will preserve his fame as an almost great poet when the hysterics and commonplace philosophy of his *Maud* and *In Memoriam* have passed out of memory, when all his Idylls are idle on the shelf, when nothing else of his save a few tender lyrics and fragments of description shall be cared for by the general public."[49]

Robert Browning, whose "vigorous and restless talents often overpower and run away with his genius so that some of his creations are left but half redeemed from chaos," had Blake's simplicity in abundant measure.[50] But Thomson greatly elaborated his views on Browning in subsequent essays to be considered in due course. In Elizabeth Barrett the element of mystical simplicity is certainly present; but Mrs. Browning has never given it fair expression. Thomson finds her works overcharged with allusions and thoughts relating to books, and her style rugged with pedantry as a consequence. She is often too vehement, "'Aurora Leigh,'" he observes, "sets out determined to walk the world with the great Shakespearean stride, whence desperate entanglement of feminine draperies and blinding swirls of dust."[51] The sonnets reveal her inmost nature to better advantage. Thomson later dedicated a poem to her memory, two of the stanzas of which have the familiar ring of Mrs. Browning's poetry:

> Soldiers find their fittest grave
>   In the field whereon they died:
> So her spirit pure and brave
>   Leaves the clay it glorified
> To the land for which she fought
>   With such grand impassioned thought.
>
> Keats and Shelley sleep at Rome,
>   She in well-loved Tuscan earth:
> Finding all their death's long home
>   Far from their old home of birth,
> Italy you hold in trust
> Very sacred English dust.[52]

But closest of all in relation to Blake, according to Thomson, stands Emerson — his verse, and his essays and lectures as well, being little else than the expression of mystical simplicity. Had he the gift of spontaneous musical utterance, he would be the supreme poet of the age. Unfortunately, "whenever he has sung a few clear sweet notes his voice breaks, and he has to recite and speak what he would fain chant."[53]

And so the survey is complete, or almost complete. There is, Thomson adds, one other author that deserves to be mentioned, a great thinker in England who may have the singing voice which Emerson has not: John Garth Wilkinson, himself an editor of some of Blake's works. According to D. G. Rossetti, Wilkinson had produced a volume of poems bearing a strong resemblance to those of Blake, but the work was not readily accessible.[54] When Thomson finally procured a copy of it, he wrote a critique, in which he expounded his own theory of artistic inspiration. We shall examine the essay in the closing section of this chapter.

Thomson ends his study with a poem in which, according to the editors of *British Prose and Poetry*, he has "caught and expressed in simple verse the spirit of Blake."[55]

> He came to the desert of London Town
>   Grey miles long;
> He wandered up and he wandered down,
>   Singing a quiet song.
>
> He came to the desert of London town
>   Mirk miles broad;
> He wandered up and he wandered down,
>   Ever alone with God.
>
> There were thousands and thousands of human kind
>   In this desert of brick and stone,
> But some were deaf and some were blind,
>   And he was there alone.
>
> At length the good hour came; he died
>   As he had lived, alone;
> He was not missed from the desert wide,
>   Perhaps he was found at the Throne.[56]

No doubt under the influence of this essay, Jacob Walter, in his *William Blakes Nachleben in der englischen Literatur*, presses the conclusion that Thomson must be considered with Rossetti, Swinburne, and Yeats, as one of the four principal continuators of the Blakeian tradition. The second of four chapters in the dissertation is devoted to an analysis of Thomson's poetic use of the "Mystic der kindlichen Einfalt"; but the author ignores the striking inversion of the Blakeian theme in the eighteenth canto of *The City of Dreadful Night*.[57]

The omission of Arnold in Thomson's review of the relations between Blake and subsequent poets is significant. Thomson was aware that the author of the "Grande Chartreuse" had experienced in himself, and had expressed in his poetry the disintegration of the romantic vision into "poor fragments of a broken world."[58] Arnold had seen the Medusa's head in the Promethean ideal of the romantic poets, and it had turned him into a hardened critic of their immoderate and therefore dangerous humanitarian expectations. What Arnold saw that silenced him as a poet, Thomson also saw — and represented with distinct vision — in his awful *Melencolia* of the concluding canto of the *City*.

The themes, images, and even the poetic personalities themselves of English romanticism loom large in the literary preparation of the author of the *City*, but that preparation is by no means exhausted in them. Thomson studied Spenser, for instance, with almost as much care as he studied Shelley. Indeed, "An Evening with Spenser," written in 1865, was Thomson's favorite among his own critical works; it alone of his long literary studies was included by him in the one volume of prose published during his lifetime. Structurally, and in many other respects, it is his best piece. He unobtrusively summarizes the judgment of recent critics of Spenser in the opening pages, cites and examines lines from subsequent poets to show the fertility of the Spenserian heritage, clarifies for the uninitiated reader some of the apparent obscurities in the design of the *Faerie Queene*, and then, after many pages of sympathetic interpretation, concludes with a glowing encomium to the spirit of the age. As writers, he remarks, the great men of the age pressed "all that they knew into their works." Drayton poured all of England, in the minutest detail, into his vast *Polyolbion*. The great dramatists put all of English and a great part of ancient history, "battles, genealogies, conspiracies, sects, schisms, factions," into their plays. And Spenser, of course, "crushes the whole Chronicle of Briton kings from Brute to Uther's reign into a canto; and all the rivers of England, together with the most famous of the rest of the world, into another, enumerating the fifty Nereids (nearly every name with a distinguishing epithet) in four stanzas."[59] Thomson's catalogue of citizens in the twelfth canto of the *City* is quite classical in manner and surely owes something to Spenser, as well as to Milton, Dante, and the ancient epic poets. His favorite readings in Spenser are the description of the House of Holiness in the tenth canto of the first Book, that of the Garden of Adonis in the sixth canto of the third Book, and the two cantos and two stanzas

following the sixth Book, which are "supposed to be a fragment of
the Legend of Constancy."[60] Spenser's Despair, who puts the dagger
of suicide into the hand of the weak and wasted Redcross Knight in
the ninth canto of the first Book, is, according to Thomson, "the
most eloquent despair . . . that has ever spoken in our language;"[61]
and the cadences of that language are certainly echoed here and
there in the *City*. He stresses the marvelous confounding of Christian and pagan terminology and values, and remarks how "like an
ancient Greek addressing a Greek audience of the Heroic Age"
Spenser invents and relates the legend of Molanna and Faunus, and
assembles all the gods on Arlo Hill. Here, as everywhere else in the
poem, "there is no indecision, no panting or straining for effect, no
hurry or slurring; no sign, in short, that the strength and knowledge
and wisdom of the mighty master are not abundant and superabun-
dant for the enterprise he has undertaken; he royally dominates his
theme; a magnificent equable composure reigns throughout."[62]

Thomson's long essay, or commentary, on the life and writings
of Ben Jonson was printed originally as fourteen monthly installments in *Cope's Tobacco Plant*. The nearly two hundred pages it occu-
pies in the posthumously published *Biographical and Critical Studies*
are filled with impressive evidence of the extent of Thomson's acquaintance with the literature of the age of Jonson and Shakespeare.
The pace of the writing is an easy ramble, full of good humor, some
sarcasm, and occasional flashes of critical brilliance. Commenting
on *Cataline, his Conspiracy*, that noble tragedy termed "a legitimate
Poem" by Jonson himself, Thomson muses:

> Macaulay, it appears, has written somewhere that "Ben's heroic
> couplets resemble blocks rudely hewn out by an unpracticed hand
> with a blunt hatchet," and that they are "jagged, mis-shapen distiches."
> This judgment, like most others of his absolute lordship, is a great
> deal too sweeping. [Thomson reproduces a portion of the Proemium
> of the Ghost of Sylla as evidence to the contrary.] If this trumpet-
> blast be uttered in "jagged, mis-shapen distiches," I make over my
> ears to the man who does the doleful elegies for *Punch*, that he may
> have a suitable second pair ready in case he should lose his own,
> which are generally recognized as the worst in the three kingdoms.[63]

But the long study is especially interesting for its peculiar "tobacconist" slant. Many delightful pages are given over to explorations
of the text of Shakespeare, for instance, to determine whether or
not the great dramatist anywhere mentions or alludes to tobacco.
There are many Shakespearean passages, Thomson writes playfully,
"which a fumous special pleader might press into the service, but I

scorn the wresting and racking of texts." Having "carefully scruti-
nized" the entire corpus of Shakespearean works, he is forced to
conclude that neither in *Othello*, nor *Macbeth*, nor *King Lear*, nor
Antony and Cleopatra, nor *Julius Caesar*, nor *Coriolanus*, is there a
trace of genuine "smoke." Nowhere is it recorded that "Hamlet ever
took a pipe to soothe his melancholy," or that Timon "offered
cigars . . . at his else sumptuous entertainments." Achilles and Ajax
always fume in *Troilus and Cressida*, but "without the aid of even a
cigarette." Shakespeare's "snuff" is never the tobacconist's, and his
pipes are without exception simply pastoral. The anti-tobacconists,
he concludes, must be allowed to exult and triumph over us: "neither in Shakespeare nor in the Bible is there sanction for such burning of incense as ours."[64] Writing the articles on Jonson was pleasant
employment indeed for the tobacco-loving "laureate of pessimism."

Swift was Thomson's favorite English "cleric." In a brief "Note
on Forster's Swift," reprinted in *Essays and Phantasies*, he wrote: "For
sheer strength and veracity of intellect, Swift is unsurpassed, and
scarcely equalled, in the whole range of English writers." For Jonson,
and Thackeray, and Macaulay, says Thomson, he was much too strong
and terrible; Scott alone was genial and large-minded enough to
appreciate him; but Scott had not the time to hunt out the informa-
tion for a good biography. As for the great mass of English readers,
"with its soft-hearted and soft-headed sentimental optimism," an intellectual genius of "such stern and unblenching insight is damned
at once and forever by being denounced as a cynic."[65] The most
interesting novelty in Forster's biography is the appendix contain-
ing the "genuine and complete text of the first one and the last
twenty-four letters" of what is called the Journal to Stella. Swift, he
comments, "was fighting Titanically a Titanic battle; and night and
morning, in bed before he rose, in bed before he slept, he found
refreshment and peace in these infantine outpourings of innocent
love." In their heart of hearts the sternest cynics, he concludes, "have
soft places . . . incomparably softer than the softness of unctuous
sentimentalists; liquid with living fountains where these are boggy
with ooze."[66] We noted earlier that many of Thomson's best satires
are Swiftian in character, and it should not be forgotten that a "stern
and unblenching insight" no less Swiftian, rather than "weakness of
will," illuminated the writing of the *City*.

We have already quoted a somber paragraph from Thomson's
early essay on Burns, written in 1859 — the one hundredth anniver-
sary year of the birth of Scotland's "royal rustic." But the piece as a

whole was a joyous rhapsody of appreciation of the full and true Burns, who reveals himself best, not in the "Saturday Night," but in the "Jolly Beggars," "Holy Fair," "Address to the Deil," "Holy Willie's Prayer," and in the tender and passionate lyrics. "Such mirth! No sourness, no selfish chuckling, but a universal laughter deep-chested, full-volumed, inextinguishable, the whole world set in tune."[67] But it is a thick trunk with deep roots that sustains this "luxuriant fruit-age"; for Burns had indeed that "dauntless magnanimity, unyielding independence, and noble defiance of hardship" that he so much admired in Milton's Satan.[68] All who knew him say that he was greater than his works. And yet a Carlyle could judge his life wasted, "gone to wreck through manifold entanglements." But no wealthy life, Thomson firmly protests, will suffer itself to be pitied: "The great conqueror wastes his heart in debaucheries in the brief intermissions of the strife. What, then, can a warrior do with his burning heart and restless brain when he is without army, cause and hope? Let him conquer himself; failing in that he is so far weak and miserable. But let not the ordinary cabman despise Phaeton because he could not control the sunsteeds: his presumption alone, not his charioteering, was ignominious in the overthrow."[69] The words might well stand as an epitaph for Thomson's own life; in fact, John Davidson (who, according to Louis Untermeyer, "identified himself with James Thomson")[70] wrote an extravagant judgment of the same sort in *The Man Forbid and Other Essays*. Nature, he wrote, "gave Thomson, let us say, passion and intellect second only to Shakespeare's; fitted him for the fullest life — not that he might occupy and enjoy, however." Nature is the supreme spend-thrift; "in order to have things stated at their worst, once for all, in English, she took a splendid genius and made him an Army schoolmaster; starved his intellect, starved his heart, starved his body, [and] took care that the very sun should smite him also."[71]

Thomson reviewed many of Browning's volumes as they appeared and wrote detailed studies of *The Ring and the Book* and *Pacchiaretto*. On January 27, 1882, five months before his death, he read a paper at the third meeting of the Browning Society — but only in order to oblige a friend who had committed him. Of the iterations and reiterations of the same terrible story in *The Ring and the Book*, he writes: "The persistent repetition is as that of the smith's hammerstrokes . . . or rather as that of the principal theme in a great Beethoven fugue, growing ever more and more potent and predominant as its vast capabilities are more and more developed through countless

intricate variations, and transmutations of tune and key and structure and accompaniment."[72] With the *Pacchiaretto* volume, however,
he was disappointed. It was scarcely worthwhile, he thought, for such
a man as Browning to fling at pigmies such contempt as is expressed
in that volume.[73] But in summing up his life-long regard for Browning Thomson says:

> I look up to Browning as one of the very few men known to me by
> their works who, with the most cordial energy and invincible
> resolution, have lived thoroughly throughout the whole of their being,
> to the uttermost verge of all their capacities, in his case truly colossal;
> . . . whereas nearly all of us are really alive in but a small portion of
> our so much smaller beings, and drag wearily toward the grave our
> for the most part dead selves, dead from the suicidal poison of misuse
> and atrophy of disuse. Confident and rejoicing in the storm and
> stress of the struggle, he has conquered life instead of being
> conquered by it; a victory so rare as to be almost unique, especially
> among poets in these latter days.[74]

Thomson's essays on Whitman have already been mentioned.
Professor Blodgett, whose general judgment we cited earlier, remarked of them, "Thomson's sketches were so effectively obscured
in these two journals [The *National Reformer* and *Cope's Tobacco Plant*]
that until recently no one seems to have noticed that the most pessimistic voice of the century had hailed the most optimistic with the
reverence due to a master."[75] The essays were republished together
as a volume in 1910 by Bertram Dobell. Only a few words and some
brief excerpts must serve here to suggest their content and character. After attempting to characterize the "majestic sense of rhythm"
and "roaring exultation" of Whitman's early songs, "which may well
shock delicate old-world ears," Thomson compares and contrasts
his measures with Heine's in the two cycles of North Sea chants, and
with Blake's in the prophetic books, where the upstirred soul of the
mystic poet heaves and foams "like a storm-tossed main."[76] But he
cannot agree with Swinburne who sees a resemblance almost amount-
ing to identity between Blake and Whitman. Drawing a number of
precise distinctions, Thomson writes:

> Blake never grasps or cares for the common world of reality, Whitman
> never loosens his embrace of it. To my mind, Burns in the same
> circumstances would have been much more like Whitman than would
> Blake. But Whitman gives no signs of the glorious humour of Burns,
> or of the wonderful lyrical faculty of either; on the rare occasions
> when he uses rhyme, he shows little facility or felicity in it. To quote
> him piecemeal is to give buckets of brine, or at most wavelets, as
> representative of the ocean. For his nature has an oceanic amplitude

and depth, its power and glory are in its immensity; nothing less than a shoreless horizon-ring can contain enough to give a true idea thereof.[77]

Whitman sings himself, Thomson adds, with an arrogance the equal of which we have not heard in ages, but to make clear his meaning he reminds his readers that "Poetry is arrogance, *Dichten ist ein Uebermuth,* chanted brave old Goethe in the *Divan*."[78] It is an arrogance claiming nothing for itself which it will not concede to every man. Elsewhere in the essay Thomson writes in defense of those who, like Whitman, celebrate the "splendid body" informed by the mighty brain:

> For how many such men are to be found in history? In our own for the last century we can perhaps cite only Robert Burns; and he perished in misery at thirty-seven. The greater part of our noblest modern poetic genius have been shrined in disease or deformity; Shelley never had good health, Keats died of consumption at twenty-four, Byron and Scott were lame, Schiller with difficulty kept alive till forty-six, Heine lay helpless in paralysis seven years before his death, Lenau died young in a madhouse, Alfred de Musset was an old man at forty, Leopardi was irretrievably shattered at twenty; and I, for one, cannot remember these, with others only less illustrious, and yet contemplate without joy and admiration a supreme poet supremely embodied."[79]

Thomson finds such consummate and suggestive art in "President Lincoln's Funeral Hymn" that he can think of nothing fitter with which to compare it "than a grand impassioned sonata or symphony of Beethoven."[80] In conclusion, he commends Whitman to all good readers, especially young ones, whose intelligence and character are still plastic to influences, "as a modern of the moderns, to counterpoise yet harmonize with the august ancients; and (if we consider Emerson as in large measure the result of old-world culture) as indisputably the greatest native voice yet heard from America."[81]

C.   Foreign Literature

Like the long essay on Ben Jonson, Thomson's essay on Rabelais is a leisurely paced piece, utterly colloquial for the most part, yet always lively and thoroughly well formed throughout, concerning the life of the man, his age, his works, and his critics. He discusses at length Coleridge's judgment, in which Pope is severely taken to task for having pictured Rabelais as "laughing in his easy-chair."[82] Thomson agrees with Coleridge that Rabelais "was among the deep-

est, as well as boldest, thinkers of his time," and that he deserves to
be "classed with the great creative minds of the world — Shakespeare,
Dante, Cervantes & c."; yet he feels bound to defend Pope's picture.[83] Profound thought and creative genius may wear a comic as
well as a tragic face, and even a mixture of both, half Thalia, half
Melpomene. Surely Democritus the laugher was no less subtle a
thinker than Heraclitus the weeper, "and our foremost scientific men
are reviving his theories after more than two millenniums." Surely
Aristophanes had as much imaginative genius as Euripides. Rabelais
was capable of great scorn and bitterness, Thomson writes, but he
was nevertheless essentially a laughing philosopher. His scorn is jolly
laughter vented in wine, whereas that of Swift, by contrast, is a *saeva
indignatio,* vented in vitriol.[84] Pursuing the comparison, Thomson
notes that both were prodigal in dirt as writers, but Swift heaped his
dirt on immorality and vileness in order to render them more repul-
sive, while Rabelais' dirt has nothing to do with morality or immorality. It is "simply the dirt of a child, such as he has described in the
infancy of Gargantua, in Book I, chap. xi." It is the dirt one finds in
Chaucer, and though offensive to many now, it is innocent compared with the vile obscenity and spurious sentimentalism in certain
French and English novels:

> — a luscious and poisonous compound, as revolting to the really pure-
> minded as that hideous Thais of Dante (*Inferno.* xviii) in that cess-
> pool of Malebolge —
>
> "quella sozza scapigliata fante,
>
> Che là si graffia con l'unghie merdose,
> Et or s'accoscia, et ora è in piede stante.
> Taida è la puttana."
>
> We may be sure that the rude and rigorous Dante, even the ineffably
> tender and ardent Dante of the *Vita Nuova* and the imparadised
> Beatrice, would have painted just such a picture of some lovely and
> fascinating countess of, say, Dumas *fils* — an exquisite and delicate
> creature, redolent of the costliest perfumes, and redolent of the
> impurest passions in the purest French.[85]

Disavowing any claim to serious competence as a judge of relative merits in French literature, Thomson nevertheless concludes
with the statement that he is inclined to look up to Rabelais as the
greatest literary genius of his country. The very finest work in that
literature was done, he believes, by Pascal, "but Pascal's finest work
is a series of fragments; and while as profound, he is narrow as an
artesian well, in comparison with the oceanic amplitude and energy,

as well as depth, of Rabelais."[86]

The essay on Rabelais, as also the long commentary on Jonson's works, was written under what Saintsbury has called the "unexpected and soothing shadow of *Cope's Tobacco Plant*" — soothing because its editors and readers were concerned not with the urgency of secularist national reform but with the enjoyments of leisurely smoking and leisurely reading. Under the same soothing shadow Thomson wrote a fascinating series of articles on the once famous humorist of the early seventeenth century — that "most jolly and genial smoker, toper, rover, soldier, and poet"[87] Marc-Antoine de Gérard, Sieur de Saint-Amant, who called himself "the fat Virgil and the Norman Democritus."[88] The piece offers twenty or more highly original and lively translations of poems of this marvelous Saint-Amant, judged by Theophile Gautier to be "assuredly a very great and very original poet, worthy to be named among the best of whom France can boast." Thomson himself says that he "would rather have ten pages of Saint-Amant than a hundred of Boileau."[89] Yet he might never have taken up a single page had it not been known that Saint-Amant was to be honored for having written "one of the earliest sonnets extant in praise of tobacco."[90]

Early in the sixties Thomson began to supply the various journals for which he wrote with occasional translations from French, German, and Italian poets and prose writers, notably Stendhal, Flaubert, Baudelaire, Lessing, Goethe, Heine, Leopardi, and Carducci. At the very least, the translations bear witness to intimate acquaintance with these authors. Of Stendhal's works he particularly enjoyed *La Chartreuse de Parma* — "an elaborate and splendid novel; a tale of North Italian political life from 1815 to 1821, with descriptions of Milanese society, Lake of Como scenery, and a realistic picture of Waterloo as witnessed by one taking part in it, which is magnificent."[91] One of the stories related in that "strange and original book,"[92] *De l'Amour*, inspired Thomson to write his long narrative, *Weddah and Om-El-Bonain*. In a brief introductory note Thomson wrote: "I found this Story, and that of the short piece following, which merit far better English versions than I have been able to accomplish, in the *De l'Amour* of De Stendhal (Henri Beyle, chap. 53), where they are given among 'Fragments Extracted and Translated from an Arabic Collection, Entitled *The Divan of Love*, compiled by Ebn-Abi-Hadglat.'" To indicate briefly the character of the long tale of love to follow — a kind of love which informs two cantos of the *City* — Thomson thus translates a fragment from Stendhal:

The Benou-Azra are a tribe famous for love among all the tribes of Arabia. So that the manner in which they love has passed into a proverb, and God has not made any other creatures so tender in loving as are they. Sahid, son of Agba, one day asked an Arab, Of what people art thou? I am of the people who die when they love, answered the Arab. Thou art then of the tribe of Azra? said Sahid. Yes, by the master of the Caaba! replied the Arab. Whence comes it, then, that you thus love? asked Sahid. Our women are beautiful and our young men are chaste, answered the Arab.[93]

In considering the influence of Dante on Thomson we shall indicate more explicitly the importance of the *Liebestod* theme in the *City*. Herman Melville wrote of *Weddah*: "It is exactly that kind of gem which some of Keats' pieces are; and what can one say more?"[94] professor G. H. Gerould has written: "Anyone who will sit down to read [it] will be captivated . . . . I cannot believe it has been much read, else its superb quality would have made it as famous and as popular as Keats' 'Isabella' with which it is fairly comparable."[95]

In a long critical study of *La Tentation de Saint Antoine* of Gustave Flaubert, Thomson reviewed and characterized the literary achievement of the great French stylist. Of *Madame Bovary* he writes: "It is a novel, so far as I am aware, unequalled for power and intensity in the fiction of his country, save by the very masterpieces of Balzac, and the supreme chapters of Victor Hugo."[96] After relating the circumstances of the book's indictment for immorality, he remarks with precision: "In such matters all turns on the tone and intention. Utter nudity may be the naked beauty and the naked truth. Or it may be shamelessly libidinous. Lasciviousness certainly cannot co-exist with profound thought, with intense imagination, with unswerving temperance, with austerest self-repression; and all these dominate throughout *Madame Bovary*.[97] He writes of the very different *Salammbò*, with its semi-barbaric opulence of color and music: "Probably the nearest analogue in French to this far-thrilling resonant music of bronze, is to be found in the poems of Baudelaire, who so thoroughly sympathized with the genius of Flaubert, and whose art also had the honour of outraging the virtuous Lower Empire."[98]

Because of its immediate relation to the *City*, Thomson's study of Italian literature is reserved for subsequent consideration. In German literature his favorite author was, of course, Heinrich Heine. But first a few words must be said about Goethe and Novalis. Thomson translated many of Goethe's poems, notably the "Prometheus," "Mahomets Gesang," and many portions of the *West-*

oestlicher Divan. "To myself," he writes in an essay on the *Divan*, "the most delightful of the work of Goethe, in addition to the choicest of the short poems, have long been *Reineke Fuchs* and the *West-oestlicher Divan*."[99] The *Divan*, he observes, is not so well known in England as it ought to be probably because it has proved so difficult to translate. "The present writer," he adds, "must confess that even in his own judgment he has quite failed in nearly every stanza thereof by him attempted." Yet the first part of *Faust* has been frequently translated and "of the second part there is a version said to be readable." But perhaps the reason for the neglect of the *Divan* is that for English readers generally "Goethe is resumed in the first part of *Faust*, and this is resumed in the operatic Margaret, with sneering Mephistopheles in the background."[100] Yet this *Divan*, darling of the vigorous old age of Goethe, is a marvelous work of perennial youthfulness; there could be "no stronger contrast than exists between the simple sunny clearness of these poems and essays, and the obscure intricacy, thick cloud with cloud inwoven, of the second part of Faust."[101]

But it was Heine's fascination with the near-eastern poets — Hafiz and Saadi especially — that had led Thomson to the *Divan* of Goethe. We have already referred to his articles on Heine which begin with a review of Stigand's book. Following that review Thomson presents a short account of Heine's life, translating many letters, and then a series of brief appraisals of the major works of the celebrated German poet. Like Novalis, and so many other contemporaries, Heine spent many years looking directly into the face of death — yet surely no other poet of the time saw so deeply into the "vast black void which underlies our seemingly solid existence." In a compact page Thomson provides what amounts to a romantic genealogy for his own representation of the abysses of living-death in the *City*:

> Of [Heine's] contemporaries with whom I am acquainted, there are three poets, all born in the decade of his birth, who have some affinity to him in this respect: Keats, with a marvelous sensuous prescience, Shelley, with a prescience more marvelously spiritual, of early death, radiated strange flashes of insight, and thrilling pulses of passion, into the depths of the obscure gulf; Leopardi, throughout a longer, though never quite helpless and motionless, agony, confronted it with a most desperate, undaunted, steadfast, and profoundest regard.

But Heine's condition was as near to total immersion in that vast black void as is possible for a living human being;

> [he] alone lay for years outstretched on a mattress grave, paralyzed in the weird border-land of Death-in-Life or Life-in-Death, a restless

and fiery mind in a passive and frost-bound body. And as he himself was fascinated with an appalling fascination by the fulness of life behind, and the emptiness of death before, so we are fascinated and appalled by what he has revealed to us of his visions from that alien and terrible point of view. And the power of the spell on him, as the power of his spell on us, is increased by the fact that he . . . was no ascetic spiritualist, no self-torturing eremite or hypochondriac monk but by nature a joyous heathen of richest blood, a Greek, a Persian, as he often proudly proclaimed, a lusty lover of this world and life, and enthusiastic apostle of the rehabilitation of the flesh.[102]

Thomson writes eloquently of the preface to the *Romancero*, "in which poetry and pathos, humour and irony, are so wonderfully intermingled";[103] of the prose *Confessions* of 1854, "a Capitolian triumph of audacious genius and truth . . . charioted by a whirling complexity of irony within irony, as dazzling as the wheels of Ezekiel's vision";[104] and of the last poems, in which "we see, as by lightning flashes in the gloom, the struggle raging between his love of life and his revulsion from his horrible tortures; nor is it easy to discern with which side the alternating victory rests at last."[105]

When Thomson's translations from Heine originally appeared with the *City* in 1880, Karl Marx, who had known Heine intimately, wrote a letter to Thomson describing the English versions as "no translation but a reproduction of the original such as Heine himself if a master of the English language would have given."[106] Stanton L. Wormley, in his *Heine in England*, marks Thomson as the English poet who most shows the influence of Heine in his own works; and of the translations he writes: "In some of the poems, those from the *Lyrisches Intermezzo* and *Die Heimkehr*, his felicity of expression is at times astonishing."[107] As an example of Thomson's re-creation of Heine's art, vivid traces of which are discernible in the language and images of the *City*, we cite a portion of his version of the beautiful "Fragen":

> What is the meaning of Man?
> Whence comes he? Whither goes he?
> Who dwells there above in the golden stars?
>
> The waves murmur their everlasting murmur,
> The wind sweeps, the clouds scud,
> The stars glitter, indifferent and cold,
> And a fool awaits an answer.[108]

Thomson wrote no critical estimate of that great favorite of his youth and early manhood, Friedrich von Hardenberg, otherwise known as Novalis. His translation of the *Hymns to Night* is extant, but

Bertram Dobell, custodian of the manuscripts, never realized his plan, announced in the preface to the *Poetical Works*, to publish them.[109] Thomson himself seems not to have considered publishing even brief selections from the work, as he did fragments of poetry and prose translated from other authors, probably because he was not satisfied with the results of what must have been an early exercise in translation. Among the papers that accompany the manuscript is a very interesting note, dated Thursday, 7/5/'66, on the art of translating. "I hold," he writes in that note, "that while adequate translation of any long poem is impossible, some short poems may be adequately translated." But even in the case of a collection of short pieces, a translator attempting all is certain to do many of them badly, no matter how skillful and sympathetic he may be. Thomson contemplates the ideal procedure:

> If each translator would attempt only his chief favorites in the collection, and of these only such as favour him beforehand with glimpses of a happy version, all the best pieces in the collection would get translated in time . . . . From the well chosen attempts of various translators, a really valuable anthology might be collected by a gardener who did not fear to engraft and prune and transplant. The system, based upon jealousy and selfishness, by which each translator must make the version of any piece wholly his own, even when fully conscious that some predecessor has given the best possible rendering of certain portions thereof, makes consummate translations far more rare than they ought to be.[110]

D.   THEORY OF ART

In many of his critical writings Thomson speculates on the nature of art. We have noted his attempt to define the essential character of poetry, and to provide a standard for measuring poetic greatness in his early essay on Shelley. In a later essay, "Open Secret Societies," he develops in somewhat extravagant and yet not invalid terms the earlier suggestions. Artistic beauty, he remarks, is related to natural beauty as the universal is related to the particular. Artistic representation has, of course, its particular aspect — sound in music and poetry, line and color in the visual arts — and that particular aspect may be studied and analyzed as one studies a piece of glass, for thickness and purity and transparency; but, as George Herbert phrased it (Thomson quotes):

> "A man that looks on glass,
>   On it may stay his eye;
> Or if he pleaseth through it pass,

And then the heaven espy."[111]

Beyond the five-fold common sense there is, in some men, a tran-
scendental sense to which the universe appears as one mighty harmony of beauty and joy, like a great orchestra comprising "all things
from shells to stars, all beings from worm to man, all sounds from
the voice of the little bird to the voice of the great ocean." Music is
the least imperfect medium for the expression of this eternal harmony. The language of men, Thomson acknowledges, is less perfect; but in the songs of truly inspired poets, as in great music, there
is "a latent undertone, in which the whole infinite harmony of the
whole lies furled; and the fine ears catch this undertone and convey
it to the soul, wherein the furled music unfurls to its primordial
infinity, expanding with rapturous pulses and agitating with aweful
thunders this soul which has been skull-bound, so that it is dissolved
and borne away beyond consciousness, and becomes as a living wave
in a shoreless ocean." There are many among the learned and the
clever, among the "educated," who hear inspired music and read
inspired poetry, and think they perfectly enjoy and comprehend;
"and they can discourse very profoundly about meters and diction
and canons of art; but they never hear the undertone, never have
vision of the interior illumination." For them the soul of music and
poetry must ever remain a "music unheard, a light unseen, a language unknown embodied in their familiar mother-tongue." In its
highest form the aesthetic experience is mystical. The highest poetic
inspiration comes from the same unutterable source that the mystic
contemplates in his moment of frenzy. There is in the highest joy of
art, intense sadness; and in the beauty, a supernatural awe. Indeed
as "Plato writes in the Phaedrus, 'He who has been recently initiated, when he sees a godlike countenance, or some bodily form that
presents a good imitation of beauty, at first shudders, and some of
the old terrors come over him.'"[112]

The poet-artist, Thomson had written in the essay on Shelley,
does not copy nature; if he is a true *poietes*, he reads the signs, and
looks to where they point, beyond materiality, space, and time. When
truly inspired, his creation surpasses anything that can be experienced in prodigal and careless nature. Echoing the thought of Plato
and the neo-platonic language of Shelley's "Defense," Thomson
writes:

> The only true or inspired poetry is always from within, not from
> without. The experience contained in it has been spiritually trans-
> muted from lead into gold. It is severely logical, the most trivial of

its adornments being subservient to and suggested by the dominant idea, any departure from whose dictates would be the "falsifying of a revelation." It is unadulterated with worldly wisdom, deference to prevailing opinions, mere talent or cleverness. Its anguish is untainted by the gall of bitterness, its joy is never selfish, its grossness is never obscene. It perceives always the profound identity underlying all surface differences. It is a living organism, not a dead aggregate, and its music is the expression of the law of its growth . . . It is most philosophical when most enthusiastic, the clearest light of its wisdom being shed from the keenest fire of its love.[113]

And then with a philosophic precision worthy of the best pages of Hegel's *Aesthetik*, he concludes exultantly that poetry of the highest inspiration, such as that of Homer, the Greek tragedians, Dante and Shakespeare, is "a synthesis not arithmetical, but algebraical; that is to say, its particular subjects are universal symbols, its predicates universal laws; hence it is infinitely suggestive. It is ever-fresh wonder at the infinite mystery, ever-young faith in the eternal soul. Whatever be its mood, we feel that it is not self-possessed but God-possessed; whether the God come down serene and stately as Jove, when, a swan, he wooed Leda; or with overwhelming might insupportably burning, as when he consumed Semele."[114]

Yet for all his enthusiastic Platonism, Thomson was by no means disposed to argue that high inspiration suffices to produce a great work of art. On the contrary, it is the character and preparation of the inspired person that determines whether or not the result of inspiration will be poetry at all. For hero, saint, and sage, no less than poet, may be inspired, and each will respond in his characteristic way, according to his preparation. In a long essay on "A Strange Book" — a study of John Garth Wilkinson's *Improvisations from the Spirit* — Thomson defines his views. A note in the volume of *Improvisations* had explained that Wilkinson considered himself to be not the author but simply the transcriber of the contents, a passive medium for the Holy Spirit. Thomson was amazed to read this note because he had freshly in mind Wilkinson's words on Blake's prophetic books — words contained in the preface to the first published version of Blake's songs, edited by Wilkinson himself in 1839. By divorcing his imagination from reason, which might have chastened and elevated it, and by spurning the "scientific daylight and material realism of the nineteenth century," — so Wilkinson's judgment of 1839 proceeded — Blake lost himself in the ruins of primitive and consummated creeds; thus the obscurity and ghastliness of his prophetic "hieroglyphics" is to be accounted for simply by the "artist's having yielded himself up, more thoroughly than other men will do, to those fantastic impulses which are common to all mankind, and which saner men subjugate but cannot exterminate."[115]

That the man who had once written such words on Blake could later suffer in himself a similar delusion was, for Thomson, astonishing. One must not doubt the sincerity of Wilkinson, he remarks, for he is not a fraud; as translator and student of Swedenborg, he has at last paid the full price of intellectual submission to Swedenborgianism. He is now unable to recognize that in conceiving his improvisations he has experienced nothing more nor less than the "fine frenzy" of Shakespeare; that his experience is of the same kind as that of all mystics —

> from the most ancient Indian gymnosophists to the Hebrew prophets and poets, to Christian apostles, as Paul and John, to Plato and Plotinus, to Mohammed and the Sufis, to early and medieval eremites and saints with their trances and ecstasies, to George Fox and his Quakers, walking by the interior light and waiting to be moved by the Spirit, to Behmen and Law, to Swedenborg and Blake, to Shelley with his opening of "Alastor," his "Hymn to Intellectual Beauty," his "Defense of Poetry," his "Ode to Liberty." The names and phrases may vary; the essential faith and doctrine is ever the same in all.[116]

Thomson then proposes to consider a few instances of mystical experience relating especially to poetry. He begins with Plato, quoting at length the passages on inspiration in the "Ion," the "Meno," the "Apology of Socrates," and the "Phaedrus." In harmony with this Platonic doctrine, he then adds, are all the serious invocations of divine aid by the loftiest earlier and later poets. When, in modern times, the appeal to the muses had become a senseless matter of routine among mediocre versifiers, Byron "did well to prick the bubble with the frank impertinence of his 'Hail, Muse! et cetera — we left Juan sleeping'" but surely Homer calling to the muses to sing, was in devout earnestness; surely Lucretius' hymn to Venus Genetrix was sincere; surely Dante in the first canto of "Purgatory" and in the first and the second of "Paradise" where he warns off those unfit to follow him, is sincere. Spenser beginning the *Faerie Queene* and in the introduction to the last complete book; Milton opening his *Paradise Lost* and *Paradise Regained*; Shelley in his best poetry and in his noble unfinished "Defense of Poetry": surely all were in earnest describing their inspiration.[117] Thomson cites the testimony of these poets at length, and then concludes that Wilkinson's experience did not differ from any of these, except in being less intense and less complete, because of his imperfect prepa-

ration as a poet. No doubt the "Spirit" visited Wilkinson. But what
reception did he accord it? "Descended into the world of flesh,"
Thomson writes, "the spirit is so far subject to worldly conditions
that its work can be furthered and hindered, its manifestations can
be made more or less clear, by the human being through which it
shines."[118] As Dante writes in his *De Vulgari Eloquentia*, anyone who
wishes to sing of the highest things must first drink deeply of the
fountains of Helicon — the waters of high inspiration. But he must
also be prepared to give orderly expression to that inspiration, and
therein consists the difficulty and true labor (*hoc opus et labor est*).[119]
Without native talent (*ingenium*), without true knowledge of the rules
of art (*ars*), and without assiduous practice (*usus*), Dante and the
ancients held, it is impossible to be a true poet. Wilkinson, Thomson
writes, with some sharpness, responded to his inspiration like a mere
registering machine, putting aside what natural *ingenium* he may have
had, and forgetting what art he may have mastered. He became a
"mere dead conduit for the metal fused by the fire of the spirit,"
with no attentive mind active to "detect the flaws." The divine invited guest enters by one door, and the host walks out by the other:
"Ah, Dr. Wilkinson, why did not you at least bring water to wash
your Lord's feet? — even the feet of many of these verses, which are
exposed, sorely blistered and bruised and dirty, through your studied neglect of the plainest duties of hospitality?"[120]

Yet a man like Wilkinson, Thomson is quick to add, could not
write a worthless volume; "Planned he ever so subtly to stultify himself, it was certain to contain much characteristic beauty and truth."[121]
And Thomson half repents himself of the severity of certain of his
strictures — though the sharpest of these were but the very same which
Wilkinson had passed on a greater genius: Blake. He is saddened
especially by what he calls the unaccountable waste of needed intellect and genius in Wilkinson's intellectual prostration. Because they
are unwilling to face boldly the harsh realities of the modern world,
too many of the best contemporary poets, saints, and sages consume
themselves like Wilkinson in the ruins of dead creeds. "I think," he
writes — "of a Maurice scourging himself with those 'forty stripes
save one,' the Thirty-nine Articles, and burying his genius in the
deathly vaults of the mouldering English Church; of a Newman dis-
membering himself of intellect and will, and perishing in the laby-
rinths of the Roman Catacombs; of a Wilkinson immolating his splendid powers on the altar built of dead men's bones, of a demented
dogmatism more implacable than the old heathen altars of mere

bodily human sacrifice."[122] And as he ponders these lives, "so frustrate of their full development and happiness in usefulness," a mournful verse from a place of "most mournful frustrate life" rises in his
memory, "a verse of Matthew Arnold's stanzas from that sepulcher
of Death-in-Life, the Grande Chartreuse: —

>   'Achilles ponders in his tent,
>   The kings of modern thought are dumb;
>   Silent they are though not content;
>   They wait to see the future come;
>   They have the griefs men had of yore,
>   But they contend and cry no more'."[123]

NOTES

1. Basil Willey, *Nineteenth Century Studies* (London, 1949), p. 252.

2. *Essays and Phantasies*, pp. 124-25.

3. *Ibid.*, pp. 127-28.

4. *Ibid.*, p. 129.

5. *Ibid.*, p. 135.

6. *Ibid.*, pp. 136-37.

7. *Ibid.*, pp. 134-35.

8. *Ibid.*, pp. 133-34.

9. *Ibid.*, p. 139.

10. George Saintsbury, *A History of Criticism and Literary Taste in Europe* (London, 1922), III, 552-53.

11. Harold Blodgett, *Walt Whitman in England* (Ithaca, 1934), p. 154.

12. Siegfried Sassoon, *Meredith* (New York, 1948), p. 125.

13. Francis Claiborne Mason, *A Study in Shelley Criticism* (Mercersberg, Pennsylvania, 1937).

14. Paul Robert Lieder, Robert Morse Lovett, Robert Kilburn Root, editors, *British Poetry and Prose*, third edition (Boston, 1950), I, 1027.

15. Thomson, "Heine," *The Secularist*, I (January 8, 1876), pp. 22-23.

16. Thomson, "Spenser, by Dean Church," *Cope's Tobacco Plant*, II, p. 432.

17. *Ibid.*, p. 492.

18. Thomson, "Notes on the Structure of Shelley's *Prometheus Unbound*," *The Athenaeum*, 1881 (November, 1881).

19. *Biographical and Critical Studies*, pp. 270-271.

20. *Ibid.*, p. 272.

21. *Ibid.*, p. 273.

22. Dante Alighieri, *Opere*, pp. 265-359 and 436-442.

23. *Biographical and Critical Studies*, p. 274.

24. *Ibid.*, pp. 275-276.

25. *Ibid.*, p. 277.

26. *Ibid.*, pp. 278-79.

27. *Ibid.*, pp. 279-81.

28. *Ibid.*, pp. 281-82.

29. Thomson, *Vane's Story* (London, 1881), front leaf.

30. Foakes, *The Romantic Assertion*, p. 169.

31. *Biographical and Critical Studies*, p. 240; see also footnote, p. 318.

32. *Ibid.*, pp. 241-42.

33. *Ibid.*, p. 243.

34. *Ibid.*, p. 246.

35. *Ibid.*, p. 251.

36. *Ibid.*, p. 253.

37. *Ibid.*, note, pp. 252-53.

38. *Ibid.*, pp. 256-57.

39. *Ibid.*, pp. 260-61.

40. *Ibid.*, p. 262.

41. *Ibid.*, p. 262; *Essays and Phantasies*, pp. 188-89.

42. *Biographical and Critical Studies*, p. 263.

43. *Ibid.*, pp. 263 and 276.

44. *Ibid.*, p. 263.

45. *Ibid.*, p. 264.

46. *Ibid.*, note, p. 260.

47. *Ibid.*, p. 264.

48. *Ibid.*, p. 265.

49. *Essays and Phantasies*, p. 163.

50. *Biographical and Critical Studies*, p. 266.

51. *Ibid.*, p. 267.

52. *Poetical Works*, I, p. 251.

53. *Biographical and Critical Studies*, p. 267.

54. *Ibid.*, p. 268.

55. Lieder, Lovett, Root, editors, *British Poetry and Prose*, I, 1026.

56. *Biographical and Critical Studies*, pp. 268-69.

57. Jakob Walter, *William Blake's Nachleben in der englischen Literatur* (Schaffhausen, 1927), pp. 27-45.

58. Foakes, *The Romantic Assertion*, p. 165.

59. *Essays and Phantasies*, p. 187.

60. *Ibid.*, p. 182.

61. *Ibid.*, p. 177.

62. *Ibid.*, p. 178.

63. *Biographical and Critical Studies*, pp. 105-106.

64. *Ibid.*, pp. 164-65.

65. *Essays and Phantasies*, note, pp. 287-88.

66. *Ibid.*, pp. 283-84.

67. *Poems, Essays, and Fragments*, p. 88.

68. *Ibid.*, p. 89.

69. *Ibid.*, p. 92.

70. Louis Untermeyer, *Modern British Poetry* (New York, 1936), p. 48.

71. John Davidson, *The Man Forbid and Other Essays* (Boston, 1910), pp. 170-71.

72. *Biographical and Critical Studies*, p. 475.

73. *Ibid.*, pp. 479-80.

74. *Ibid.*, pp. 456-57.

75. Blodgett, *Walt Whitman in England*, p. 154.

76. James Thomson, *Walt Whitman, the Man and the Poet* (London, 1910), pp. 28-29.

77. *Ibid.*, p. 29.

78. *Ibid.*

79. *Ibid.*, pp. 18-19.

80. *Ibid.*, pp. 36.

81. *Ibid.*, p. 37.

82. *Biographical and Critical Studies*, p. 33.

83. *Ibid.*, pp. 34-36.

84. *Ibid.*, p. 37.

85. *Ibid.*, pp. 37-38.

86. *Ibid.*, pp. 45-46.

87. *Ibid.*, p. 47.

88. *Ibid.*, p. 79.

89. *Ibid.*, p. 69.

90. *Ibid.*, p. 78.

91. Thomson, "Henri Beyle (otherwise De Stendhal)," *The Secularist*, XXV, New Series (February 14, 1895), 107.

92. *Ibid.*, p. 107.

93. Thomson, *Vane's Story*, p. 68.

94. Cited by James Billson, *The Nation and the Athenaeum*, XXXIX, 712, 713.

95. Gordon H. Gerould, *op. cit.*, p. xvii; H.S. Salt, in *Seventy Years Among the Savages* (London, 1921), p. 108, reports Meredith's judgment that Thomson's Weddah was the best narrative poem in the English language; William Van Doorn, in *Theory and Practice of English Narrative Verse since 1833* (Amsterdam, 1932), p. 130, writes that when Thomson wrote *Weddah* ["his imagination set on fire by a mere anecdote in Stendhal's *De l'Amour*"] in ottava rima, "he challenged comparison with Keats' 'Isabella or the Pot of Basil,' telling a better story and telling his story better than the man he emulated." Doorn concludes that Thomson's *Weddah* is the best narrative poem produced in England since 1833.

96. Thomson, "La Tentation de Saint Antoine par Gustave Flaubert," *The Secularist* (September 30, 1876), p. 214.

97. *Ibid.*, p. 215.

98. *Ibid.* (November 4, 1876), p. 292.

99. *Poems, Essays, and Fragments*, p. 205.

100. *Ibid.*, pp. 205-206.

101. *Ibid.*, p. 206.

102. Thomson, "Heinrich Heine," *The Secularist*, I (February 12, 1876), 101.

103. *Ibid.*, p. 67.

104. *Ibid.*, p. 102.

105. *Ibid.*, p. 101.

106. Salt, *Life*, p. 263.

107. Stanton Lawrence Wormley, *Heine in England* (Chapel Hill, 1943), p. 51.

108. Thomson, *Poetical Works*, I, 335.

109. *Biographical and Critical Studies*, p. v.   Novalis' *Hymns to Night*, as well as his *Heinrich von Ofterdingen*, directly influenced some of Thomson's early writings (see pp. 221-24). In the *City*, especially in the imagery of Canto X, the values that Novalis ascribes to night, the "mother of love," are inverted.

110. Salt, *Life*, p. 262.

111. *Essays and Phantasies*, p. 207.

112. *Ibid.*, pp. 205-206.

113. *Biographical and Critical Studies* pp. 279-80.

114. *Ibid.*

115. *Ibid.*, pp. 307-308.

116. *Ibid.*, pp. 326-327.

117. *Ibid.*, pp. 327-32.

118. *Ibid.*, p. 336.

119. Dante Alighieri, *Opere*, p. 412.

120. *Biographical and Critical Studies*, pp. 336-37.

121. *Ibid.*, p. 352.
122. *Ibid.*, p. 370.
123. *Ibid.*, p. 371.

IV. PHILOSOPHIC PESSIMISM

In his youthful essay on Shelley, Thomson had professed to believe, as we noted, that "the essence of poetry and philosophy is communication with the Infinite and Eternal," and that "to be strongly inclined to such communication is to be gifted with the first requisite for a poet and a philosopher."[1] Although the poet's way of beauty and the philosopher's way of wisdom may be widely separated at first, they are bound to meet at last, the young critic argued, as certainly as meridians far removed at the equator are bound to meet at the poles. A few years later, in "Open Secret Societies," written to serve as a serious counterpoise to the satirical "Per Contra: The Poet, High Art, Genius," Thomson coupled the brave and the pure with the beautiful and the wise, proclaiming with Emersonian enthusiasm the ultimate "identity of the masculine ideal of the Hero and the Philosopher and the feminine ideal of the Poet and the Saint."[2] According to Thomson, each of these ideals has its open secret society of adherents, not to be confounded with the professional armies, churches, schools of philosophy, and literary academies of the world, although occasionally members of the latter may be genuine heroes, saints, sages, and poets. Each society has its meridian to follow, or *scala amoria* to climb, but only the "very flower and crown" of the membership — "Saints of Saints, Heroes of Heroes, Philosophers of Philosophers, Poets of Poets" — actually scale the heights to the point of unity where the mysteries of bravery, purity, wisdom, and beauty are dissolved momentarily in an ineffable experience of infinite love.[3]

A. THE LIMITATIONS OF PHILOSOPHY

Thomson the poet was certain in his own mind that he had experienced the *ecstasis* of Platonic, or, to use Plato's term, erotic love, and that the experience qualified him to distinguish genuine heroes, saints, sages, and poets from the many who have "parodied and counterfeited and traduced" their ideals through the centuries.[4] We have noted, in examining his moral and religious satires and critical essays, with what presumption of authority he pronounced judgments in these spheres. No less presumptuous was he in judging philosophers. In the loftiest experience of philosophers — so he wrote in "Open Secret Societies" — there is an "identity of the purest faith and the purest skepticism; the extremes not only meet, they intermingle and grow veritably one."[5] In the "universities and colleges

and schools" many men are honored as philosophers and are sala-
ried to lecture and write "about ideas, archetypes, dialectics, realism, nominalism, and so forth,"[6] who yet know nothing of this high
and terrible ecstasy of philosophical eros — terrible because, in the
flash of a trembling glance, it reveals to man's spirit the source of
highest happiness and then thrusts him back into the world of shadows with a quickened spiritual desire which nothing in this world
can satisfy. The ordinary man experiences such a fall only once, in
that birth which is a sleep and a forgetting. "How is it," Thomson
questioned in 1862, "that the creeds and systems wherein the wisest
and purest men profess to have found repose and satisfaction, never
satisfy the young and ardent souls?" Part of the answer is, no doubt,
that youth demands the excitements of pursuit and aspiration; but
the chief reason is that "in most cases the creed of a mature man,
however earnest and honest he may have been, is more the refuge
of a spirit sick and weary than the palace-temple of a spirit triumphant." Without philosophic training, the ordinary youth "feels the
illusion and falsehood, though, perhaps, he cannot expose it, even
as he feels the inadequateness of nearly all the world's poetry and
painting." But as the years go by, as he sinks ever deeper into the
sleep of this world of shadows, acquiring "much knowledge of the
rules and artifices which he would fain account valuable knowledge,"
the ordinary man attempts to persuade himself and others that he
has found repose and contentment in some hole that he has bur-
rowed for himself on a lowly step of the grand stairway that winds
steeply up out of the world of genesis and decay into the realm of
abiding ideas.[7] But the true philosophers, who never forget that this
world of common place and time "is but a poor expression of
thought," and that "action is but a rude hieroglyph of soul," cannot
so easily maintain the illusion of repose.[8] Having been thrust back in
the full maturity of their intellectual faculties, they feel like prisoners sunk in a cavernous dungeon, condemned to work out their own
"system" of salvation or escape by tying one little idea securely to
another, until they have woven, out of sheer thought, "a faithful
counterpart of the world, a microcosm the perfect image of the
macrocosm."[9]

Since that great turning point in the history of western thought
when Plato's Socrates astounded Glaucon with his assertion that the
highest good — the idea of ideas — transcends thought as well as
being,[10] the wisest of men have struggled to explain how the
profoundest spiritual anguish is somehow coupled with the supremest

joy, the loftiest hope intermingled and made one with the deepest despair, in the experience of that sublime paradox. Some, perhaps to deaden in themselves the sense of loss, have dwelt on the excitement of the anticipation of ecstasy; others, perhaps to keep vivid the impression of light in their minds, have traced and retraced upon it the darkest images of this shadowy world. The former, Thomson writes, have stressed the "truth of summer and dazzling noonday"; the latter have stressed the "truth of winter and black night"; but the ultimate experience itself transcends both truths, utterly confounding the midnight and the noon and the beholder of the vision.[11] In the dozen or more philosophic essays written in the course of his journalistic career, Thomson has explored this dialectical paradox; in many of his minor poems in verse and prose he has represented some of the dizzying effects of the rapid alternation of visions of light and darkness; in the *City* he has attempted to picture, in Dantesque language, this world which lies before us like a land of dreams, so various, so beautiful, so new, as it appears to one who has just sunk back into it from the highest experience of erotic ecstasy.

In an essay entitled "On the Worth of Metaphysical Systems," written shortly after completing the *City*, Thomson attacked the pretensions of "dedicated" philosophers, even as he had satirized the pretensions of moral and religious reformers in his "Proposals for the Speedy Extinction of Evil and Misery," and of literary saviors of the world in "Per Contra: The Poet, High Art, Genius." A system, he had said in his essay on Spenser, is "a little strait-waistcoat wrought by some little man, and in which he would fain confine" the entire universe of Titanic Nature; Nature at first laughs with immense good humor at the puny fellow, "but if he seriously persists in attempting to force it on her, she inevitably makes him fit for a strait-waistcoat himself."[12] That some of the "profoundest intellects and noblest spirits of mankind" have been fascinated by system-building, he writes in the later essay on the worth of systems, is not to be wondered at, for "no fascination can be stronger to such intellects and such spirits than the hope of securing certitude beneath the transitory and illusive shows of this world and life." Indeed, so intense is the fascination that it has bewitched many good and able men, who despaired of attaining certitude by rational means, into "abjuring their reason, strangling their doubts, and seeking peace in blind faith and abject submission to authority, mutilating their minds as Origen mutilated his body." But the builders of systems cannot abjure reason, and will not despair. The keenest-minded of them recognize quite clearly the practical trustworthiness of what the natural or relative sciences have established within their limits; but they cannot endure the utter blank immeasurable beyond those strait limits, the formless void unfathomable beneath their thin surface. They see plainly what many of the triumphant and triumphing natural philosophers do not see at all, that even the most obvious and commonplace so-called facts are undermined by deepest metaphysical doubts. Admitting the relative truth, they must seek the absolute basis; acknowledging the limited fact, they hunger for the universal law.[13]

These subtle thinkers cling to the belief that the laws and processes of the human intellect correspond with those of the universe. With incredible self-sufficiency each of them labors at his task, unaffected by the manifest failures of others who have labored before him, never doubting that his mind is a valid mirror of the world, "though he sees that its reflections are more or less different from those of all other minds."[14]

The value of these great systems, Thomson argues, consists almost altogether in the great thoughts and noble sentiments embodied in them, and these are "not improved but injured by the incorporation." As the immense structures into which they are built become ruins, the great thoughts and sentiments remain "as precious marbles, goodly for use in edifices less vast but less imperfect, more humble but more habitable."[15] Unfortunately, these precious marbles are often so chipped and hacked to his purpose by the ancient builder that their forms make them inconvenient for anything else. A system builder discovering some new truth, or some new aspect of an old one, Thomson writes, invariably "strains and distorts it trying to expand it into a complete system."[16] There is much, for instance, that is fresh and stimulating, and little if anything metaphysical, "in the greater part of what is called the Idealism of Berkeley." But the distorting pressure of system-building enters, it is immediately felt, "when he brings in the Eternal and Infinite Mind to give permanence to the ideal world." Similarly there is "nothing metaphysical in Kant's demonstration that time and space are but constant forms of our sensibility"; metaphysics enters "when beyond the phenomena of our perceptions he predicates the noumena or things in themselves of which we know nothing."[17] For the system-builder the new truths are not as marvelous jewels which he may "cut and polish," and mount according to his pleasure in some equally marvelous star-shaped or cross-shaped setting. That is the work of the poet. The philosopher feels that he must cut and set his jewels "in the sole best form and order, harmonious with the form and order of sun and moon and stars, and failing in this he damages them for other use."[18]

But it is strange, Thomson concludes, that we have to appeal to

the record of history — the wearying cycle of system succeeding system century after century — to show the worthlessness of "absolute"
systems. In a very modern "existentialist" vein he asks:

> How can man, an infinitesimal atom in the infinite universe, embrace
> that infinity? How can man, whose life is an inappreciable moment
> in eternal time, comprehend the laws of that eternity? A critic may
> be very small, and a philosopher or theologian very great (according
> to our petty human standards), yet the former in relation to the
> latter must be immeasurably greater than the latter in relation to the
> universe he has the audacity to expound . . . . During many milleniums
> some of the best and wisest of our race have devoted themselves to
> teaching us all about God and our immortal souls; yet when one
> comes to reflect on the matter it is overwhelmingly certain that not
> one of these men has ever really known anything about such things,
> or whether they really exist or not.[19]

Even the most stupid of men is therefore justified in rejecting
any absolute system without examination — for beyond doubt it must
be ludicrously inadequate . . . . Thomson imagines a colony of mice
in a great cathedral, lviing on Communion crumbs and taper-drop-
pings, attempting by deep speculation to understand the origin, the
plan, the purpose of the cathedral, the significance of the altar, the
clashing of the bells, the trepidation of the organ. The thought is
absurd; "yet a mouse explaining the final cause of all these things
would be incomparably less absurd than a divine or sage expound-
ing the mysteries of Nature or God." With due adroitness and agility
most of us can manage to pick up a living out of "this shoreless and
fathomless ocean of being" in which we find ourselves; but we are
deluded to the point of insanity when we imagine that we have actually succeeded in charting its main currents and boundaries.[20]

In a subsequent essay, "A Few Words on the System of Spinoza,"
Thomson illustrates his thesis by the example of a particular system,
"choosing for this purpose the most profound, the most rigorously
enunciated, and the most influential of all modern philosophies, that
of Spinoza as expounded in his Ethics."[21] All the great German sys-
tem-builders, Kant, Fichte, Schelling, Hegel, and Schopenhauer,
whose philosophies are "among the most elaborate and absolute ever
constructed," have acknowledged their dependence on Spinoza.
Thomas cites Hegel's words: "Thought must absolutely raise itself to
the level of Spinozism ere mounting yet higher . . . . Would you be
philosophers? commence by being Spinozists, else you can accomplish nothing." Without pretending to review in a brief article a philosophy elaborated through decades of secluded life, Thomson raises
some critical questions regarding its foundations. He grants that the
system is utterly consistent within itself, and asks only whether it

truly corresponds "in plan and elevation with the living world."[22] Thomson's critique, interestingly enough, strikes with Kantian precision at the masked "ontological argument" of Spinoza's system, which maintains that "the order and connexion of ideas is the same as the order and connexion of things" and that, as a corollary, "all that follows objectively from the infinite nature of God, follows subjectively from the idea of God in the same order and with the same connexion."[23] That these arguments are true within the system, and subject to its definitions, axioms and postulates, one need not doubt; but there is "complete lack of demonstration and even of presumptive evidence" that they are true beyond the system, in the universe of life. And even within the system itself there are doctrines, such as that of intermediary causes emanating from God, that are, according to Thomson's understanding, patently "irreconcilable with the root-ideas of Spinozism." In the doctrine of emanation, Thomson remarks (and his words recall Hegel's critique of Spinoza in the *History of Philosophy*) "we have evil and imperfection resulting from infinite and eternal perfection, a contradiction even more glaring than in the Christian scheme, where the fictions of creation and free-will shroud it in comparative obscurity."[24]

And yet great thoughts and sentiments abound in the system of Spinoza perhaps more than in any other that has been built in Christendom. Whatever one may say of the discursive connections, there is certainly sublimity in the dominating conception of the unity of Substance — a "conception that in no narrow sense amply merits the high eulogy of Hegel." Thomson then proceeds to examine some of the many gems of elevated thought imbedded in the *Ethics*. There can be no doubt that Spinoza, "whose life was a long trance and ecstasy of contemplation," has disclosed in his sublime utterances "immense and serene horizons beyond the huddled and sordid tumult of our common life, clouded with low creeds, bounded by narrow thoughts, turbid with selfish passions." Not the pure philosophic vision of such a man, only the system of discursive and geometric reasoning into which he tortured its memory, is worthless.[25]

B. The Ethics of Schopenhauer

Thomson characterized Spinoza as "this most subtle Oriental genius recluse in the Occident." In the philosophy of Schopenhauer he found an even more thorough-going Orientalism; yet he was never able to admire the brilliant German pessimist as he admired Spinoza.

Paul Neugebauer, in his study of the literary influence of Schopenhauer in England, has remarked that Thomson, despite his profound
pessimism and long acquaintance with the works of the German "vol-
untarist," is not to be counted among the many in England who
reflect a direct influence in their writings.[26] In his long essay on the
life and works of Schopenhauer, published in five installments, and
in the companion pieces on two of Schopenhauer's favorite themes,
"Suicide" and "Sympathy" — in which he arrives at conclusions contrary to those of the German philosopher — Thomson himself has
indicated the limits of his sympathy and interest.

He owed his first acquaintance with the German philosopher, he
says, to the widely-known "article in the *Westminster Review* for April,
1853, generally attributed to Mr. John Oxenford."[27] His long review
of the life and works, written almost twenty years later, opens with a
reminder to his readers that Schopenhauer had not wished his biography to be written, so that his life might be identified with his works.
And yet his works, so full of import for practical life, inevitably awaken
interest in the man, and excite curiosity about his actual conduct of
personal affairs. Schopenhauer had repeatedly confessed his moral
inadequacy to friends, maintaining that he was satisfied only with his
intellectual character and conscience. He held that every philosophy
has its corresponding ethical religion, and that Buddhism corre-
sponded to his own. The four "sublime truths" of Buddhism — that
existence is pain, that the cause of pain is desire, that pain or desire
may cease by Nirvana, that Nirvana is attained by contemplation
and, finally, by ecstasy — contain, Thomson explains, the essence of
Schopenhauer's ethics.[28] They are not to be confounded, however,
with the fundamental principles of his philosophy, which are specu-
lative or theoretical in character, not practical. The German sage
insists that the ultimate object of his system is the ordering of true
knowledge, not good behavior or beautiful artistry, though, of course,
some theoretic account of the good and the beautiful must ever be
an essential part of any complete system of the true. Thomson ac-
cepts the distinction; and yet, he observes, the emphasis on the *will*
in the theoretic system, the primacy given to it even in the title of
Schopenhauer's chief work, *Die Welt als Wille und Vorstellung*, leads
inevitably to curiosity about the state of the author's will. Schopenhauer has expressly said that genuine "theoria," pure intellectual
contemplation, is impossible until man has crushed in himself the
will to live; he himself has carefully catalogued the various stages of
the process, which begins, Thomson notes, "when a man ceases to

draw an egotistic distinction between himself and others, and takes as much part in their sorrows as in his own." Once the distinction gives way, the individual, recognizing his own self in all beings, comes to regard the miseries of other persons as his own, and appropriates to himself the sorrows of the entire world. His knowledge of the world then becomes a *quietus* of the will, a "state of voluntary renunciation" which is the transition from virtue to asceticism. Beyond sympathetic asceticism is the higher *quietus* of artistic, will-less contemplation of beauty (which is the secret of the beauty of homely objects represented with abnegation of will by the masters of still-life); and beyond that, the total *quietus* of absolute intellectual contemplation or "theoria," which transcends thought as well as being.[29]

But when we turn from Schopenhauer's system to his biography, to see how far he actually got in the process of self-abnegation, we cannot help marvelling, Thomson observes, how complex a thing is the soul of man, and how inexpressive are the meager hieroglyphs of action by which it manifests its substance. Assuredly, he writes, the philosopher's life and character, as revealed in his conduct, "were wholly at variance with his doctrine." Instead of turning from life with his will, he seems to have clung to it "desperately and even abjectly, fleeing in blind panic from the cholera and hoping to live till a hundred after his life's work was done." Instead of merging himself in others by abnegation of will, he "took pride in keeping himself apart from them; and when accused of misanthropy answered that he did not hate men, he only despised them." So far from making their griefs his own —

> he abhorred, because they perturbed his sublime tranquility, men goaded to revolt by unbearable injustice and oppression, hailed the advent of the oppressors who secured his selfish peace . . . . So far from renouncing desire, he clung to the goods of the world with a clutch more vehement than that of those whom common men called worldlings; and the threatened loss of his fortune almost unhinged his mind. So far from acquiring lofty and unselfish calm by contemplation, he was continually storming against his contemporaries and the mass of mankind as despicable idiots . . . ; and the Pessimism on which he had insisted so much and so long, as the essential, universal, everlasting and supreme truth, melted away like a morning mist in the first sunbeams of fame that struck upon his own forehead.[30]

But if this were all there were to Schopenhauer, the man would not be worth writing about. It is an error to confound the biographical accounts with the works, for, in fact, Thomson insists, the author had a truly "splendid and capacious intellect" and also the "clear intellectual conscience" of which he boasted. One cannot read many pages of his masterpiece and essays without being persuaded that he would, as he said, rather have "sent a bullet through my brain" than submit to earning a philosopher's living, by conforming his doctrine to official restrictions. In that respect, at least, according to Thomson, the German sage reached the height of a "much nobler spirit, Giordano Bruno," who had declared in his lofty and energetic manner: "Of all poor wretches the most miserable are they who philosophize for their bread." Regardless of what one thinks of Schopenhauer the man, therefore, one may be assured of the "absolute sincerity and grandeur of his main thoughts" as recorded in his chief works. He remains, after all, Thomson asserts, "the most intelligible and concrete of German philosophers; his style not only clear, but racy, pungent, and vigorous, full of the most various illustrations, drawn from here, there and everywhere." The marvelous quotations he introduces, page after page, "would richly furnish a commonplace book, which would be anything but common place." And almost as remarkable as his philosophical subtlety is the worldly wisdom with which he "discusses or comments on countless curious and interesting matters." Thus, Thomson concludes: "even those who like myself have small liking or esteem for systems which profess to expound the universe, may read him with pleasure and profit. Buddhism, the venerable, the august, the benign, so tender, so mystic, so profound, so solemnly supernal, came to us with a very poor heart if a very rich brain, and the opulent splendours of the East were no longer in its soul, when it came to us heralded and incarnate in Schopenhauer. Yet even thus impoverished and disennobled, how well worthy of admiring study!"[31]

Students of the philosophy of Schopenhauer know with what severity he judged the ancient Stoics, condemning especially their doctrine of suicide as antithetical to his own doctrine of ascetic sympathy. His opposition to suicide seems, however, to involve him in a paradox. He notes, with derision, that the Jews alone in antiquity condemned suicide as a crime, despite the fact that even in the Old Testament there is no forbiddance of it, or even positive disapproval. None of the other ancient peoples condemned it. Schopenhauer cites the arguments of Pliny, the ancient Stoics, Aristotle (who to be sure, said that "suicide is wrong against the state, although not against the person"), the Hindoo and Chinese sages, all of whom defended it as a fundamental right of the individual. And yet, after rejecting the Judeo-Christian attitude, which he says is altogether unthinking, and probably founded on a superstitious prudence that fears to offend the God who created the world and saw that *it was all good*, Schopenhauer is forced to declare his own opposition, based on grounds which are, he insists, at the greatest possible remove from those of Judaism and Christianity. "The only valid reason existing against suicide," he writes, summarizing the moral doctrine elaborated in his major work, "is this: that suicide thwarts the attainment of the highest moral aim, by the fact that, for a real release from this world of misery, it substitutes one that is merely apparent." For that reason Schopenhauer judged the ethics of the Stoics to be essentially one of moral callousness, void of that true sympathy with the griefs of the world which is a necessary phase in the will's perfect abnegation of self.[32]

In his essays "On Suicide" and "Sympathy," Thomson carefully distinguishes his own views from those of Schopenhauer, though without indicating specifically the source of the arguments he is criticizing. In the first, he maintains that, for the ancients at least, suicide was not a way of release from the griefs of this life. It was not a sudden, crazed leap from a window, but a very deliberate, philosophically calculated self-destruction. He reminds his readers of Leopardi's profound remark (in the *Storia del Genere Umano*) that suicide is rarely contemplated by those whose lives are most wretched; that, indeed, "those who suffer are usually sanguine of an improvement in their condition, and therefore desire to live, believing that they would be altogether happy could they overcome the evils which afflict them." Surely it is a poor argument to insist that, for the sake of "sympathy," a man who feels that "his life is useless or worse than useless to himself and others . . . especially if he has reason to expect that it will grow more miserable, more dependent, more ignoble, more vicious, with advancing years," ought to preserve it. Suicide is essentially the hero's way of self-abnegation, not the poet's or saint's or sage's. Yet it is not therefore any the less admirable as a moral act.[33]

But what becomes, then, of the doctrine of ascetic sympathy? In the first part of his essay on the subject, subtitled "With Others," Thomson attempts to assess with minute critical care man's capacity to participate in the feelings of another. True sympathy, he writes, is, of course, not to be confounded with beneficence, or fidelity, or sentimentality. A man is kind to the needy, true to his friends, tender with the feeble, more often as the result of a process resembling the solution of an algebraic problem than as the result of sympathy. One sees a blind beggar. Does one feel with him instinctively? Certainly not. Subconsciously, or habitually, one applies a formula: blindness is X, misery is Y, together they mean inability to work, privation of common pleasures, and so claim one's help and pity. But an ordinary little boy, unfamiliar as yet with the formula, might express his "sympathy" by attempting to "trip or trick the blind man, and if the attempt succeeded, would certainly approve it as a jolly lark."[34]

Indeed, what we ordinarily call sympathy, may be termed more accurately, "*autopathic sympathy*, a contradiction in terms precisely suited to a contradiction in ideas." Thus a man in business can "sympathize" with another who has become bankrupt; a mother, with another whose husband or child is ill; a young man, with a wounded or decorated soldier; a nubile maiden, with a bride — though we all know how easily such autopathic sympathy can be "changed by fortune into jealousy or contempt."[35] The dramatist, or novelist, Thomson reminds his readers, is surely better able than our friends to arouse such sympathy in us; for we usually leave behind our most serious personal concerns when we take up a book or sit expectantly, "open to receive and avid to drink in emotion," at the theater.[36]

Shelley had argued in his *Defense of Poetry* that, to be truly great and good, a poet must "imagine intensely and comprehensively; he must put himself in the place of another and of many others; the pains and pleasures of his species must become his own." A corollary of this, Thomson reasons, would seem to be that intense and comprehensive sympathy is as rare as intense and comprehensive imagination.[37] Is it in fact so rare? After testing the "richest ores" through several pages, Thomson concludes:

> So rare and priceless is genuine sympathy, in and for itself, whether effectuated in action or not; so much purer and higher must be the nature that can fulfill the precept, "*Love thy neighbor as thyself,*" than that which may obey the commandment, "*Do unto others that which ye would they should do unto you;*" so true is it that "*Her sins, which are many, are forgiven; for she loved much;*" that there are sentimentalists whom we cherish for their sentiments alone more dearly than the great working philanthropists, whom history orders us to love, but whom we only manage to esteem. To a prisoner who knew the life and works of Goldsmith, this poet was probably more dear than was Howard himself, though Howard had ameliorated that prisoner's doom. Despite her austere Calvinism and his free Paganism, Scotland cherishes Burns as the very idol of her inmost heart, because his

sympathy was so broad and deep. And we love and reverence Shelley above all other famous men of his generation, because these lines in *Julian and Maddalo* are true to himself above all those other men: —

But *me,* whose heart a stranger's tear might wear
As water-drops the sandy fountain stone;
Who loved and pitied all things, and could moan
For woes which others feel not, and could see
The absent in the glass of phantasy,
And near the poor and trampled sit and weep,
Following the captive to his dungeon deep;
Me who am as a nerve o'er which do creep
The else-unfelt oppressions of this earth.[38]

The second part of the essay considers the capacity of man to sympathize with his past self; and it is here that Thomson presses his analysis to a conclusion opposed to that of Schopenhauer. Intense and enduring self-sympathy, he asserted, "is really as rare as intense and enduring sympathy with others." How many of us can really sympathize with what we were in childhood? "In our maturity successive years seem to sympathize deeply with each other; but not days, and still less hours." And when we look into ourselves more closely we find that even the years and decades are not joined "each to each" with what we may call real sympathy.[39] Thomson proposed to consider first the hours and days. Surely in two moods of two several hours a man's relations to the most serious problems of life may be, and often are, essentially opposite. One mood may burn with hope and faith, the other may lower black with doubt and despair; and there is no possibility of conciliating the antagonism in a philosophic sense, since the two moods are mutually unintelligible. To illustrate his meaning, Thomson cites the exclamation of George Herbert in Giddiness, 99:

O what a thing is man! how far from power,
From settled peace and rest!
He is some twenty several men at least
Each several hour.[40]

Turning to consider the relations of longer periods, years and decades, in a single life, Thomson observes that while a man of thirty may more easily sympathize with the thoughts and sentiments of a *present* friend than with his own thoughts and sentiments of ten and twenty years earlier, he nevertheless cherishes a much stronger, even tyrannical interest in "his own peculiar individuality, as *one* from childhood," than in that of his present friend. It is not easy to analyze this sense of life-long personal identity, but surely it owes its being to a very complex network of external as well as internal circumstances. "Readers of the *Arabian Nights* and *The Taming of the Shrew*, Thomson writes, "must have been struck by the ease and readiness with which Abou Hassan and Christopher Sly are persuaded that their real past lives were delusive dreams, and that the present delusions are realities." The story-teller and the dramatic genius seem obviously to have "considered the conviction of personal identity . . . as being very much at the mercy of those around us!" Although we hear so much of its intuitive character and necessary truth, that conviction, Thomson concludes, is by no means an axiomatic one, anterior to experience, above and inaccessible to logic, as many philosophers have claimed. It is not simple, but compound; and an extended analysis of it may very well "reduce it to the rank into which the analysis of Hume reduced the idea of causation, the analysis of Berkeley the belief in the independent exterior existence of matter, the analysis of Kant the belief in the universal existence of space and time.

> We are such stuff
> As dreams are made of, and our little life
> Is rounded with a sleep."[41]

C. STOICISM

As a practical ethics, in which men can actually be trained to live, the doctrine, crowned with suicide, of the ancient Stoics is incomparably superior, in Thomson's view, to Schopenhauer's doctrine of sympathy, which attempts to subordinate a gift as rare as the loftiest poetic imagination to practical ends. In 1870, just after he had begun the *City*, Thomson wrote a long essay, published in three installments, on the so-called "Meditations" of Marcus Aurelius Antoninus; shortly after completing his masterpiece, he wrote a long review of Long's translation of *The Discourses of Epictetus*. Much that Thomson says in these essays is echoed or anticipated in his *City*, especially in the nineteenth canto, on suicide, and in the final vision of the *Melencolia*.

Ancient Stoicism, Thomson reminds readers of his "Marcus Aurelius Antoninus," emerged in the decay of Paganism, even as "in the decay of Christianity we have now a Stoical school." Stoicism is not a philosophy for periods of bodily or spiritual health. The old Pagan ideal, in the glorious days of Greece and Rome, "was a healthy mind in a healthy body, the utmost enjoyment of this life, any future life being very doubtful and at best very shadowy." The old Christian ideal, in the holiest days of Christendom, "was a chastened mind in a mortified body, this life being worth nothing in itself, and only important as giving opportunity to secure the future life of eternal bliss." The Pagan seeking to avoid disease, relapse, and cure, cherishing health of mind and body as an absolute good, was "quite rational in his conduct, for this life to him was all." The Christian poisoning his soul with the sense of sin, stabbing it with terrors of judgment, and living a maimed, half-starved life here so as to obtain, through the cure of faith, full fruition in heaven, was "no less rational on his premises, for the next life to him was all."[42] Stoicism did not emerge until the ancient ideal of earthly well-being was corrupted. The Greeks, conquered by Macedon, sent out to rule and inhabit oriental lands, lost the sense of flourishing health that had made mere existence delightful for their ancestors; and the bold Romans, when they mastered the lands of Alexander's empire, inherited the malaise. It is when "corruption and falsehood abound, and the air is charged with pestilence," that men of noble character must "brace themselves to endure, fronting life and fate not with hope but with suppression of fear; keeping the body subject to the mind and the mind ever vigilant, seeking tranquility not enjoyment, staking as little as possible in the game ruled by fortune." Ancient Stoicism was thus a half-way station between old Paganism and Christianity, having neither the health of the former nor the faith of the latter, "which compensates misery here by eternal bliss hereafter." It was "stern manhood" succeeding the joyous youth of Paganism, just as modern Stoicism is "hopeless manhood following the deluded youth of Christianity."

But the Stoicism of Marcus Aurelius, Thomson notes, has not the original sternness of the sect; it is Stoicism of a gentler type, "as of one used and reconciled to suffering." Resignation becomes, in it, a free acceptance of all that nature brings; it "loves and pities mankind while not hoping much to improve him, finds satisfaction and even joy in strict obedience to conscience, and performs energetically all social and political duties." Among the chief tenets of the Stoic Emperor's philosophy, there is one that coincides marvelously with a major tenet of that great champion of modern Stoicism, Thomas Carlyle. Both feel intensely, Thomson writes, "that 'All dies and is for a time only; is a Time-phantasm, yet reckons itself real.'" Yet both feel with equal intensity that life is, nevertheless, "most earnest and momentous, that moral purity in life is of supreme ineffable significance, and that moral worth is proved in action not in thought." One cannot help remarking, Thomson adds,

> that if life be so ephemeral and phantasmal, nothing pertaining to it can be of substantial importance; that whether it be moral or immoral, pure or impure, noble or vile, malignant or loving, wise or foolish, brave or cowardly, matters little or nothing, all its attributes being at least as vain, void, and illusive as itself. The fact is that human nature, a life, is seldom or never logical and self-consistent; that hostile convictions which ought to be mutually self-destructive may inhabit it together . . . . In this case we can but say that two of the best and wisest men we know have each held these contradictory convictions, reconciled in fact by living co-existence and co-efficience, and leaving logic little to say but, "So much the worse for the facts."[43]

At the close of the essay, Thomson comments generally on the utility of the old manuals of behavior that used to be written to assist men in the conduct of their lives and in the purification of their consciences. In modern times, the want of such manuals is especially felt by those who, rather than violate the integrity of their thought, have sternly renounced the communion and fellowship that Churches can afford. In the literature of Christendom, many excellent manuals are to be found, of great worth "even to the extreme infidel who aspires to live a good life." This should not surprise the free-thinker, for any great system of religion which, in addition to its peculiar spiritual content, "has gathered to itself the spoils of older religions and philosophies," must naturally absorb into its communion the best persons of the age in which it flourishes — "before criticism has sapped its authority and the higher intellect evacuated its dogmas and moved into strange regions." Thomson especially recommends the *Imitation of Christ*, attributed to Thomas à Kempis, and *A Serious Call to a Devout and Holy Life*, by William Law, as books that may be used with such profit even by "an atheist, although he must ignore a good deal of them as not essential but transitory, the old fashions of a creed which itself is going out of fashion." But much more suitable for such men are the Emperor's *Thoughts* which make up not a volume to be read and set aside, but a manual for daily and then weekly or monthly use, from which one may constantly draw "strength and courage for the stern unintermitted warfare of life."[44]

Thomson's essay on the *Discourses of Epictetus* has much in it of the same vein; yet it is especially significant from the point of view of this study because of the comparisons it introduces between ancient Stoicism and the modern varieties encountered in Leopardi and Pascal. Thomson notes that among the mature works of Leopardi there is a translation into Italian of the complete manual or "enchiridion" of Epictetus, introduced by a brief but weighty preface. In that preface the Italian pessimist argues that contrary to the general opinion, which is that the "Stoic philosophy is not suitable, nor even possible, save to those who are beyond measure virile and robust," the philosophy of Epictetus is especially adapted to such men "as by nature or habit are not heroic, nor very strong, but tempered and endowed with mediocre strength, or are even weak; and therefore to modern men yet more than to the ancient." The utility of the indifference, or coldness of heart preached by Epictetus and the other Stoics, springs solely from the fact that "man cannot in his life by any means either attain happiness or avoid continual unhappiness." For if he could possibly attain these ends, it would certainly not be useful or rational to refrain from seeking them. The strong persist in the quest, urging fierce and mortal war against Destiny, like the *Seven Against Thebes* of Aeschylus. The weak only can learn to surrender in the face of Necessity, and for that reason they are especially able to profit from the manual of Epictetus. Pascal, too, teaches that Stoicism is a discipline not of strength but of weakness, not of "self-sufficiency" but of "insufficiency." It is a philosophy, Thomson concludes that uplifts the weak and humbles the proud, and the proof is to be found in the very pages of its chief spokesmen, Epictetus, the slave, who acquires an insistent and imperious character, and Antoninus, the Emperor, who resigns his imperial dignity in recording his most intimate thoughts.[45]

D. Pascal and Leopardi

Thomson's translations from Leopardi, most of which had appeared serially in the columns of the *National Reformer* during the eighteen-sixties, were collected and published posthumously in 1905, by Bertram Dobell in a volume entitled *Essays, Dialogues and Thoughts of Giacomo Leopardi*. Included in the volume are a sixty-page introductory memoir made up of translations of the most important letters of the Italian poet, an essay comparing his pessimism with that of Pascal, an excerpt from Thomson's essay on Epictetus, a translation of Leopardi's major work in prose, the *Operette Morali*, and a complete version of the fragmentary "Pensieri." At the close of the introductory memoir, Thomson translates Schopenhauer's brief tribute to Leopardi, inserted in the 1859 edition of his *Die Welt als Wille und Vorstellung*, under the heading "On the Nothingness and Anguish of Life." "No one else," Schopenhauer had written, "has treated this subject so fundamentally and exhaustively as in our days

Leopardi. He is wholly filled and pervaded with it; throughout he makes the mockery and woe of this existence his theme, on every page of his works he dwells upon it, yet with such multiplicity of forms and applications, with such wealth of imagery, that he is never tedious, but on the contrary is always interesting and affecting." Thomson also cites with approval the judgment of Count Platen, who had said that "the grand Italian poetry, born on the lips of Dante, died at length on those of Leopardi."[46]

In the fragmentary "Parallel Between Pascal and Leopardi," Thomson observes that "Leopardi has been termed, not without reason, the Pascal of Italy," though in fact he is "more virile or less feminine, although supremely a poet, than the Pascal of France." But the two have surely this in common — that, by the "grandeur of their genius and the enduring intensity of their suffering," they are

> perhaps the most remarkable victims in our modern literature of that tragedy in which Nature seems to delight, the tragedy of a powerful and energetic spirit in an imbecile body. Chatterton and Keats suffered bitterly, but not for long; Marlowe fell in lusty youth; Shelley's pains and sorrows were drowned before he could reach his prime, and moreover he had lived and loved; Alfred de Musset was prematurely outworn, but at least he was "a young man with a fine past"; Novalis faded away early after his ideal beloved, and he was gentle and pietistic and about to marry another; Heine lay for seven years tortured and helpless on his mattress-grave; but not until he had freely enjoyed a youth and manhood of the richest life.[47]

Pascal and Leopardi alone seem to have had scarcely any life of genuine childhood, and none at all of spirited youth and manhood. They endured a continuous death-in-life of disease, languor, hypochondria and infinite weariness, the potent spirit disabled by the impotent flesh, in an "agony prolonged to the verge of the fortieth year."[48] Pascal, as a mere boy, accomplished in pure and applied mathematics what would have sufficed to crown with glory a full life of genius; Leopardi, as a youth, acquired such mastery of Greek and Latin philology that he astounded the leading scholars of Europe, with his forgeries first, and then with his precise scholarship. Yet both soon renounced their first studies, and "by their writings of general interest, written in brief intermissions of agony," rather than by their specialized talents, made their indelible impressions on subsequent generations. The best pages of Pascal's *Thoughts*, Thomson asserts, "are probably the finest for simple and noble beauty in the whole range of French literature; and the best in Leopardi's *Moral Essays* (which are his equivalent for Pascal's *Thoughts*, his own *Thoughts*

moving principally on a lower plane) can hardly be paralleled in
Italian save by the noblest in Dante's *Vita Nuova*."[49]

After examining the diversity of style "which is due as much to
the difference of the languages as of the men," Thomson turns to
consider the intellectual similarities and divergences. The Christian
no less than the pagan rationalist, he writes, sees with preternatural
clearness "the nature of man in all its strength and weakness and
marvelous inconsistency." But from this point of coincidence the
two men diverge, one to become an ascetic saint, the other a stoical
pessimist. Pascal studies the Bible so that he knows every word of it,
and in that study renounces all the light of his critical intelligence,
hating and torturing himself to become a perfect Christian. Leopardi,
more masculine in soul, gazes steadfastly on the "dreadful truth,"
refusing to the very end the "fond consolations of religious and other
dreams." It is important to stress, Thomson says, that both Leopardi
and Pascal "were wretched; the sublime infidel equally with the sublime Christian." It is not faith or lack of it that is responsible for
human misery in its most intense forms. "When life in the flesh is a
long agony," he concludes, "life is miserable; in whatever creed or
system it may clothe itself."[50]

In a prose essay, or rather fable, entitled "Storia del Genere
Umano" ("Story of the Human Race" in Thomson's version),
Leopardi epitomized his pessimistic view of mankind's lot in the
world. The chief Italian critics, from De Sanctis to Giovanni Gentile,
have stressed the importance of the work as a key to the unity of
thought running through the entire corpus of Leopardi's writings.[51]
Each of its sentences has been analyzed to show how it contains, in
germ, the substance of one or another of the chief Leopardian poems and dialogues, some of which were written earlier, some later.
Thomson has pressed its full substance into the verses of his masterpiece, but has altered, or rather inverted its meaning through the
device of locating his *City* imaginatively on the edge of the Christian
hell of Dante's poetic universe. To appreciate the intellectual and
religious, as well as literary significance of the inversion, or transvaluation, of values that results from the juxtaposition of proud pagan despair and desperate Christian hope (for the worldly Christian
hope of Dante is surely desperate) in the *City*, one has only to come
to it with an accurate statement of Leopardian pessimism in mind.
And such a statement, full of verbal anticipations of the language
and imagery of the *City*, may be read in Thomson's version of the
"Storia del Genere Umano."

De Sanctis has remarked with what classical reserve Leopardi recites his fable — as if he were a being altogether unacquainted with the ordinary feelings of the race of man whose history he is relating.[52] The first men to people the earth, he says,[53] were formed at the same time, all infants, on a world much smaller, far less various than it is now. Yet, as they grew, with childish willingness to be pleased they rejoiced in every aspect of it, deeming every new or unfamiliar thing marvelous, majestic, vast. And even more exciting than present enjoyments were their hopes for the future. In time, however, the novelty wore away; they realized that the earth was not really vast, that they could easily explore all its parts, and that the parts as well as the inhabitants were really all very much alike. As they had been inordinately happy when they were children together, so, in growing old together, they became inordinately unhappy, many of them spontaneously putting an end to their existence.

To renew their interest in life, Jove expanded the creation, varied the shape and composition of the earth, introduced strange sounds in forests, winds and caverns, mixed the generations of men, and troubled their sleep with dreams. These changes restored the charm of human existence for a time, but again familiarity led to tedium. Men began perversely to mourn the event of birth and to celebrate that of death; and the gods, angered by such perversion, punished the entire race with the flood of Deucalion in which only a pair of mortals survived. Too disdainful of life to endure the work of generation, the survivors had to be taught to repeople the world by throwing stones over their shoulders.

But Jove, by now, had come to know the true nature of men — that they "desire always and in whatever condition the impossible," and that they "torment themselves the more with imaginary evils the less they are afflicted with real ones." He therefore plagued them with diseases, earthquakes, storms, compelling them to take endless care in feeding, sheltering, and clothing themselves; he instructed Mercury to stimulate song and the other arts, to found great cities, introduce rivalries, discords, and diversities of language, so as to complicate communication; and he himself introduced laws and certain phantasms of "excellent and superhuman nature . . . called Justice, Virtue, Glory, Patriotism and the like." With so many petty and difficult problems confronting them, with so many "ideals" to pursue, men were truly saved from boredom and disdain of life — until their marvelous inventiveness enabled them to solve most of the difficulties, and familiarity and leisure once again led to satiety and contempt.

But the real source of the decline of the state "we are now wont to call antique" was the seductive influence of the phantasm known as Wisdom, which daily promised men that it would "show them Truth, which it said was a very great genius and its own master, never yet seen upon the earth, but dwelling with the gods in heaven." The mere phantasm of Wisdom could not, of course, make good its promise, but it so excited the minds of men that they began to cry out against the heavens, upbraiding the deities for withholding from them the benefits to be derived from the presence of Truth in the world. In a moment of supreme ill-will toward men, Jove satisfied their demand; Truth was sent to take up permanent residence in their midst. And the result was the condition of men as we have it now. The harm was incalculable for thereafter nothing could appear more profoundly true to men than the falsity of human blessings and the vanity of everything except their suffering. The old phantasms fled at the approach of Truth. No longer able to pride themselves on love of justice, virtue, country, men began again, as in the beginning, to "account themselves citizens of the world, making professions of universal love towards all their species," though in reality the race consisted no longer of communities, but of individuals, and these, "having no native country to be specially loved and no foreign one to hate," turned to hating everyone else, each loving himself alone.

So cruel did man's lot thereafter seem, that the gods themselves were moved to pity. Jove then decided to make the phantasm Love impervious to the destructive force of Truth, so that men might find some solace in that shadow. And later, when he observed that some men here and there managed to maintain integrity of conduct even while "afflicted by the hard domination of Truth," he relented further, and asked the gods whether any of them were disposed to visit men in person to comfort them as they had formerly been accustomed to do. "Whereon all the others keeping silent, Love, the son of the Celestial Venus," like in name to the earthly phantasm, but in virtue most unlike, offered himself, as he had never done before, to leave the companionship of the gods for brief times. Only very rarely has Love actually descended to earth. When he does, he takes up abode in the "amiable and tender hearts of generous and magnanimous persons," filling them with a strange and wonderful serenity. Sometimes he unites two such souls with reciprocal ardor — but Jove seldom permits him to gratify their desires. Yet "merely to experience in one's self the presence of this divinity is a happiness such as transcends all others that have ever been known to mankind." For the duration of the visits of Love, Truth itself is impotent; the beautiful phantasms that usually fly from its presence resume their former place, shielded by Love's power. Thus, in the stern rule of Truth, men experience the justice of the gods, and in the fleeting contentment of Love's visits, their mercy.[54]

In 1882, a few months before he died, Thomson attempted to render something of the thought and mood of this fable in English verses worthy of the lyric song of the Italian poet. The result was the posthumously published "Proem" which begins with a very Leopardian cry of anguished nostalgia:

> O antique fables! beautiful and bright
> And joyous with the joyous youth of yore;
> O antique fables! for a little light
> Of that which shineth in you evermore,
> To cleanse the dimness from our weary eyes . . . .[55]

Favole antiche, Leopardi had written in an explanatory subtitle for his plaintive early poem "Alla Primavera."[56] But Thomson is here echoing also the sentiments and words of Theseus in the lines of *A Midsummer-Night's Dream* which begin: "I never may believe / These antique fables, nor these fairy toys."[57] For Theseus, no less than for Leopardi, the bright wonders of old are but the imaginings of madmen and frantic lovers, shaped by the poet's pen which gives to airy nothing a local habitation and a name. But unfortunately the past is not all wondrous fables. Rapidly, Thomson's "Proem" reviews the "burden" of Leopardi's history of man's unhappiness:

> We stagger under the enormous weight
> Of all the heavy ages piled on us,
> With all their grievous wrongs inveterate,
> And all their disenchantments dolorous,
> And all the monstrous tasks they have bequeathed;
> And we are stifled with the airs they breathed;
> And read in theirs our dooms calamitous.

Nothing of their dreams and phantasms, only the burden of their very real deeds survives. "No deities in sky or sun or moon, / No nymphs in woods and hills and seas and streams." Ancient scientific thought of the time of Empedocles had stripped the Greek world of such dreams, analyzing all that is or has been into "mere earth and water, air and fire"; and with the modern renaissance of analytical science the dreams of the Judeo-Christian world have fared no better:

> No God in all our universe we trace,
> No heaven in the infinitude of space,
> No life beyond death — coming not too soon.

Modern men have tried to reanimate the universe with myths of their own, but they have failed; their souls have been stripped of the faculty to hope and dream as men hoped and dreamed in the past. "Our souls," the poet writes, "are stript of their illusions," and our hopes, at best, are placed

> in some far future years
> For others, not ourselves; whose bleeding feet
> Wander this rocky waste where broken spears
> And bleaching bones lie scattered on the sand;
> Who know *we* shall not reach the Promised Land; —
> Perhaps a mirage glistening through our tears.

The Land of Promise seems powerless to be born — like the new world of Matthew Arnold. But what if all our expectations were realizable? And if there be this Promised Land indeed, the poet cries —

> Our children's children's children's heritage,
> Oh, what a prodigal waste of precious seed,
> Of myriad myriad lives from age to age,
> Of woes and agonies and blank despairs
> Through countless cycles, that some fortunate heirs
> May enter, and conclude the pilgrimage!

There is, Thomson came to believe with Leopardi, a terrible callousness, or want of moral cultivation, as John Stuart Mill might have said, in hopes that see a promised land in the eventual alleviation of poverty, in the eventual conquest of disease, in the eventual elimination of war, of oppression, of inequality, of prejudice — as if the well-being thus to be enjoyed by generations to come could really compensate for, could really "justify," the myriad myriad lives of woes and agonies and blank despair that have gone before. If the sufferings of the past are of no account, neither are present sufferings, for they will soon be past. In his "Proposals for the Speedy Extinction of Evil and Misery," Thomson had elaborated the thought, showing that good men cannot, like mad tyrants, be happy while knowing that others are not, cannot be, or have never been happy. To contemplate seriously what must be the consequences of the realization of such worldly hopes, therefore, is to see those very hopes emptied, punctured, shriveled into nothing. Thus, writes Thomson,

> Our last illusion leaves us wholly bare,
> To bruise against fate's adamantine wall,
> Consumed or frozen in the pitiless air .

It is the moment of the Everlasting No, the vision of the Medusa's head, which consumes the heart of man, or "freezes" it into stone. All hopes dead, the naked will, left directionless, turns inward, concentrating all its animating power, all its capacity to desire, upon itself. "Ah love," Arnold wrote, in his own precious experience of the crisis, "let us be true / To one another!" — and the reason for his plea for truth in the name of love is that there really is no love, no certitude, no light, no hope, no help. Thomson's Leopardian "Proem" cries inwardly:

> In all our world, beneath, around, above,
> One only refuge, solace, triumph, — Love,
> Sole star of light in infinite black despair.

And with this anguished acknowledgment of the lingering power of the son of Celestial Venus, this epitome of the Leopardian spiritual experience, spirals back upon itself in the final stanza:

> O antique fables! beautiful and bright,
> And joyous with the joyous youth of yore;
> O antique fables! for a little light . . .

A few weeks after completing the "Proem." Thomson plunged himself with abandonment — so his friends report[58] — into the last volcanic whirl of drunken oblivion that sent him reeling, homeless and destitute, through London streets, jails, and hospitals, to burial in the unconsecrated ground of Highgate Cemetery, where his body, with the bodies of many other brave secularists — George Eliot, George Henry Lewes, Karl Marx — moulders and dissolves, as he himself expressed it, "to merge afresh, in earth, air, water, plants and other men."[59] Having paid a final tribute to Leopardi's much-worshipped deity, he seemed, in that Empedoclean plunge, to be saying:

> Unarm, Eros; the long day's task is done,
> And we must sleep.

E. Liebestod

According to Henry S. Salt, one subject clearly predominates in all Thomson's writings. It is, he says, that "great struggle between Love and Death, the pessimistic view of which must present itself, in certain moods, and at certain times, to the mind of every thoughtful person."[60] Thomson's preoccupation with the subject was occasioned, it is alleged, by his youthful grief over the death of Matilda Weller, a girl of fifteen, whom he dearly loved. "This was a crisis in his fate,"

Salt writes, "on which, as far as is known, he uttered no word in his after-life, even to his most intimate associates."[61] Yet, with all his reticence about the personal significance of the event, Thomson made no effort to conceal the literary excitement he experienced in discovering how many other poets in English, French, German, and Italian literature had been moved by similar encounters with death to write poetry of the kind that had been wrenched out of him by his grief.

It was probably Carlyle's essay on Novalis that first introduced Thomson to the author of the "Hymnen an die Nacht" and *Heinrich von Ofterdingen*.[62] The Sophia of the former glorified in the Mathilda of the latter — that "visible spirit of song" who becomes, after her youthful death, the inmost soul, the "guardian spirit" of the poet's "holy fire" — fascinated his imagination.[63] Later he read and was further fascinated by the account in *The Romantic School* of Heinrich Heine's meeting with Novalis' angelic muse, just before she died. She held in her hand, when he saw her, a gilt-edged volume, bound in red morocco. It was *Heinrich von Ofterdingen*, which she had read and re-read "until its pages had inoculated her with consumption, and now she looked like a luminous shadow."[64] But Heinrich Heine, too, like the hero of Novalis' romance, loved a Matilda, the lively mistress and wife whom he called by that name probably because she had come to him in innocence and was destined, he immediately knew, to remain with him, through "days good and evil," praying for his soul and nursing his body until the hour of his death.[65]

The importance of the name Matilda in the lives of Novalis and Heine led Thomson to identify himself with the German poets. He adopted Novalis' name, translated the "Hymnen an die Nacht," and, in his autobiographical *Vane's Story*, written in 1864, identified his own Matilda with Heine's. The hero of that Heinesque poem tells the story of a dream in which his beloved returns from death transfigured to chide him for having failed to achieve the good things "youth pledged ripe manhood to attain."[66] Many verses of Heine are introduced and translated in the course of the story and, in a long footnote, Thomson quotes the lines addressed to "mein Kind, mein Weib, Mathilda," from the *Letzte Gedichte*, in which Heine cries out in dismay at the thought that his death ("Mich ruft der Tod") will leave Mathilda alone among the vicious and sick beasts that inhabit

> Paris, die leuchtende Hauptstadt der Welt
> Das singende, springende, schone Paris,
> Die Holle der Engel, der Teufel Paradies.

The note also contains remarks that indicate the direction of Thomson's thoughts on the theme of his early *Doom of a City*. "Babylonische Sorgen," the title of Heine's last songs on death, love, and Paris, suggests, Thomon writes:

> and may have been especially suggested by, that great verse of Jeremiah li. 7: "Babylon hath been a golden cup in the Lord's hand, that made all the earth drunken: the nations have drunken of her wine; therefore the nations are mad."
>
> So Bèranger, in his *Jean de Paris*:
>
> > "Quel amour incroyable,
> > Maintenant et jadis,
> > Pour ces murs dont le diable
> > A fait son paradis!"
>
> And he who knew his Paris best, Balzac the Terrible: "Cette succursale de l'enfer."— *Melmoth Reconcilié.*
> Again, "Paris a été nommé un enfer. Tenez ce mot pour vrai." — *Le Fille aux Yeux d'or.*" — (Histoire desTreize.)
> And yet again, "Ce Paris qualifié d'antichambre del'enfer." — *Balzac, to the Abbé Eglé.*[67]

In her final transfiguration, Thomson's Matilda will lead him through an antichamber or limbo of hell that will be a mighty Babylon, indeed, resembling haughty London, however, rather than "Das singende, springende, schone Paris."

In Leopardi's beautiful "Amore e Morte," and in that masterpiece of Platonic psychoanalysis, "Alla Sua Donna," Thomson found an almost perfect mirroring of his deepest thoughts and feelings about love and death.[68] But it was Shelley who had shown him, long before, where to look for the ultimate poetic unraveling of love's mysteries. Shelley, too, had fallen in love with a Matilda — with that supreme Matilda of all literature, caretaker of Eden's innocence on the summit of Dante's seven-storied mountain of Purgatory. Students of the influence of Dante in English literature have remarked the correspondence between Shelley's doctrine of love and that of the *dolce stil novo*, which culminates in the Matilda scene of Purgatory. That Shelley recognized in Dante's Matilda the prototype of the "soul out of my soul" which he rashly sought "in many mortal forms," is attested by the fact that the one portion of the *Divine Comedy* he undertook to translate was the vision of the *bella donna* of the earthly paradise.[69] Although his friend Medwin was at a loss to explain why Shelley should have preferred that passage above all others in the *Divine Comedy*, the reason is quite obvious.[70] The Matilda of Purgatory is, as Grandgent remarks in his text of the *Commedia*, "the embodiment of Innocence, who, by the remission of sin through Lethe and Eunoë, restores innocence to Dante."[71] After drinking of Lethe, which causes him to forget his fall from innocence and all the painful steps of his progress toward recovery, Dante is shown an awe-inspiring vision of the meaning of history; and only after the vision is complete is he made to drink of the waters of Eunoë, which restore the memory of all the good he has experienced, separated completely from the evil that may have occasioned it and the pain that may have accompanied it. Shelley aspired, as he wrote in the "Triumph of Life," to represent

> a wonder worthy of the rhyme

> Of him who from the lowest depths of hell
> Through every paradise and through all glory,
> Love led serene, and who returned to tell

> The words of hate and awe; the wondrous story
> How all things are transfigured except Love; — [72]

but he died prematurely, without having heard an inspired answer to his question, "what is life?" and without having drunk of the healing waters of Eunoë. Concerning the relationship between Shelley and Dante, Thomson wrote to William M. Rossetti in 1873: "While agreeing with you in ranking *The Witch of Atlas* very high, I cannot agree with you in preferring it to the *Epipsychidion*. It has always seemed to me that Shelley never soared higher than in this poem, which I find full of supreme inspiration. It is his *Vita Nuova*, tender and fervid and noble as Dante's; and his premature death has deprived us of the befitting *Divina Commedia* which should have followed."[73] Shelley, according to Thomson, had reached the garden of Dante's Matilda and had died there; his own Matilda, Thomson dared to believe, had led him beyond the "Triumph of Life" to a wondrous vision truly worthy of the rhyme of Dante.

Another letter addressed to William H. Rossetti, from Colorado City, U.S.A., where, in 1872, Thomson spent six months as representative of an English mining company, reveals what poetry was foremost in his mind during the years in which the *City* was taking final shape. Responding to a request for additional critical comments on Rossetti's text of Shelley's poems, Thomson writes: "I cannot say anything about the Shelley notes now, as the only books I could find room for in my portmanteau were the Globe Shakespeare and Pickering's diamond Dante (with Cary's version squeezed in for the notes and general assistance)."[74] On the question of Thomson's relation to Shelley and Dante, his publisher and friend, G. W. Foote, wrote in 1884:

> I remember how cordially he agreed with me when I dissented from
> Miss Simcox's comparison [in the *Academy*] of his style with Shelley's.
> His great master was Dante; and Dantesque is the only proper word
> to describe the strongest characteristics of his style in *The City of
> Dreadful Night*. He possessed for many years the little Pickering edition
> of Dante, and he knew it almost by heart. Ruskin calls the great
> Florentine poet "the central intellect of all this world." "When," said
> Thomson to me, "I first read this sentence I thought it an
> exaggeration, but now I regard it as correct and true." I may here
> remark in passing, that Thomson, who was a masterly satirist, wrote
> a terrible piece of grave irony on the late Lord Lytton in the *terza
> rima*, which is what Dante might have written himself if he lived in
> our age and had a talent for such work.[75]

The piece on Lord Lytton to which Foote refers was written in 1870
and bears the title "Supplement to the Inferno." It consists of forty-
one *terzine* and imitates particularly the "opening of Canto V., and
the close of Canto XXI" of Dante's original, to which Thomson refers his readers. Like the passages it imitates, the "Supplement" is
gross in language and imagery. Poor Bulwer, confronted by Minos,
is forced to cast off the wondrous dress of his literary career piece by
piece:

> Cloak, tunic, surplice, toga, mangle, cape,
> Hood, bonnet, hat, boot, slipper, buskin, sock,
> Bulged slowly to a heap that well might drape
> A college of professors with their flock,
> And furnish 'guises for a masquerade,
> And still leave six old clo' men ample stock.[76]

The "great soul" stripped naked is revealed to be, in George Eliot's
words, "a great bladder for dried peas to rattle in." Minos refuses to
judge such a creature, and so it is thrown aside. But Graffiacave, one
of the prankish demons of Malebolge, pierces it with a hook and
offers it to Malacoda, the demon whose infernal task it is to blow
signals for the comings and goings of damned spirits. "Look!"
Graffiacave cries, "If thy sweet lips are moist with trumpeting, /
Here is a rag to wipe them!" In support of the line on the trumpeting of Malacoda, Thomson notes: "'Et egli avea del cul fatto
trombetta.' — A verse too easy to translate. Note that the austere
Dante so enjoys this Aristophanic touch that he chuckles over it, not
grimly, through twelve lines of grave burlesque opening the following Canto XXII, the only case of such self-indulgence I remember in
the *Divine Comedy*."[77]

Thomson was thus acquainted with the depths as well as the soaring heights of Dante's art. He knew the "ineffably tender and ardent Dante of the *Vita Nuova* and the imparadised Beatrice," but also this "rude and rigorous Dante" of the "hideous Thais . . . in the cesspool of Malebolge," who scratches herself "con l'unghie merdose."[78] In his *City* he occasionally attempts to be ineffably tender as well as rude and rigorous, but he strives especially to match the art that shaped the

> magnificent Sordello of the *Purgatorio* (vi.), defined, solid, massive, as if cast colossal in bronze, the most superb figure, I think, in all Dante; him who leaps from his haughty impassibility to embrace Virgil at the one word "Mantuan," kindling the Florentine to the fulgurant invective, *Ahi serva Italia*; the Sordello of that noble passage, not to be rendered into English: —

> "Ma vedi la un'anima che posta
>   Sola soletta versa noi riguarda;
> Quella ne'nsegnerà la via più tosta.

> Venimmo a lei; O anima Lombarda,
>   Come ti stavi altera e disdegnosa,
> E nel mover degli occhi onesta e tarda!

> Ella non ci diceva alcuna cosa,
>   Ma lasciavene gir, solo guardando
> A guisa di leon quando si posa."

> "But look and mark that spirit posted there
>   Apart, alone, who gazes as we go;
> He will instruct us how we best may fare.

> We came to him: O Lombard spirit, lo,
>   What pride and scorn thy bearing then expressed,
> The movement of thine eyes how firm and slow!

> No word at all he unto us addressed,
>   But let us pass, only regarding still
> In manner of a lion when at rest."[79]

Thomson makes no attempt here, in his version of the untranslatable, to render the latent undertone of Dante's poetic music, which is not to be confused with the sounds of the Italian syllables. A competent musician ("first clarinet" at the Caledonian and Royal Military asylums)[80] he was never persuaded as critic or poet that the mere sound of words, apart from their sense, can have a high degree of musical beauty. The beauty of intelligible words, poetically ordered, addresses itself, according to Thomson, not to the external senses, but to the mind and heart, which can be reached through the eyes as well as the ears. It is in the mind and heart, not in the external senses, that words can produce the most marvelous musical effects without sound, even as they can paint with color, fashion statues and palaces without stone, and animate living men and women without flesh and blood. In characterizing the inner music of Dante's poetry, Thomson almost invariably refers to Beethoven — on whose "forehead broods the frown of thunder, but [whose] smile is so ravishing and sweet that naught can compare with it save the tenderness and sternness of Dante the Divine."[81] In a beautiful poem on music, in which he characterizes with technical accuracy the thematic work of Beethoven's piano sonatas, the "arising and passing-away of the several motives," that so fascinated von Bulow,[82] he sings of a mind and heart filled with

> colossal Beethoven, the gentlest spirit sublime
> Of the harmonies interwoven, Eternity woven with Time;
> Of the melodies slowly and slowly dissolving away through
>   the soul,
> While it dissolves with them wholly and our being is lost
>   in the Whole;
> As gentle as Dante the Poet, for only the lulls of the stress
> Of the mightiest spirits can know it, this ineffable gentleness.[83]

Yet there are also mighty silences in Dante, vast visible silences, throbbing with the noiseless clamor of restless frustrated wills. In his posthumously published "Insomnia," which is the gloomiest of his poems, and in the early "Mater Tenebrarum," Thomson has attempted to reproduce such silences. "Insomnia" pictures the silent hours of sleepless night as so many "hideous Malebolges" cut deep into the "hollow night's dominions" transforming it into an infernal maze of dreams.[84] "Mater Tenebrarum" written in 1859, is the earliest of the series of poems and poetic essays, including *Vane's Story*, "To Our Ladies of Death," "A Lady of Sorrow," and the *City*, in which a woman transfigured in death returns to the poet to reveal the mysteries of love. She is represented in the early poem as she first appeared to the poet when his spirit was still too stunned to be more than barely conscious of her presence, sitting black-veiled beside him, "speaking not a word, as the friends of Job sat silent at first, for they saw that his grief was great." But the poet at length prays for an end to silence and for a lifting of the veil. "Come down!" he cries in the mood of the *Vita Nuova* —

> O come! come serious and mild
> And pale, as thou wert on this earth, thou adorable child!
> Or come as thou art, with thy sanctitude, triumph and bliss
> For a garment of glory about thee; and give me one kiss,
> One tender and pitying look of those pure loving eyes,

> One word of solemn assurance and truth that the soul
>   with its love never dies![85]

This prayer of the poet is answered in *Vane's Story* where the trans-figured woman returns as an embodiment of purest love — the Matilda of Eden's innocence. The "splendour of her beauty" makes him blind, and poet tells us; but his mind grows bright, and his heart begins to long for Death to bear him through Lethe into her "deep-est cave under the Sea," where, like the hero of *Heinrich von Ofterdingen* and his Matilda, he and his beloved, in a death-embrace, may be cleansed for resurrection in a new life of everlasting bliss.

But death has many aspects, three of which are distinguished in "To Our Ladies of Death," written in 1861. Thomson notes that the "Three Ladies" of the poem "were suggested by the sublime sister-hood" of De Quincey's "Suspiria de Profundis," and that the seven-line stanza was "moulded under the influence" of Robert Browning's "The Guardian Angel."[86] Although he longs, at first, to see Death as "Our Lady of Beatitudes . . . garmented in purest white," the poet shrinks from her when she appears in that form:

> Would that me
> Though hadst upgathered in my life's pure morn!
> Unworthy then, less worthy now, forlorn,
>   I dare not, Gracious Mother, call on Thee.[87]

She appears next as "Our Lady of Annihilation." Thomson's presen-tation of this aspect of death provides a gloss for his picture of the *Melencolia* in the concluding canto of the *City*. In this early poem the poet is unaware that his "Lady of Annihilation" has marked him for her own. He pictures her as of "mighty stature," — a royal sorceress

> Upon whose swarthy face and livid brow
> Are graven deeply anguish, malice, scorn,
> Strength ravaged by unrest, resolve forlorn
> Of any hope, dazed pride that will not bow.[88]

Rolled round her body like a chain is a serpent of two heads, one stinging her brain, the other her heart. In one hand she wields a rod of serpents, in the other, a cup of raging fire; her lidless eyes, her wings, her clothes and hair are dark as the grave. She is, the poet says, "Night essential radiating night" — a colossal "statue of Despair." The poet is aware that to hearts and minds dominated by her she appears "young and warm, / Pard-beautiful and brilliant," like the *lonza leggiera . . . di pel maculato* of Dante's *selva oscura*.[89] But he is not yet caught in the web of the inscrutable enchantress:

> The evil passions which may make me thine

> Are not yet irrepressible in me;
> And I have pierced thy mask of riant youth,
> And seen thy form in all its hideous truth:
> I will not, Dreadful Mother, call on Thee.[90]

Ten years later Thomson will depict this dreadful mother not as she appears to those who long for Eden's innocence, or who are swayed by evil passions, but as she appears to the brave and honest Carlyles and George Eliots of the modern world, who, though shut out from the light and love of the Judeo-Christian God, labor incessantly, with indomitable will, to improve the spiritual lot of mankind. Here it may be noted, as a further gloss on the meaning of Thomson's *Melencolia*, that, in his response to George Eliot's letter of 1874 in which she expressed the hope that the author of the *City* would "soon give us more heroic strains with a wider embrace of human fellowship in them," Thomson had written: "I ventured to send you a copy of the verses (as I ventured to send another to Mr. Carlyle) because I have always read, whether rightly or wrongly, through all the manifold beauty and delightfulness of your work, a character and an intellectual destiny akin to that grand and awful Melancholy of Albrecht Dürer which dominates the City of my poem."[91] In the poem of 1861, however, the poet is not yet ready to — will not, he says — acknowledge himself a child of that dreadful "Lady of Annihilation." He there longs for death to come in the form of that "throneless queen . . . of human stature," whose eyes are shadowed wells of Lethe waters, and whom he calls "Our Lady of Oblivion." To her the poet prays:

> O sweetest Sister, and sole Patron Saint
>   Of all the humble eremites who flee
> From out life's crowded tumult . . .
> Take me, and lull me into perfect sleep
> Down, down, far hidden in thy duskiest cave . . . .[92]

It is the death the poet prayed for in *Vane's Story*, the death of reunion with innocent love that Novalis celebrates in the *vita nuova* scenes of *Heinrich von Ofterdingen*.

But in "A Lady of Sorrow," Thomson's principal prose writing which he placed first in the 1881 volume of *Essays and Phantasies*, the poet comes to know that his pursuit of love beyond the grave is leading in a direction the very opposite of Dante's in the *Divine Comedy*. Dante's vision of dead-love, Beatrice, leads him from the innocence of an earthly paradise to a heavenly love full of transcendent joy: "Amor di vero ben, pien di letizia; / letizia che trascende ogni dolzore."[93] Yet surely the world knows another kind of love, and another kind of death, and a union of the two, that does not lead to transcendent joy. Thomson quotes the lines of Leopardi:

> Fratelli, a un tempo, Amore e Morte
> Ingenerò la sorte.
> Cose quaggiù sì belle
> Altre il mondo non ha, non han le stelle.[94]

In what way does the love-death worshipped by Leopardi differ from Dante's? So little seems to be required to transform the love of a Paolo for a Francesca — the personal love so intense that the beloved must reciprocate — into that *amor di vero ben* which gives transcendent joy. And yet even in Dante, who cherished both forms of love as a poet, they are placed a universe apart. Shelley's love for that "soul out of his own soul," Leopardi's love for that marvelous woman he dared not hope to see in life, Thomson's love for his young Matilda, all had power to raise such lovers high above this world of genesis and decay to a vision of that source of all beauty, all goodness, all truth which moves the world by being loved, even as a magnet, itself unmoved, moves metal filings. Dante seems to present just such an "erotic" ascent in his *Divine Comedy*. He proceeds, from the circle of carnal love, through the hellish center of the earth, where he learns to see through the glittering surface of sin, and then up through Purgatory, where the encrustations of sin are removed from his eyes and its stains, from his soul. On the summit of Purgatory he is restored to innocence by the mysterious Matilda, and is at last pure and disposed to rise, in union with his dead Beatrice, to the stars. Only here and there in his long ascent of Platonic eros does the Christian poet give any indications of the operation of another kind of love, or of the efficacy of another kind of death. Rarely is it more than suggested in the *Divine Comedy* that the love-death that saves the Christian poet is, ultimately, not that of Beatrice but that of the Son of Mary on the Cross. Earth as well as heaven (*e cielo e terra*),[95] Dante confessed, had contributed to the writing of his sacred poem; love dictated it to him, he said to Buonagiunta in Purgatory,[96] but it was, plainly, a double love, and precisely how much was due to earth and how much to heaven in the finished work cannot easily be discerned.

In "A Lady of Sorrow" Thomson reveals that the high path of erotic love through death has led him to the antithesis of Dante's joy. In the "brilliant morning of a joyous holiday," he says, a transfigured woman who was neither Love nor Death suddenly appeared to him. Her advent had been long before announced, but now she

came to take possession, "absorbing every thought and feeling to
her devotion, and compelling even the dreams and visions of both
day and night to worship her; the darkly beautiful Queen, the disin-
herited Titaness, the Pythia of an abandoned and ruined shrine, the
wild, passionate, tender-hearted, desolate, sorcery-smitten Sorceress;
Sorrow, the daughter of Love and Death."[97] Like her parents, Sorrow suffers many transformations. Slight changes affect her every
moment, decided changes every hour. Only three of her "multitudinous and still evolving variations" does the poet attempt to picture;
and these correspond to the aspects of love and death he has pictured in "Mater Tenebrarum," *Vane's Story*, and "To Our Ladies of
Death." But Sorrow's task is to instruct. Like the transfigured Beatrice
on the summit of Purgatory, Sorrow comes to reveal the profoundest
secrets of the history of mankind — secrets that will enable the poet
to justify in poetry his long pursuit of love through the regions of
death. But before revealing those secrets, Sorrow draws a confes-
sion out of the poet. He knows that Love, the mother of Sorrow, is
dying; and therefore, to make him confess it, she pours into his soul
a melody of "overwhelming sorrow," and transforms herself into a
"foul wrinkled hag," who clings to him with mocking endearments
until he is driven, by the horror of putrefaction crawling about his
body and writhing like a swarm of worms in his brain, to implore
and imprecate "rest, unconsciousness, annihilation."[98]

Having driven him to seek Annihilation, Sorrow returns as a formless shadow to instruct the poet by leading him "hour after hour of
dusk and night through the interminable streets" of the vast Metropolis of London, "which was become a vast Necropolis, desolate
as a Pariah." Thomson here returns to the theme of the *Doom of a
City*. As he wanders through the "streets of this great and terrible
city," he becomes aware of the movements, the running after some
goal, of its myriad inhabitants:

> The ever-streaming multitudes of men and women and children,
> mysterious fellow-creatures of whom I know only that they *are* my
> fellow-creatures — and even this knowledge is sometimes darkened
> and dubious — overtake and pass me, meet and pass me; the
> inexhaustible processions of vehicles rattle and roar in the midst;
> lamp beyond lamp and far clusters of lamps burn yellow above the
> paler cross shimmer from brilliant shops, or funereally measure the
> long vistas of still streets, or portentously surround the black gulphs
> of squares and graveyards silent; lofty churches uplift themselves,
> blank soulless, sepulchral, the pyramids of this mournful desert, each
> conserving the Mummy of a Great King in its heart; the sky overhead

lowers vague and obscure; the moon and stars . . . are as wan earthly
spectres, not radiant rejoicing spheres whose home is in the heavens
beyond the firmament.[99]

In the midst of this Necropolis, not in a garden of innocence, Sorrow displays her pageant of life. She draws for her wisdom not on
the Old and New Testaments, as Beatrice is able to do in the earthly
paradise, but on the great chronicles of nature and of human history, in which the material constituents of the universe and the generations of men have told their stories. Out of the latter she draws
the chief figures of her pageant. All of human kind "that have ever
lived, with all that are now living and all that are being born into life,
all the members of the aeon of humanity, compose the solemn procession." Far in advance of the rest "gleam stately figures in ample
Oriental robes, 'dusk faces with white silken turbans wreathed,' from
whose midst sway the long necks of highbacked camels." Then follow medieval knights, kings dark-bearded and queens trailing brilliant retinues; hooded monks in sombre gowns; barbarians with limbs
and features weirdly tatooed; nomad tribes with their flocks; —

> legions on legions countless of all history's soldiery, from the heroes
> who fought around Troy to the warriors of Waterloo; the chariots
> and the spoils of a Capitolian triumph; "elephants endorsed with
> towers;" the silent flash of Maenads who run as they ran upon the
> Thracian mountains; dim crowds in the garb of our own time and
> country: and, as upon an unseen river flowing down the mid-stream
> of the swollen river of the peoples, glide forward galleys and galleons
> and ships of all seas and centuries: all come sweeping by, thronged
> and intermingled yet unconfused, in ghostly silence; and their
> trampling does not shake the earth beneath their feet: not more
> silent is the procession of the stars.[100]

Dante, on the summit of purgatory, sees a vision of the history of
Christianity from the time of the establishment of the Church in the
world to his own era. It appears to him as the history of a tremendous conflict, with banners confused in the fray, foul made fair and
fair become foul; a tragic history, beginning with glad tidings of
great joy for all mankind, and ending, or apparently on the verge of
ending, in complete disaster. Dante's vision ends with the head of
the Church transformed into a harlot prostituting herself for worldly
gain, forced to become a courtesan of a national monarch. To see
this tragic vision, Beatrice tells Dante,[101] he has been led through
hell and Purgatory; he has learned why, and to what extent, the world
lives ill, and must now continue on his journey — his long Odyssey —
to God, in whose countenance he will read how the tragic conflict

between the Church and the World may be brought to a happy reso-
lution, so that earthly and heavenly ideals may co-exist in peace and
harmony. Thomson's Lady of Sorrow reveals a pageant of tragedy in
which the history of Christianity is but an episode. Her pageant proceeds accompanied by a vague echo of music from a sphere remote.
To interpret its meaning she chants and recites some of the "briefer
human anthem-words and collects," which the loftiest singers in the
pageant have themselves composed. In the original version of this
essay, printed in the *National Reformer*, Thomson cited at length
twenty-eight such anthem-words in verse, and twelve in prose, limit-
ing himself to those written or well-rendered in English. From the
poetry of Chaucer, the early Scottish ballads, Spenser, Shakespeare,
Webster, Chidich Tychborne, James Thomson of the *Seasons*, Byron,
Shelley, Poe, Emily Bronte, Tennyson, Arnold and Browning; from
Job, Ecclesiastes, Plato, Raleigh, Bacon, Thomas Browne, De Quincey,
Garth Wilkinson and Carlyle, page after page come the answers to
Shelley's question in the "Triumph of Life" and to Heine's "Fragen" —
life's but a walking shadow, a tale told by an idiot, signifying noth-
ing.[102]

At the close of the essay Thomson is on the verge of turning the
lesson of Sorrow inside out, on the verge of glorying in despair. He
had read that thought of Leopardi which was to enable the great
"actionist" philosopher of the fascist era, Giovanni Gentile, to find
in the pessimism of the faithless poet an inexhaustible source of
spiritual comfort for godless young men and women.[103] Thomson
himself had translated the "thought" which so marvelously anticipates the creed of Bertrand Russell in "A Free Man's Worship." "To
be unable to find satisfaction in any earthly thing," Leopardi wrote:

> to consider the inestimable amplitude of space, the number and
> astonishing mass of the worlds, and find that all is little and petty to
> the capacity of our soul; to imagine the number of the worlds infinite,
> and the universe infinite, and feel that our soul and our desire would
> be still greater than such a universe; always to accuse things of
> insufficiency and nullity, and endure that want and emptiness which
> we call life-weariness [noia]; this seems to me the greatest sign of
> grandeur and nobleness which human nature presents. Let it also be
> noted that life-weariness is scarcely known to insignificant persons,
> and very little or not at all to the lower animals.[104]

Leopardi had sung this truth in his last poem, "La Ginestra";
Schopenhauer had grudgingly acknowledged it at the close of his
great work; but, according to Thomson, its spirit operated most marvelously not in the pessimism of the Leopardis and Schopenhauers,

where it leaps up paradoxically at the close, but in the Carlyles and Mills, and Matthew Arnolds, and George Eliots of the world, who, after having caught but a glimpse of the Medusa's head, boldly buckle on their belts to confront the enemies of man in the modern world with as much abandon as Macbeth showed in preparing himself for his last desperate fight.

What saved Thomson from — but perhaps one should say, deprived him of — the renewal that is worked in men after they have seen the Gorgon's head, no one can ever know for certain. But certain it is that he experienced no such transvaluation of values. In the last part of "A Lady of Sorrow," Thomson wonders whether the form in which the daughter of Love and Death then appeared to him would be the final form. He suspects, he says, that there are deeper mysteries of erotic love to be explored, and that, therefore, "a successor or successors" will appear.[105] Just as Beatrice, in the closing scenes of the *Paradiso*, must step aside and allow the jongleur of the Virgin to present Dante to the Mother of Jesus, Queen of the City of God,[106] so the transfigured Lady of Sorrow steps aside finally and allows the "pure sad artist" of "three centuries and threescore years ago"[107] to present Thomson to a mighty mother, the winged *Melencolia*, "Patroness and Queen" of *The City of Dreadful Night*.

NOTES

1. *Biographical and Critical Studies*, p. 274.

2. Essays and Phantasies, p. 207.

3. *Ibid.*, p. 211.

4. *Ibid.*, p. 197.

5. *Ibid.*, p. 208, note.

6. *Ibid.*, p. 204.

7. *Poems, Essays and Fragments*, pp. 256-57.

8. *Essays and Phantasies*, p. 203.

9. *Ibid.*, p. 298.

10. See Plato's *Republic*, the closing paragraphs of Book VI.

11. *Essays and Phantasies*, p. 2; see also Thomson's letter to George Eliot, cited in Salt, *Life*, p. 82.

12. *Essays and Phantasies*, p. 302.

13. *Ibid..*, pp. 297-98.

14. *Ibid.*, p. 298.

15. *Ibid.*, p. 299.

16. *Ibid.*, p. 300.

17. *Ibid.*, p. 297.

18. *Ibid.*, p. 300.

19. *Ibid.*, pp. 300-301.

20. *Ibid.*, p. 301.

21. *Ibid.*, p. 303.

22. *Ibid.*, p. 304-305.

23. *Ibid..*, p. 306.

24. *Ibid.*, p. 307.

25. *Ibid.*, p. 312.

26. Paul Neugebauer, *Schopenhauer in England*, mit besonderer Berücksichtigung seines Einflusses auf die englische Literatur (Berlin, 1932), p. 25.

27. Thomson, "Arthur Schopenhauer," *The Secularist*, I (1876), 121.

28. *Ibid.*, p. 173.

29. *Ibid.*

30. *Ibid.*, pp. 173-74.

31. *Ibid.*, p. 174.

32. Arthur Schopenhauer, *Studies in Pessimism*, selected and translated by T. Bailey Saunders (London, 1890), pp. 47-48.

33. *Poems, Essays, and Fragments*, pp. 248-52.

34. *Essays and Phantasies*, p. 230.

35. *Ibid.*, p. 233.

36. *Ibid.*, pp. 234-35.

37. *Ibid.*, p. 228.

38. *Ibid.*, p. 237.

39. *Ibid.*, p. 238.

40. *Ibid.*, pp. 238-42.

41. *Ibid.*, pp. 243-49.

42. Thomson, "Marcus Aurelius Antoninus," *The National Reformer*, XVI (1870), 274.

43. *Ibid.*, pp. 274-75.

44. *Ibid.*, pp. 274 and 259.

45. *Essays, Dialogues and Thoughts of Giacomo Leopardi*, translated by James Thomson (London, 1905), pp. 320-24.

46. *Ibid.*, p. 85.

47. *Ibid.*, p. 91.

48. *Ibid.*, pp. 92-93.

49. *Ibid.*, pp. 93-95.

50. *Ibid.*, pp. 95-96.

51. See especially Giovanni Gentile, *Manzoni e Leopardi* (Firenze, 1937), pp. 115-72.

52. Francesco De Sanctis, *Antologia Critica sugli Scrittori D'Italia* a cura di Luigi Russo (Firenze, 1931), pp. 164-65.

53. *Essays, Dialogues, and Thoughts of Giacomo Le*opardi, p. 97.

54. *Ibid.*, pp. 97-111.

55. *Poetical Works*, II, 61.

56. Giacomo Leopardi, *Tutti le Opere*, I (Milano, 1940), 31; Thomson cites the poem in *Satires and Profanities*, p. 105.

57. Act V, Scene 1, 11. 2-3; Thomson cites six lines of Theseus' speech to illustrate the meaning of poetic inspiration, the poet's "fine frenzy," in *Biographical and Critical Studies*, p. 327.

58. See especially William Stewart Ross, *Roses and Rue* (London, 1890): "I shall never forget the last time I ever met Thomson . . . . I told Mr. Salt of the meeting; but he has deemed it, as I told it him, too tragically realistic for his pen — and, in all its details, it is too morbid and ghastly for mine . . . . The hand of death was on the poet's shoulder . . . met by a calm and suffering, rather than a fierce and defiant, despair . . . . I thought I descried in his eye a twinkle of desperate satisfaction when I assured him — I have heard it whispered that my prediction was verified — that unless he took precautions, he would bleed to death . . . . It mattered not. That shoulder, red with brick-dust, could carry the coffin, and those old slippers could walk to the grave. This was their last and awful duty, and it was upon them" pp. 24-25.

59. *Poetical Works*, I, 155; Thomson was buried in the grave of Austin Holyoake.

60. Salt, *Life*, p. 166.

61. *Ibid.*, p. 12.

62. Thomas Carlyle, *The Works of Thomas Carlyle*, XXVIII (London, 1899), 1-55.

63. Frederick Hiebel, *Novalis* (Chapel Hill, 1954), p. 108.

64. Havelock Ellis, *The Prose Writings of Heinrich Heine* (London, 1887), p. 128.

65. Hugo Bieber, editor, *Heinrich Heine, A Biographical Anthology* (Philadelphia, 1956), p. 344.

66. *Poetical Works*, I, 7.

67. *Ibid.*, pp. 38-39, footnote.

68. Leopardi, *Opere*, I, 94 and 61. Leopardi's "donna" is of the golden age, or resembles nothing on earth, or is one of the eternal ideas.

69. Shelley translated *Purgatorio*, XXVIII, 11. 1-51. See *Poetical Works*, edited by Thomas Hutchinson (New York, 1933), pp. 719-21.

70. Corrado Zacchetti, *Shelley e Dante* (Napoli, 1922), p. 209.

71. C. H. Grandgent, editor, *La Divina Commedia* (Boston, 1933), pp. 581-82.

72. Hutchinson, editor, *Poetical Works,* pp. 514-15.

73. Quoted in Salt, *Life,* p. 67.

74. *Ibid.,* p. 59.

75. G. W. Foote, "James Thomson," *Progress,* III-IV (1884), 253.

76. *Poetical Works,* I, 308.

77. *Ibid.,* pp. 311-12, footnote.

78. *Biographical and Critical Studies,* p. 38.

79. *Ibid.,* pp. 440-41.

80. Salt, *Life,* p. 5.

81. Salt, *Life* (first edition), p. 148.

82. Hans von Bulow, editor, *Ludwig van Beethoven, Sonatas for the Piano,* II (New York, 1923), 441, footnote.

83. *Poetical Works,* II, 46.

84. *Ibid.,* p. 43.

85. *Ibid.,* p. 388.

86. *Poetical Works,* I, 112.

87. *Ibid.,* p. 115.

88. *Ibid.,* p. 116.

89. *Inferno,* I, 11. 32-33.

90. *Poetical Works,* I, 117.

91. Quoted in Salt, *Life,* p. 82.

92. *Poetical Works,* I, 119.

93. *Paradiso,* XXX, 11. 41-42.

94. *Essays and Phantasies,* p. 9.

95. *Paradiso,* XXV, 1. 2.

96. *Purgatorio,* XXIV, 11. 52-54.

97. *Essays and Phantasies,* p. 4.

98. *Ibid.,* pp. 14-15.

99. *Ibid.,* p. 18.

100. *Ibid.,* p. 19.

101. *Purgatorio,* XXXII, 11. 103-104.

102. *Essays and Phantasies,* pp. 27-34.

103. Giovanni Gentile, *Manzoni e Leopardi* (Firenze, 1937), pp. 31-217.

104. *Essays, Dialogues, and Thoughts of Giacomo Leopardi,* p. 365.

105. *Essays and Phantasies,* p. 17.

106. *Paradiso,* XXXI, 11. 59-69.

107. *Poetical Works,* p. 171.

V. THE CITY OF DREADFUL NIGHT

> Yet the wisest of men might well devote his whole
> life to the study of this marvellous London, in
> all its streets and courts and squares, in all its
> professions and trades and scoundrelisms, in its
> pleasures and its miseries. Its mighty gloom is
> more impressive and fascinating than all splen-
> dors. Yet what was said of Babylon must be said
> of London, of Paris, of New York, of every su-
> preme city: "Babylon hath been a golden cup in
> the Lord's hand, that made all the earth drunken:
> the nations have drunken of her wine; therefore
> the nations are mad."[1]

A. SUBJECT MATTER

Although it is not a "religious" poem in the sense that Tennyson's
In Memoriam is sometimes said to be religious, *The City of Dreadful
Night* is, nevertheless, an essentially Christian work of art. Not a glimmer of faithful assent is discernible in its 1123 lines; yet, from beginning to end the poem insists, with a fervor reminiscent of the
profoundest pages of St. Augustine or Luther, on the utter deprav-
ity of man's condition — on the thorough worthlessness of his intelligence, moral goodness, and humanitarian sense of fellowship —
apart from the gifts of Christian Faith, Hope, and Love, which cannot be earned.

Having read Pascal and Schopenhauer, Thomson was aware that
moral pessimism of the extremist kind has a place in the traditional
Christian doctrine. Schopenhauer, in the closing sections of *Die Welt
als Wille und Vorstellung*, acknowledges that his view of man, however much it may differ from the teachings of modern Christianity
which has "forgotten its true significance and degenerated into dull
optimism," accords with and is in fact contained in the ancient
dogma.[2] One of the essential doctrines of original Christianity, he
writes — a doctrine "which Augustine, with the consent of the leaders of the Church, defended against the platitudes of the Pelagians,
and which it was the principal aim of Luther's endeavor to purify
from error and re-establish, as he expressly declares in his book, *De
Servo Arbitrio*" — is that the will of man has an original bias toward
evil, and that, as a consequence, all deeds motivated by his will are
necessarily evil, no matter how "righteous" they may appear from a
worldly, external point of view.[3] It is a doctrine anticipated in the

Old Testament, especially in the dilemma of "upright" Job whose good intentions and good behavior have no merit in the eyes of God, and who is rewarded finally only because he acknowledges their worthlessness; but it is in the epistles of St. Paul that the doctrine is for the first time explicitly defined. That Thomson is concerned in his *City* with precisely the doctrine foreshadowed in Job's dilemma — namely, that the best deeds of men motivated by their own wills are utterly worthless — is indicated with sufficient clarity in the poem itself. His limbo, Thomson explains in the eleventh canto, includes none of the "wicked" who "have their proper hell"; it is a place reserved for persons of "upright" character who have "much vision," "much goodness," "much patience," quite like Job.[4] But the notebook in which Thomson originally wrote the verses of his *City*, carefully dating original drafts, major revisions and minor refinements, leaves no room for doubt concerning its "Jobean" subject matter. Above the poem's title, the first time it occurs in the manuscript,[5] is the concluding verse of the tenth chapter of *Job*: "A land of darkness, as darkness itself, and of the shadow of death, without any order, and where the light is as darkness." Job's expostulations with God in that famous tenth chapter include the characteristic charge: "Thou knowest that I am not wicked . . . yet thou dost destroy me." The *Old Testament* martyr asks only to be let alone for a time before he must go whence he shall not return, "even to the land of darkness and the shadow of death." The chapter is an admirable gloss for the *City*.[6]

On the same page of Thomson's notebook, just below the title of the poem, three lines of the *Inferno* are quoted (III, 11. 1, 3, 9):

"Per me si va nella città dolente:
. . . .
Per me si va tra la perduta gente
. . . .
Lasciate ogni speranza voi ch'entrate."

Following these are two lines from *Titus Andronicus* (Act. III, Sc. 1, 12, 13): "In the dust I write / My heart's deep languor and my soul's sad tears"; and, at the bottom of the page, two lines from Shelley's "Triumph of Life"; "And others mournfully within the gloom / Of their own shadow walked and called it death."[7] Each of the passages quoted relates, in its original context, to the problem of the apparent purposelessness of much of human suffering. Thomson had noted them as possible captions for his *City* in 1870; in 1873, having already determined to use passages from Leopardi, he made several new notations on that original page, crossing out the lines from

Job and Shelley, as well as two of the three lines from Dante, and indicating that the lines from *Titus Andronicus* were to be used in the "last section" — which became, in the final version, the introductory "Proem."[8]

From a theological point of view it is extraordinary that Thomson should have chosen to project his modern interpretation of "Job's dilemma" upon the Limbo of Dante's poetic universe. Although he managed to keep within the limits of Christian orthodoxy in his great poem, Dante had little inclination to support the position of moral pessimism illustrated by the story of Job and fully elaborated finally by St. Augustine in his polemic against the Pelagians. He conceded that moral virtue of itself, without Christian grace, cannot raise a man to heaven; but, at the same time, he defended with vehemence the position that, except in the rare instances of saintly ascetics who have special gifts, saving grace itself cannot make a Christian good if he does not practice the pagan moral virtues.[9] Moral virtue of itself cannot scale the heights of heavenly bliss, but it can earn the second best spiritual reward — fellowship in the marvelous company of pagan heroes, prophets, poets and sages who inhabit the noble castle of Limbo, which is not, as he pictures it, a "land of darkness, as darkness itself," but an Elysian field enveloped by a gracious hemisphere of soft and honorable light.[10]

By venturing to substitute for Dante's noble castle a city large enough to include all the modern as well as ancient virtuous pagans, and by shrouding that city in dreadful night, the author of *The City of Dreadful Night* is, in effect, disputing the permanent validity of Dante's moral optimism. But his actual intention is perhaps better indicated by saying that, in his *City*, Thomson offers a revision of the earthly approaches to hell such as Dante himself might have provided had he been recalled to life in the eighteen-seventies, just after the Franco-Prussian War, when England's popular imperialism was making London a mighty Babylon indeed, when the wearer of the purple mantle of Christ's vicar was being kept prisoner in a tiny and not very honorable limbo of the great world of national states, and when events were occurring in Italy that would lead many to predict as certain and imminent the final disappearance of the traditional Church of Christ from the face of the earth. Had the *City* appeared in the eighteen-seventies as the work of some despondent cleric raging against triumphant secularism, or had it been found among the papers of some self-effacing Trappist, its Christian significance and Dantean implications could hardly have escaped notice. It appeared, instead, in the columns of a blatantly secularist journal addressed to the most irreligious audience London could

then provide. And yet it was, in a sense, the work of a religious
recluse who had pledged himself twenty years earlier in response to
the "Stanzas from the Grande Chartreuse" to wait in darkness beside the dead body of Christ — a recluse who had, perhaps, gained a
profounder insight than is allowed most men into the meaning of
those dreadful words uttered by the Jew of Nazareth as he lay dying
on the Cross: "My God, my God, why has though forsaken me?"

B. Structure, Characters, Thoughts and Sentiments, and Language

One learns from the notebook preserved in the British Museum
that, as originally designed in 1870, the *City* was to consist of fifteen
cantos. Clearly indicated in the earliest outline is the obvious distinction between the odd-numbered cantos, which are all of the same
stanzaic form, and the even-numbered, which vary in form — the
poet's intention having been, evidently, to produce through the external structure something of the effect of a musical "rondo." The
original sequences were:

II.	Dead faith, dead love, dead hope
IV.	As I came through the desert
VI.	The festival that filled with light
VIII.	Refused entrance into hell
X.	The search for the broken clue
XII.	The conversation
XIV.	The Sphinx and the Angel
I.	The City
III.	How he arrives there none can surely know
V.	Although lamps burn along the silent streets
VII.	What men are they who haunt these fatal glooms?
IX.	Some say that phantoms haunt those sombre streets
XI.	It is full strange to him who hears and feels
XIII.	The River of Suicides
XV.	Why and for whom written[11]

Both sequences underwent a number of revisions before Thomson
brought the poem's design to completion in 1873, adding the six
cantos ("to come in about the middle" he simply notes at first)[12] that
make up the grand "cathedral scene," shifting what was originally
the final canto (Why and for whom written") to the position of introductory "Proem," and crowning the whole with his vision of the
"Melencolia statue."[13]

In the odd-numbered sequence, to which the "Proem" belongs,
the poet-narrator describes his psychological experience first as a

visitor wandering without a guide through the streets of the City,
later as a newly-initiated citizen, and finally as a practiced worship-
per of the "Melencolia." In the even-numbered sequence, he represents a series of dramatic encounters with typical citizens, the occasion of his own initiation, and finally a vision of the tragic pattern of
human history. Like many of the characters portrayed by Dante, the
chief figures of Thomson's *City* are shaped artistically by mere sug-
gestion, the indication of a typical utterance, gesture, or pose. Dante's
characters, however, are usually distinguished further by names and
personal histories, so that when one of them has formed itself in the
reader's imagination and has passed into his memory, the name alone,
or a detail of the history is thereafter enough to evoke the original
image in its entirety. The ethical scheme of the *Divine Comedy* required that main figures be specifically and memorably identified,
for, as Cacciaguida cautions in the seventeenth canto of *Paradiso*:

> L'animo di quel ch'ode non posa
> Ne ferma fede per esempio ch'aia
> La sua radice incognita e nascosa.[14]

In the scheme of Thomson's poem quite the contrary was required.
The narrator has nothing to teach, no secret to disclose to any who
divined it not before. Indeed, the characters he encounters are all in
the process of losing whatever personal identity or significance they
may once have had. They have the *will* of personality but have been
deprived of the power to actualize that will. According to R. A. Foakes,
one may discern among them frustrated or impotent equivalents of
all the leading English Romantic and Victorian poets.[15] Other critics
have identified equivalents of Bradlaugh, Carlyle, Novalis, Leopardi,
Heine, Poe, among their number. But in fact one sees what one
brings — for Thomson, with deep insight into the mysteries of the
will, has succeeded in representing the bare principle of personality
as it exists in potency, stripped of particularity, requiring but brief
contact with a reader's imagination to shape for itself a semblance of
identity. The citizens of the City are united in their incapacity, or
"unwillingness" to subordinate their human wills to a higher will. In
ordinary language such incapacity is known as pride; in the language
of Christian pessimism it is called *amor sui*, the antithesis of *amor
Dei*.[16] Such pride makes men scorn to be "selfish" in their love, which
is always love for another, or others. Its ideal is not the narrow human selfishness of the egotist but mankind's full-hearted, full-souled,
full-strengthened love of all mankind, which is, according to St. Augustine at any rate, human selfishness raised to the nth power.[17] None

of the inhabitants of Thomson's City is a mere egotist incapable of loving "another," and yet they are all animated by *amor sui*. Indeed, represented among them is the entire range of such man-centered love, extending from the instance of the sole professed Christian there who repeats Adam's sin, renouncing with moral nobility all choice of life or death so that he may remain forever at his beloved's side, to that of the large-hearted preacher of universal fellowship who after having searched the heights and depths of the universe to find some solace for the wild unrest of his fellow men, vainly asks them to rejoice in the glad tidings that there is no God, no fiend with names divine to torment them.[18] By such love (*amor sui usque ad contemptum Dei*), in its infinite varieties, is the City of dreadful night built.[19]

We noted in the introductory chapter how well the coupling of quotations from Dante and Leopardi in the poem's caption serves to indicate its underlying paradox of thought and feeling. From Leopardi's "Canto Notturno," Thomson quotes the complaint of a solitary shepherd contemplating the night sky:

> Poi di tanto adoprar, di tanti moti
> D'ogni celeste, ogni terrena cosa,
> Girando senza posa,
> Per tornar sempre la donde son mosse:
> Uso alcuno, alcun frutto
> Indovinar non so.[20]

In Dante's time the motion of the stars was accounted the perfect symbol of the purposefulness of all things in the universe, a symbol so perfect that Dante chose to end each *cantica* of the *Divine Comedy* with the same word: *stelle*. But of course Dante lived long before Galileo, Newton, and the celestial mechanics, and Leopardi long after. Intelligence and purpose had long since been banished from the heaven of Leopardi's shepherd — banished by intelligent man, perhaps for the purpose of arrogating them finally to himself as an exclusive possession.

The second Leopardian quotation in the caption comes from his magnificent "Coro di Morti," the chorus of mummies, long dead, who comment on the meaning and value of life as they try to recall some trace of the vital sensation that was once their habitual experience. The message of their song is as old as Silenus, but infinitely more tragic in significance after eighteen hundred years of Christianity:

> Sola nel mondo eterna, a cui si volve

> Ogni creata cosa,
> In te, morte, si posa
> Nostra ignuda natura;
> Lieta no, ma sicura,
> Dall'antico dolor . . . .
> Però ch'esser beato
> Nega ai mortali e nega a'morti il fato.[21]

In a purposeless universe, death is the sole comforter of men. Although such pessimistic appraisals of the meaning of human existence seem at first to belittle man in his own estimation (Freud, for instance, argues that the Copernican, Darwinian, and "Freudian" revolutions have humbled proud man), they really enable him, ultimately, to glorify himself above all the minerals, vegetables, animals, planets, stars and cosmic spaces that have been, are, or can be, as the only being in the universe capable of thinking, willing, and loving. What alone prevents such an inversion of the underlying pessimistic thought and feeling of Thomson's *City* is the constant reminder that its inhabitants are confined to an edge of Dante's Christian universe, with a heaven full of luminous thought and love soaring above them and a hell of physical anguish and chaos yawning below.

Although the language of the poem is filled with echoes of many poets, Thomson's intention was obviously to write an allegory in the style of Dante, appealing to the "visual imagination." T. S. Eliot has reminded modern readers that, in order to make his audience "see what he saw," Dante employed "very simple language, and very few metaphors, for allegory and metaphor do not get on well together."[22] That Thomson's language is simple, offering few verbal or syntactical puzzles, and allegorical rather than metaphorical, even the severest critics of his art will allow, for they charge it against him as a defect. Thomson's poetry is, indeed, hardly poetry at all, when judged according to the standard of that still prevalent theory of "poetic technique" which Cleanth Brooke sums up as "the rediscovery of metaphor and the full commitment to metaphor."[23] But theories and tastes have their seasons; and in the long run the specialized training that cultivates a taste for images and verbal transfers in every line must give way before the pressure of general culture, which knows that greatness in poetry consists in the capacity to create for the imagination grand visions of cities, ages, and worlds.

But in order to illustrate these general remarks about Thomson's language, as well as our earlier remarks about the thoughts and feelings, characters, structure, and subject matter of the poem, we must now turn to consider in detail the evidence of the text.

C. ANALYSIS:
PROEM[24]

In the "Proem" that introduces the twenty-one numbered cantos, the poet explains "why and for whom" he has written his *City*
and also raises his voice in what amounts to a religious invocation, a
prayer for divine sustenance in his task. But how — if indeed the
muses are gone from the world, if there is no longer a bright Apollo
in the sky, no blessed lady attentive in heaven, and no omnipresent
living God — how shall an exiled Scottish Dante pray? How then shall
they call on him in whom they have not believed?[25]

> Lo, thus, as prostrate, "In the dust I write
>   My heart's deep languor and my soul's sad tears.

Thomson's first utterance, quoting the prayerful words of Shakespeare's Titus Andronicus,[26] may recall, in the internal hearing of a
sympathetic reader, the great leap and chords sounded impetuously
in the opening measures of Beethoven's *Opus 106*; and not the first
utterance alone, but the entire "Proem" as it develops, closely paral-
lels the rhythmic and melodic movement in the opening pages of
that great Sonata. That Thomson should have attempted, in imitat-
ing the poetic language of Dante, to parallel the musical effects of
Beethoven, which he himself heard in Dante's poetry, should not
occasion surprise; at any rate, once the lines of the "Proem" are
connected in the imagination with the opening pages of the "Ham-
mer-Klavier," it is not easy to disassociate the two. When Beethoven's
sudden outburst exhausts itself abruptly, a lyrical figure, carried lightly
on single notes, succeeds. But soon this new, seemingly apologetic
figure begins to twist and coil about itself, and then sweeps up suddenly to shatter itself on a peak of emotional intensity. Every nu-
ance in the music up to that point is paralleled in Thomson's "Proem."
After the cry of the opening lines he writes:

> Yet why evoke the spectres of black night
>   To blot the sunshine of exultant years?
> Why disinter dead faith from mouldering hidden?
> Why break the seals of mute despair unbidden,
>   And wail life's discords into careless ears?
>
> Because a cold rage seizes one at whiles
>   To show the bitter old and wrinkled truth
> Stripped naked of all vesture that beguiles
>   False dreams, false hopes, false masks and modes of youth;

Because it gives some sense of power and passion
In helpless impotence to try to fashion
  Our woe in living words howe'er uncouth.

Having explained why he has written his poem, the poet proceeds to limit his audience; and his lines, like the parallel measures of Beethoven's sonata, move with a gradually accelerated rhythm that mounts to a peak and precipitates itself into a verbal equivalent of a cascade of octaves:

Surely I write not for the hopeful young,
  Or those who deem their happiness of worth,
Or such as pasture and grow fat among
  The shows of life and feel nor doubt nor dearth,
Or pious spirits with a God above them
To sanctify and glorify and love them,
  Or sages who foresee a heaven on earth.

The stanza is typical of Thomson's rhetorical manner in direct statement, yet not typical of the poem, as a whole. It is perhaps worth noting how the sound and rhythm of each line enhance the sense, and how the sense turns emotionally on apparently insignificant words: the broad "surely" in the first line, "deem" in the second, the harsh "such as" and "grow fat" in the third, the bantering feminine rhymes in the fifth and sixth, and the abrupt antithetical "earth" at the close. But here is Thomson's cascade of octaves:

For none of these I write, and none of these
  Could read the writing if they deigned to try:
So may they flourish, in their due degrees,
  On our sweet earth and in their unplaced sky.

Non ragionam di lor! After his brief but rigorous display of power, the poet returns to his original prayerful mood. He does not expect to be read sympathetically by a very large audience:

If any cares for the weak words here written,
It must be some one desolate, Fate-smitten,
  Whose faith and hope are dead . . . .

Yes, here and there some weary wanderer
  In that same city of tremendous night,
Will understand the speech, and feel a stir
  Of fellowship in all-disastrous fight;
"I suffer mute and lonely, yet another
Uplifts his voice to let me know a brother
  Travels the same wild paths though out of sight."

The "Proem" has accomplished its purpose — or very nearly. Beethoven often reminds listeners, by means of musical reminiscences, that others have labored in the field before him, and that full appreciation of his work is possible only for those who know the tradition on which he was nurtured. Thomson writes simply:

> O sad Fraternity, do I unfold
>   Your dolorous mysteries shrouded from of yore?
> Nay, be assured; no secret can be told
>   To any who divined it not before:
> None uninitiate by many a presage
> Will comprehend the language of the message
>   Although proclaimed aloud for evermore.

So the "Proem" ends. Of its seven-line stanza, Edmund Blunden, perhaps mindful of Coleridge's account of poetic motion, has written: "this recurrent, slow-uncoiling, backward coiling stanza, with the overhanging rhymes towards the close only suggesting a freedom of movement in order that the close may be more ironically definite, is the pulse of the City."[27] Thomson uses the same stanzaic form in all the odd-numbered cantos, and its recurrence after each dramatic episode of the even-numbered sequence produces, as we noted, the effect of a "rondo" movement in a piano sonata. The heavy use of sonorous Latinate diction that characterizes many of the "returning" stanzas accentuates harmonically the melodic return — though, when the sense requires, Thomson is quite capable of stringing twenty low words in two dull lines:

> To fill our so-short *roles* out right or wrong;
>   To see what shifts are yet in the dull play.[28]

I

The opening stanza of the first numbered canto forewarns the reader that the somber city of the poem can have been a reality only in the hemisphere of night:

> The moon and stars may shine with scorn or pity;
> The sun has never visited that city,
>   For it dissolveth in the daylight fair.

And yet, how certain are we of the reality even of our daylight world? For long centuries mankind's pursuit of true knowledge has been illuminated not by the certain light of heaven, but by man-made lamps, which do not have the power to dispel phantoms. Even the best man-made lamps, the great lamps of Germany, produce a strange light that beguiles the mind and distorts the simple vision. Who among us now is sure of his vision? Who among us can discern a dream from real life in aught, if that dream persists night after night through many weeks, and if such weeks recur each year for several years?

> For life is but a dream whose shapes return,
>   Some frequently, some seldom, some by night
> And some by day, some night and day: we learn,
>   The while all change and many vanish quite,
> In their recurrence with recurrent changes
> A certain seeming order; where this ranges
>   We count things real; such is memory's might.

Obviously the conscious artist is at work here preparing his modern audience to read and *see* imaginative poetry. By exposing the weakness of dull empiricism in its own stronghold — in the testimony of the senses — and by enveloping his subject in the magic light of German philosophy, which shows through the shadowy surfaces of things, the poet turns the reader's skepticism against itself and seizes the occasion of compounded doubt to gain a subtle control over his imaginative vision. But having gained this precious control, the conscious artist immediately retires, and the narrator, the pilgrim in the poem, is left in his place to weave the veil of allegory.

The narrator's task is difficult, but he sets himself studiously to it, reporting every circumstance of his phantasmagoric experience; not only what he sees and hears, but also what he feels and thinks and how he checks one sense against another, and against the common sense and reason, to be sure he is not beguiled. It is this constant preoccupation with the testimony of the senses that enables the narrator to recreate imaginatively the sensuous reality of his vision. And the sympathetic reader, following the process of recreation, soon finds himself seeing and feeling his way after the narrator through the heavy atmosphere of the City. Gradually he comes to realize that he is being taught how to read a serious allegory; but not until he has recognized in the person of his guide a personification of his own imaginative vision is he likely to appreciate fully the fine art of his teacher.

The phantasmagoric City first appears on the horizon as a mighty Babylon, a great temple of commerce, distinctly visible with its towers, great piers and causeways, island suburbs, noble bridges. Upon an easy slope it lies, rising to a long curved crest two leagues from the river marge:

> A trackless wilderness rolls north and west,
> Savannahs, savage woods, enormous mountains,
> Bleak uplands, black ravines with torrent fountains;

And eastward rolls the shipless sea's unrest.

Surely it is not the world of "Nature" to which the early Romantic poets fled from the weariness of city life. Perhaps Thomson had in mind that "selva selvaggia e aspra e forte" of Dante's opening lines.[29] Entering the City itself, the narrator observes that it has somewhat of the aspect of modern London. "The city," he writes

> is not ruinous, although
> Great ruins of an unremembered past,
> With others of a few short years ago
> More sad, are found within its precincts vast.

But there is a silence there which benumbs and strains the sense and fills the soul with awe. Where are the inhabitants of this great City? Are they sleeping in the "ranged mansions dark and still as tombs"; or are they dead, "or fled from nameless pestilence"? —

> Yet as in some necropolis you find
> Perchance one mourner to a thousand dead,
> So there; worn faces that look deaf and blind
> Like tragic masks of stone.

Mature men, chiefly, women rarely, now and then a child! They speak to one another seldom. Each rapt in his own doom, they wander, murmuring to themselves, or "sit fordone and desolately ponder through sleepless hours." Their woe broods inwardly and "scorns to wreak itself abroad." And

> if at whiles it grow
> To frenzy which must rave, none heeds the clamour,
> Unless there waits some victim of like glamour,
> To rave in turn, who lends attentive show.

One is reminded of the night-London of Engels or of Dickens. Surely the mass of common men in that great commercial city were then as wretched and as sad as these. But this is not London, and these are not common men. These have other cares, other thoughts:

> They leave all hope behind who enter there:
> One certitude while sane they cannot leave,
> One anodyne for torture and despair;
> The certitude of Death, which no reprieve
> Can put off long; and which, divinely tender,
> But waits the outstretched hand to promptly render
> That draught whose slumber nothing can bereave.

The men of this City live under an everlasting shroud of darkness, in a night more dreadful than ever the Cimmerians knew, for it is the night of Godlessness.

II

In the second canto the pilgrim relates the first of a series of dramatic incidents recollected from previous visits to the City of Night. Now he is familiar with the scene, but once he too had been a stranger there, not knowing how or why he had come, or where to turn. He remembers distinctly how, once, while he was standing at the corner of a great square, awed by the silence and darkness, a frail and shadowy figure "wrapt in thought as in a veil" (*tutta in sè romita*, as Dante says),[30] suddenly moved out of the shadows close by. The figure passed in silence; but because it seemed to walk with an intent, the pilgrim followed, hoping that, like Dante's pilgrim, he followed a guide: "Thus step for step with lonely sounding feet / We travelled many a long dim silent street." *Allor si mosse, ed io gli tenni dietro.*[31]

At length our pilgrim and his guide passed near a black mass towering in the night. The "huddled stones of grave and tomb" at its base marked it as "some old God's acre, now corruption's sty" — like Dante's *cimitero*, which is reduced to a "cloaca . . . della puzza."[32] The guide paused for a moment, murmuring "to himself with dull despair, / Here Faith died, poisoned by this charnel air." Then "turning to the right," he went on until he reached an open door in a low wall, beyond which the lights of a villa gleamed through dense foliage. Again he paused and "muttered with a hard despair, / Here Love died, stabbed by its own worshipped pair." With the pilgrim-narrator still at his heels, he moved on once more, traversing many streets and lanes, until

> on stooping through a narrow arch
> We stood before a squalid house at length:
> He gazed, and whispered with a cold despair,
> Here Hope died, starved out in its utmost lair.

At these words, the pilgrim, "perplexed by something in the signs of desolation" he had seen and heard in the course of "this drear pilgrimage to ruined shrines," inquired earnestly: "When Faith and Love and Hope are dead indeed, / Can Life still live? By what doth it proceed?" And the guide, in answering, supplies the first major poetic figure of the poem:

> As whom his one intense thought overpowers,
> He answered coldly, Take a watch, erase
> The signs and figures of the circling hours,
> Detach the hands, remove the dial-face;

> The works proceed until run down; although
> Bereft of purpose, void of use, still go.

Poor little man on earth! He must ever be the heavenly microcosm, even in the universe of the Philosophes! "Then turning to the right" (like T. S. Eliot's hero turning up the stairs in "Ash Wednesday") the guide paced on again, leading the pilgrim through squares and streets whose gloom seemed more and more familiar, until at last they passed again "that sullen temple of the tombs." Again the guide paused and murmured as before, "Here Faith died, poisoned by this charnel air." But this cannot be Dante's guide! this cannot be the poetic voice of reason:

> I ceased to follow, for the knot of doubt
>   Was severed sharply with a cruel knife:
> He circled thus for ever tracing out
>   The series of the fraction left of Life;
> Perpetual recurrence in the scope
> Of but three terms, dead Faith, dead Love, dead Hope.

Thus the first dramatic episode of the poem ends. The pilgrim-narrator has experienced vicariously the merry-go-round of Godless men that St. Augustine describes in Book XII of the *City of God*.[33] But, so that even the dullest reader might not mistake the symbolic significance of the canto, the poet adds a bizarre footnote, giving the fraction left of life: "Life divided by that persistent three = LXX/333 = .210 . . . . " The attentive reader, of course, is reminded of the thought of Leopardi cited in the caption. And he does not fail to notice, moreover, that it is the hero of the dramatic scene, not the narrator, who pronounces this first somber judgment on the meaning of the "human journey" in a Godless universe.

III

The characteristic seven-line stanza which had yielded to a less tortuous form, consisting of six lines rhyming ababcc in the preceding dramatic episode, reappears in the third canto as the poet resumes his description of the current scene in the City of Night:

> Although lamps burn along the silent streets;
>   Even when moonlight silvers empty squares
> The dark holds countless lanes and close retreats;
>   But when the night its sphereless mantle wears
> The open spaces yawn with gloom abysmal,
> The sombre mansions loom immense and dismal,
>   The lanes are black as subterranean lairs.

Streets, squares, retreats, wears, abysmal, dismal, lairs — the rhymes resounding in the ear cut like an engraver's tool. Throughout the poem, and especially in the descriptive sequences, the poet uses rhymes thus as Dante does, to support the figurative sense. In the remaining stanzas of this third canto, for instance, as the narrator proceeds to study carefully the reactions of his senses in the darkness of the City, reporting first how "the eye a strange new vision learns," then how the ear too "becomes familiar though unreconciled," the burden of the meaning is carried primarily by the rhyme words: learns, dense, discerns, sense, obscurely, surely, intense; deep, unreconciled, asleep, wild, derision, vision, beguiled; awe, thing, law, king, terror, error, wondering.

The object of this brief canto is to prepare the reader for the phantasmagorically distinct sensations of shadowy figures perceived in shadows, of black edifices perceived in blackness, of soundless sobs, murmurs, conversations perceived in silence which are to be represented in subsequent cantos. The poet works very consciously to produce the impression that moved Paul Elmer More to write: "In the sharpness of its outlines, in the balance of its members, there is something in *The City of Dreadful Night* that borders on the geometry of delirium."[34]

IV

Here a new dramatic personality, very unlike the frail and shadowy figure of the second canto, is introduced. The narrator tells us that he encountered this new figure, where he was wont to stay, in a spacious square, declaiming "as if large multitudes were gathered round." Erect he stood, with uncovered head and streaming hair: "A stalwart shape, the gestures full of might, / The glances burning with unnatural light." But like the earlier figure, this new one also is here celebrating the dialectical crisis of his life — doomed to re-enact forever his part in the romantic agony of disordered love. Love had been snatched from him by death, and the loss causes him such pain that at last, in a rage, he turns his back on all the goods of the world, on heaven and hell, and on all the fatal powers. He has much to say and therefore the poet, after having used the six-line stanza of the second canto to introduce him, allows him to speak in a distinctive stanza of his own:

> As I came through the desert thus it was,
> As I came through the desert: All was black,

> In heaven no single star, on earth no track;
> A brooding hush without a stir or note,
> The air so thick it clotted in my throat;
> And thus for hours; then some enormous things
> Swooped past with savage cries and clanking wings:
>> But I strode on austere;
>> No hope could have no fear.

And so through six stanzas of his mad-song the enraged lover describes his striding through the spiritual desert of life. Twisted creatures, throbbing with starved desires (like T. S. Eliot's shapes "twisted on the banister" in "Ash Wednesday"), clutched after him, he says, with "fleshless fingers cold"; meteors crossed their javelins in the bleak sky-span; dreadful thunderbolts jarred earth's fixed frame; then —

>> Air once more,
> And I was close upon a wild sea-shore;
> Enormous cliffs arose on either hand,
> The deep tide thundered up a league-broad strand;
> White formbelts seethed there, wan spray swept and flew;
> The sky broke, moon and stars and clouds and blue:

but the enraged lover went striding on. Even when the rising sun "stopped and burned out black" (like the sun of *Revelations* 6.12), "except a rim, / A bleeding eyeless socket, redf and dim" — still he strode on austere; "no hope could have no fear." And then suddenly a change:

>> From the right
> A shape came slowly with a ruddy light;
> A woman with a red lamp in her hand,
> Bareheaded and barefooted on that strand;
> O desolation moving with such grace!
> O anguish with such beauty in thy face!
>> I fell as on my bier,
>> Hope travailed with such fear.

Plainly it is his dead love returning from the grave. But who does not know this man? Who does not recognize the pagan lover of Astarte, of Ulalume and Anabelle Lee, of the lost Ann, of Cathy of Wuthering Heights, of Clair, and of Vera, and the fatal Sonja — and of the many other mysterious dark ladies of the nineteenth century? As the dead woman draws near, the mad-lover is literally beside himself with anguish:

>> I was twain,
> Two selves distinct that cannot join again;
> One stood apart and knew but could not stir,
> And watched the other stark in swoon and her;

. . . .
A large black sign was on her breast that bowed,
A broad black band ran down her snow-white shroud;
The lamp she held was her own burning heart,
Whose blood-drops trickled step by step apart:
. . . .
She knelt and bent above that senseless me;
Those lamp-drops fell upon my white brow there,
She tried to cleanse them with her tears and hair;
She murmured words of pity, love, and woe,
She heeded not the level rushing flow:
        And mad with rage and fear,
        I stood stonebound so near.

As I came through the desert thus it was,
As I came through the desert: When the tide
Swept up to her there kneeling by my side,
She clasped that corpse-like me, and they were borne
Away, and this vile me was left forlorn;
I know the whole sea cannot quench that heart,
Or cleanse that brow, or wash those two apart:
        They love; their doom is drear,
        Yet they nor hope nor fear;
        But I, what do I here?

Betraying in a phrase the utter vanity underlying this triumph of Godless love, the mad-lover ends his song. He will sing it again and again, but the pilgrim will not stay to hear.

    This mad-song is especially interesting for its literary allusions. It echoes Poe in "Annabelle Lee," pledging that nothing "shall ever dissever" the lover's soul from that of his beloved; Dante in the *Vita Nuova*, seeing Beatrice eat his own heart in a dream vision; De Quincey in his "Dream-Fugue," shrieking warnings to the young girl, with the diadem of white roses, as she approaches the quicksands; and in his "Confessions" where he wakes in struggles from a dream of his lost Ann, to cry aloud, "I will sleep no more!" R. A. Foakes observes that the canto combines in its development two of the major Romantic images — "the journey of life and the vision of love" — but thoroughly inverts their values.[35] The journey out of the desert of life is frustrated at its completion: the woman who comes to the wayfarer as a savior is herself lost, and there is only a "ghastly parody of the Romantic vision of unity in the union of two corpse-like figures floating out on that ocean which only seems to be an extension of the desert."[36] A number of critics have noted the similarities between this song and Browning's "Childe Roland to the Dark Tower Came" — although, of course, in Browning's poem the hero's journey is crowned with light and reunion with his friends in death, whereas the journey of this fourth canto leads the hero, or rather the vile half of him that survives, from a dreadful desert to the even more dreadful spiritual desert of the City of Night.

V

Again the narrator resumes his effort to confound vision and actuality in the reader's imagination. No one, he explains, who visits the City of Night can know clearly how he arrives or how he leaves, for "memory swoons in both the tragic acts." It is as Dante says of his own entry into the "selva oscura": *non so ben ridir com'io v'entrai.*[37] But once there, one feels a citizen; escape seems hopeless: "Can Death-in-Life be brought to life again?" And yet release does come. There comes a morn when the visitor, who thought himself lost, wakes to find the world so changed for him that "he is verily as if new-born." Scarcely able to believe that he has actually been freed, "he weeps perchance who wept not while accurst." Never again, he vows, will he so much as think of that accursed place, now that its evil spell is broken. Never again will he leave the daylight of his home, his babes, his wife, his friends whom he loves "more than death and happy life." Never again will he . . . alas! — "Poor wretch! who once hath paced that dolent city / Shall pace it often." He must renounce all blessings of the daylight, and steal forth again, as before, to haunt that builded desolation "of woe and terrors and thick darkness reared."

VI

But even tragic earnestness can have an almost comic aspect. Even as he considers the tragic plight of the citizens who can never escape from the City of Darkness, the narrator is reminded of an almost amusing incident. He had been sitting by the river-side — watching the bridge-lamps glow like stars "above the blackness of the swelling tide," listening to the "heave and plashing of the flow" against the river wall — when gradually he became conscious of "strange voices joined in stranger talk" near by; especially strange, because there had not been the sound of approaching feet. Two voices were discussing the possibilities of escape from the City of Night. Indeed, one of the speakers had actually attempted to escape and had failed, and was just then explaining to his companion the

circumstances of his failure. He had made his way to the very edge
of the "selva oscura," but there all ways were barred:

> I reached the portal common spirits fear,
> And read the words above it, dark yet clear,
> "Leave hope behind, all ye who enter here;"

> And would have passed in, gratified to gain
> That positive eternity of pain,
> Instead of this insufferable inane.

> A demon warder clutched me, Not so fast;
> First leave your hopes behind! — But years have passed
> Since I left all behind me, to the last . . . .

He himself cannot give the name of hope to that black despair which
drives him to the pit. The Dantesque warder, therefore, snarls at
him:

> What thing is this which apes a soul,
> And would find entrance to our gulf of dole,
> Without the payment of the settled toll?

The warder shows an open chest outside the gate where unblest
souls must pay their fees. It is Pandora's box, which will be shut
forever when hopes have filled it; "but they are so thin that it will
never glut." Being unable to pay the required fee, the wayfarer stands
aside in dejection and watches the passing spirits pause and fling off
hope before entering at the gate. Dante himself could not have drawn
a more Dantesque picture:

> When one casts off a load he springs upright,
> Squares back his shoulders, breathes with all his might,
> And briskly paces forward strong and light:

> But these, as if they took some burden, bowed;
> The whole frame sank; however strong and proud
> Before, they crept in quite infirm and cowed.

From each passing spirit the disconsolate observer begs a morsel of
hope, that he might pay his entrance fee. Not one will resign a tittle,
though each knows that in a few moments all must be resigned for
evermore. Therefore in despair the wayfarer has returned to his City:

> Our destiny is fell;
> For in this Limbo we must ever dwell,
> Shut out alike from Heaven and Earth and Hell.

His companion, having heard the sorrowful news, sighs:

> Yea; but if we grope
> With care through all this Limbo's dreary scope,
> We yet may pick up some minute lost hope;

> And, sharing it between us, entrance win,
> In spite of fiends so jealous for gross sin:
> Let us without delay our search begin.

This wryly humorous episode serves to connect *The City of Dreadful Night*, alike geographically, morally, and dramatically, with the *Divine Comedy*. Dante's hell, with its demons, belongs to another age, and unless we suspend disbelief we can hardly help laughing. But in this City on the edge of hell, the laughter of disbelief rings rather hollow; one rather wishes there were such demons.

After being introduced by the narrator, who employs the usual six-line stanza reserved for himself in the even-numbered cantos, the two voices speak, as we have seen, in rhyming tercets of iambic pentameter that resemble the *terza rima* of Dante about as much as they resemble the shorter tercets of Tennyson's "Two Voices." Although clearly identified as two by the narrator, the voices are so united in thought that the same stanzaic form suffices for both of them. In the next even-numbered canto the narrator will introduce a real "conversation," in which the speakers will be assigned distinctive forms of poetic utterance.

VII

It is no uncommon thing in the City to hear bodiless voices or to see insubstantial shadows flit and roam. Some visitors say

> that phantoms haunt those shadowy streets,
> And mingle freely there with sparse mankind;
> And tell of ancient woes and black defeats,
> And murmur mysteries in the grave enshrined:
> But others think them visions of illusion,
> Or even men gone far in self-confusion;
> No man there being wholly sane in mind.

The narrator himself has seen "phantoms there that were as men, and men that were as phantoms," and has heard voices when no living creatures were near. But can he rely safely on the testimony of his senses? Can he trust appearances? Things often seem fantastic here; but that frail despondent creature of the first scene, and the desperate wild man chanting his mad-love song, and those dreary "optimists" searching for a scrap of hope — surely they were real men! —

> And yet a man who raves, however mad,
> Who bares his heart and tells of his own fall,
> Reserves some inmost secret good or bad:

The phantoms have no reticence at all:
The nudity of flesh will blush though tameless,
The extreme nudity of bone grins shameless,
    The unsexed skeleton mocks shroud and pall.

VIII

While he still lingered on the river-walk, after overhearing the conversation reported in the sixth canto, the pilgrim heard another couple speak, and presently saw them also —
                    to the left hand in the gloom
    Seated against an elm hole on the ground,
    Their eyes intent upon the stream profound.

One of them is heard complaining of his personal misfortune. He has never known another man on earth, he says, "but had some joy and solace in his life," — some chance of triumph; only he, it seems, has had unmitigated misery and failure. His companion tries to correct his pathetic error:
    "We gaze upon the river, and we note
    The various vessels large and small that float,
    Ignoring every wrecked and sunken boat."

But the repiner will not hear. He has asked precious little of life, not wealth or fame, only homely love, common food and health, and "nightly sleep to balance daily toil;" but not even that little has been granted him. His companion, who listened patiently at first, now turns away, mockingly, as if addressing a third person:
    "This all-too humble soul would arrogate
    Unto itself some signalising hate
    From the supreme indifference of Fate!"

But the complainer's only response to this gesture of reproof is a heightened rhetorical tone:
    "Who is most wretched in this dolorous place?
        I think myself; yet I would rather be
        My miserable self than He, than He
    Who formed such creatures to His own disgrace.

    "The vilest things must be less vile than Thou
        From whom it had its being, God and Lord!
        Creator of all woe and sin! abhorred,
    Malignant and implacable! I vow

    "That not for all Thy powers furled and unfurled,
        For all the temples to Thy glory built,
        Would I assume the ignominious guilt
    Of having made such men in such a world."

Such eloquence might have delighted Longinus himself, had he lived to hear it. These three quatrains alone would have provided him with examples of many if not most of the rhetorical devices described in his essay. Here first is the leading question, and the answer with its striking antithesis; then, in order, the pointed reiteration of "than He," the sudden change of person from "He" to "Thou" for the indictment of the implacable fiend, the subtle asyndeton and the shifting point of view in the list of fiendish epithets, and finally, the defiant oath and grand recapitulation which reverberates to the close of the passage. The speech itself is almost worthy of a Prometheus or a Capaneus, but the speaker here is obviously not of their parties. This pretentious fellow, whose lineage is betrayed by his Miltonic diction, knows that he is "safe" in his blasphemy. There will be no vultures to gnaw at his side, no thunderbolts to strike him dead. The fiend he contemns is as impotent as he himself. Therefore his companion mocks him as before:

"As if a Being, God or Fiend, could reign,
At once so wicked, foolish, and insane,
As to produce men when he might refrain!

"The world rolls around for ever like a mill;
It grinds out death and life and good and ill;
It has no purpose, heart or mind or will."

Here also is eloquence, but eloquence contrasting sharply with the florid speech of the repiner. The very sound of these tercets is like the clanging of a great bell announcing the one sad gospel which is true for the hollow men of this citadel of frustrate wills. In the concluding stanzas, the clanging resolves itself into silence:

"While air of Space and Time's full river flow
The mill must blindly whirl unresting so:
It may be wearing out, but who can know?

"Man might know one thing were his sight less dim;
That it whirls not to suit his petty whim,
That it is quite indifferent to him.

"Nay, does it treat him harshly as he saith?
It grinds him some slow years of bitter breath,
Then grinds him back into eternal death."

IX

The pilgrim has no sooner finished relating the preceding episode, when he is suddenly startled by the "booming and the jar of ponderous wheels, / The trampling clash of heavy ironshod feet."

He is about to resume his slow narrative, but the noise distracts him.
Who can this be, riding in the City of Night? What omen? At last the
cause of the thundering noise rolls into view. And as it passes, the
horses snort and strain, the harness jingles. It is an overloaded van.
On the shaft the driver sits, nodding, three parts asleep, despite the
jarring, as the ponderous wheels roll into the night again . . . .

> What merchandise? whence, whither, and for whom?
>   Perchance it is a Fate-appointed hearse,
> Bearing away to some mysterious tomb
>   Or limbo of the scornful universe
> The joy, the peace, the life-hope, the abortions
> Of all things good which should have been our portions,
>   But have been strangled by that City's curse.

Epitomizing with a flourish the basic theme of spiritual and cultural
exhaustion, the canto rises and falls, like one of those dissonant abor-
tive melodies that the mature Brahms loved to weave into his most
intricate and delicate webs of music.

X

To hear the booming of wheels and the clash of ironshod feet in
the dark deserted streets of the City is full strange; but more than
strange, even portentous there, is such a sight as the narrator now
describes. One night he had come upon a mansion standing apart
on its own grounds. Its massy iron gates were open, "And every window of its front shed light, / Portentous in that City of the Night."
"But though thus lighted," the place "was deadly still." Softly the
narrator entered the open door:

> The hall was noble, and its aspect awed,
>   Hung round with heavy black from dome to floor;
> And ample stairways rose to left and right
> Whose balustrades were also draped with night.

The visitor paced "from room to room from hall to hall," but met no
life in all the maze. Yet in every room where tapers burned he found
a picture or a statue or a bust enshrined; all copied from one form
of dust — *das schönste Bild von einem Weibe*[38] — a woman very young
and very fair: "Alike as stars, all beautiful and bright, / These shapes
lit up that mausoléan night."

At length, pursuing a faint "murmur as of lips," the visitor reached
an open oratory overhung with heaviest blackness. And there, upon
a low white bed, beneath a fuming censer, lay the Lady of the Images! —

                                            supine,
    Deathstill, lifesweet, with folded palms she lay:
    And kneeling there as at a sacred shrine
        A young man wan and worn who seemed to pray:
    A crucifix of dim and ghostly white
    Surmounted the large altar left in night.

A crucifix? a Christian in the City of Darkness? What sort of Christianity is it that can survive in the very citadel of Godlessness? But perhaps this pale Novalis gasping a rhymeless prayer to his beloved will enlighten us. His speech comes faint and breathless, but the accent is clear:

    The chambers of the mansion of my heart,
    In every one whereof thine image dwells,
    Are black with grief eternal for thy sake.

    The inmost oratory of my soul,
    Wherein thou ever dwellest quick or dead,
    Is black with grief eternal for thy sake.

Not in a mansion have we been pacing from room to room from hall to hall, but in the very heart of this man. As he continues his litany, we seem to hear faint choes of Hölderlin, Novalis, Heine, Lenau . . . .

    I kneel beside thee and I clasp the cross
    With eyes for ever fixed upon that face
    So beautiful and dreadful in its calm.

    I kneel here patient as thou liest there;
    As patient as a statue carved in stone,
    Of adoration and eternal grief.

    While thou dost not awake I cannot move;
    And something tells me thou wilt never wake,
    And I alive feel turning into stone.

    Most beautiful were Death to end my grief,
    Most hateful to destroy the sight of thee,
    Dear vision better than all death or life.

    But I renounce all choice of life or death,
    For either shall be ever at they side,
    And thus in bliss or woe be ever well. —

    He murmured thus and thus in monotone,
        Intent upon that uncorrupted face,
    Entranced except his moving lips alone:
        I glided with hushed footsteps from the place.
    This was the festival that filled with light
    That palace in the City of the Night.

"How can I live without thee," Milton's Adam had cried: "from thy State / Mine never shall be parted, bliss or woe."[39] Thomson's mastery of literary allusion is on a level with that of Virgil and Dante, for in these stanzas, lines of the *Old Testament* and Milton and the fifth canto of the Inferno are woven together transparently. And, though he had read nothing of St. Augustine, the poet also vies with him here, in this delicate representation of the heart of sin, condemning to his City of Darkness this peculiar Christian love that seeks and finds its beatitude not in the will of God, but in itself. So darkly wretched are all things else in Thomson's doleful City, however, that even the meanest sort of Christianity appears there as a festival of light.

XI

Here, at the mid-point of the poem, the working out of the scheme we discussed in our general remarks on the structure becomes apparent. The poet has clearly developed his theme from the outset along two lines: discursively, as a connected personal experience, in the odd-numbered cantos; and episodically, as a vicarious or cultural experience, in the even-numbered cantos. But now, in the eleventh canto, the two lines converge: the narrator becomes aware that his episodic contact with the men of the City has been a kind of education for him. His understanding has gradually deepened, so that he is no longer troubled by the dubious testimony of his senses. Now, when he asks himself, for the reader's sake, what manner of men these are who, having pierced life's veil of pleasant error, now haunt the streets of the City wherein the lamps of Hope and Faith expire, his answer reads like a paragraph epitomizing St. Augustine's thought on the lot of virtuous pagans:

> They have much wisdom yet they are not wise,
> They have much goodness yet they do not well,
> (The fools we know have their own Paradise,
> The wicked also have their proper Hell);
> They have much strength but still their doom is stronger,
> Much patience but their time endureth longer,
> Much valour but life mocks it with some spell.

These men are rational, and yet insane; behind their outward madness is a clear but impotent reason which sees the sadness and foresees "plainly the ruin in its path," and yet tries vainly "to cheat itself refusing to behold." They are men from every station of life:

> And some are great in rank and wealth and power,

And some renowned for genius and for worth;
And some are poor and mean, who brood and cower
And shrink from notice, and accept all dearth
Of body, heart and soul, and leave to others
All boons of life: yet these and those are brothers,
　　The saddest and the weariest men on earth.

XII

But the reader need not imagine for himself the identity of the various men of the City, or the nature of the bond which unites them in their sad brotherhood. The narrator has heard them identify themselves and confess their sodality, and he can report their very words.

Once, in the recent past, he had been surprised to see many more inhabitants of the limbo than he had ever seen together before, moving thoughtfully in a long loose line across the broad cloistered square toward the City's great cathedral, where, one by one, they vanished into the darkness of the western front. In the cathedral porch a shrouded figure "with deep eyes burning through a blank white hood," welcomes each man with the challenge: "Whence come you in the world of life and light / To this our City of Tremendous Night?" The narrator, who out of curiosity has joined the "long loose line" on the cathedral steps, hears the solemn challenge and listens attentively as, one after another, the men entering the porch give their answers:

From pleading in a senate of rich lords
For some scant justice to our countless hordes
Who toil half-starved with scarce a human right:
I wake from daydreams to this real night.

From wandering through many a solemn scene
Of opium visions, with a heart serene
And intellect miraculously bright:
I wake from daydreams to this real night.

From making hundreds laugh and roar with glee
By my transcendent feats of mimicry,
And humour wanton as an elfish sprite:
I wake from daydreams to this real night.

From prayer and fasting in a lonely cell,
Which brought an ecstasy ineffable
Of love and adoration and delight:
I wake from daydreams to this real night.

From ruling on a splendid kingly throne

A nation which beneath my rule has grown
Year after year in wealth and arts and might:
I wake from daydreams to this real night.

From preaching to an audience fired with faith
The Lamb who died to save our souls from death,
Whose blood hath washed our scarlet sins wool-white:
I wake from daydreams to this real night.

Each passing speaker might be named, were there a place for names in such a catalogue. The theme is the ancient one of the vanity of human wishes. But here it is not the lesson of one man's lifetime. This inverted litany is not the chant of a world-weary Solomon surveying the course of his earthly fortune, or of an imprisoned Boethius thoughtfully consoling himself in the face of death, or of an eighteenth-century rationalist scoffing at the ways of the world, or of an insatiable Faust forever indulging an appetite for new passions. The actors in this procession of vain delights, like their fellow citizens elsewhere in the City, know nothing of resignation or consolation or prudence or new passions. They speak as men still in the throes of spiritual conversion — still in the agony of that dialectical moment, when, having turned from one way of life, they are yet unable to discover another. The poet allows each of them only three lines and a refrain in which to concentrate the frustrate passion of a lifetime. And three lines apparently suffice, for the high level of emotional intensity attained in the opening quatrains is sustained to the close of this solemn procession:

From drinking fiery poison in a den
Crowded with tawdry girls and squalid men,
Who hoarsely laugh and curse and brawl and fight:
I wake from daydreams to this real night.

From picturing with all beauty and all grace
First Eden and the parents of our race,
A luminous rapture unto all men's sight:
I wake from daydreams to this real night.

From writing a great work with patient plan
To justify the ways of God to man,
And show how ill must fade and perish quite:
I wake from daydreams to this real night.

From desperate fighting with a little band
Against the powerful tyrants of our land,
To free our brethren in their own despite:
I wake from daydreams to this real night.

It is a catalogue of the vanity of human wishes worthy of St.

Augustine's nineteenth book of the *City of God*. Structurally, it serves, like Virgil's lecture on the classification of sinfulness in the eleventh canto of the *Inferno*, to orient the reader. But the poet does not interrupt the progress of his drama in order to effect this orientation. He extends his "long loose line" of men through the canto — and then gives it a slight snap at the close:

> Thus, challenged by that warder sad and stern
>   Each one responded with his countersign,
> Then entered the cathedral; and in turn
>   I entered also, having given mine;
> But lingered near until I heard no more,
> And marked the closing of the massive door.

"I entered also, having given mine"! The poet has been describing the moment of his own initiation as a citizen in the City of dreadful night. When he joined the long loose line of men entering the cathedral, he thought he was still that curious spectator of the early dramatic episodes, prying — like a student of literature — into the intimate lives of other men. But actually, after the many preliminary encounters, it was inevitable that he should have come to that square at the appointed time to be initiated. Having entered imaginatively and sympathetically into the pulsing hearts of so many God-forsaken creatures, it was inevitable that at length he should have entered with them into the innermost temple of their City.

XIII

At the close of the preceding canto, the first of six that constitute the "cathedral scene," the narrator tried to pass lightly over the manner of his own initiation into the brotherhood of the City; but immediately, in the next canto, the significance of that disclosure becomes apparent. Heretofore the poet has been obliged to speak of his fellow citizens as "they" so as not to anticipate the order of progress in his story. Now, in the thirteenth canto, he can for the first time speak freely of "we." His speech is therefore like a sigh of relief. For a moment he can almost feel again the first thoughtless pleasure of new-found fellowship. But what possible pleasure can such men in such a world enjoy together? The answer is plain: it must be a pleasure like the wild thrill of the transvaluation of values, like the wisdom of old Silenus, like the peace of Epicurus, or like the fixed willfulness of primitive stoicism: or the beatitude of Leopardi's mummies whose word the poet cited in the caption. Yes, it is indeed a pleasure, when men commune in the City of Darkness, to think how man beguiles himself about the meaning of life and time and change and death. Man is ever-complaining "How time is deadly swift, how life is fleeting, / How naught is constant on the earth but change." Yet how often he finds the hours, the days, the months, scarcely bearable, and dreams of sleeping "through barren periods" and of arousing only

> at some longed-for date of pleasure;
> Which having passed and yielded him small treasure,
> He would outsleep another term of care.

But in his fancy man makes quick wings for time; for time which, in reality, crawls round the earth and ocean like a monstrous snake, slow, blind, "condemned to circle ever thus." And wretched little man, who does not know how to use aright what little time is granted him on earth, yet claims to inherit "the everlasting Future, so that his merit / May have full scope." The narrator now interrupts his discourse with an apostrophe on the length of the intolerable hours, and of the full Time of Life, "whose woeful vanities remain immutable" through all centuries and in all regions. We — the newly-initiated citizen suddenly exclaims, using the pronoun for the first time — we do not complain of Life's speed and variance:

> *We* do not ask a longer term of strife,
>   Weakness and weariness and nameless woes;
> We do not claim renewed and endless life
>   When this which is our torment here shall close,
> An everlasting conscious inanition!
> We yearn for speedy death in full fruition,
>   Dateless oblivion and divine repose.

The thought is thoroughly Leopardian.

XIV

The narrator immediately resumes the story of the twelfth canto. Inside the City's great cathedral, after the closing of the massive door:

> all was hush: no swelling organ-strain,
>   No chant, no voice or murmuring of prayer;
> No priests came forth, no tinkling censers fumed,
>   And the high altar space was unillumed.

A hollow church for hollow men! But this vacancy is a real want, more earnest perhaps even than that of Arnold's "Grande Chartreuse," verses of which the poet here echoes.

Men and shadows lean against the clustered pillars, or hold dark corners; others seem to brood "bent or recumbent in secluded stalls."

All silently await the coming of the preacher. At length there is a stir
in the dark pulpit; two burning eyes appear, "Two steadfast and
intolerable eyes / Burning beneath a broad and rugged brow." Then
a great sad voice resounds swaying the rooted congregation:

> O melancholy Brothers, dark, dark, dark!
> O battling in black floods without an ark!
>   O spectral wanderers in unholy Night!
> My soul hath bled for you these sunless years,
> With bitter blood-drops running down like tears;
>   Oh, dark, dark, dark, withdrawn from joy and light!

A mighty Carlyle, Ingersoll, or Bradlaugh in full panoply! The
prophet of the free-man's worship has begun his harangue. The
battling in black floods without an ark echoes Dante's "nave senza
nocchiero in gran tempesta";[40] and the opening and closing lines of
the stanza make use, as we noted earlier, of Samson Agonistes' cry:

> O dark, dark, dark, amid the blaze of noon,
>   Irrecoverably dark, total eclipse
>   Without all hope of day![41]

More interesting than the allusions, however, is the grand new figure, the mighty humanitarian preacher who, like ancient Epicurus,
has "searched the heights and depths, the scope of all our universe,"
to find some solace for mankind's wild unrest. "Omne immensum
peragravit mente animoque," wrote Lucretius, "unde refert nobis
victor."[42] Thomson's preacher says:

> And now at last authentic word I bring,
> Witnessed by every dead and living thing
>   Good tidings of great joy for you, for all;
> There is no God . . . .

A hollow preacher for hollow men! *And the angel said unto them, Fear
not: for, behold, I bring you good tidings of great joy, which shall be to all
people.* But that was the old gospel, the "dark delusion of a dream";
and we must all be glad that it was a dream, that dreadful curse-
promise of everlasting life. Our wretched weary souls do die; no
awful eternity of Being confronts us. The preacher continues:

> This little life is all we must endure,
> The grave's most holy peace is ever sure,
>   We fall asleep and never wake again;
> Nothing is of us but the mouldering flesh
> Whose elements dissolve and merge afresh
>   In earth, air, water, plants, and other men.
>
> We finish thus; and all our wretched race
> Shall finish with its cycle, and give place
>   To other beings, with their own time-doom.

There is no "special clause of cruelty or kindness, love or hate" for man in the universal laws which govern him as they govern all other things. Man is but a passing form of that same eternal substance which is in all things, ever struggling, living, changing, through countless shapes, by "countless interactions interknit." All times and forces act to make man what he is, and nothing in the world can prevent what befalls him in life. "I find no hint," the preacher solemnly avows,

> throughout the Universe
> Of good or ill, of blessing or of curse;
> I find alone Necessity Supreme;
> With infinite Mystery, abysmal, dark,
> Unlighted ever by the faintest spark
> For us the flitting shadows of a dream.

But are these good tidings? What comfort does this epitomizer of Lucretius propose? Will he dare to suggest to such a congregation the old hedonism of Epicurus? Or will he presume, like the Bertrand Russell of "A Free-Man's Worship," to ask them to treat their fellows "humanly" after he has so systematically denied their "humanity" in his materialistic philosophy? No, this hollow preacher, preaching to hollow men in a hollow church, offers a hollow comfort, nothing more:

> O Brothers of sad lives! they are so brief;
> A few short years must bring us all relief:
>   Can we not bear these years of laboring breath?
> But if you would not this poor life fulfill,
> Lo, you are free to end it when you will,
>   Without the fear of waking after death. —
>
> The organ-like vibrations of his voice
>   Thrilled through the vaulted aisles and died away;
> The yearning of the tones that bade rejoice
>   Was sad and tender as a requiem lay:
> Our shadowy conjuration rested still
> As brooding on that "End it when you will."

And when the powerful voice of this mighty preacher carried across the years to William James, it caused that serious man to brood and to quote its words at length against the claims of a sanguine optimism.

XV

When serious men assemble to pledge themselves in brotherhood, they at once feel gratified and comforted, for men are social animals. But if they hold communion long, the immediate gratification wears. For fellowship is not sufficient in itself, but must have some higher outlet, some end and cause beyond itself, or it will soon make torments of its comforts. In this fifteenth canto thoughts and sentiments enough to fill a book of Wordsworth's *Prelude* are compressed into a few lines:

> Wherever men are gathered, all the air
>   Is charged with human feeling, human thought;
> Each shout and cry and laugh, each curse and prayer,
>   Are into its vibrations surely wrought;
> Unspoken passion, wordless meditation,
> Are breathed into it with our respiration;
>   It is with our life fraught and overfraught.
> So that no man there breathes earth's simple breath,
>   As if alone on mountains or wide seas;
> But nourishes warm life or hastens death
>   With joys and sorrows, health and foul diseases,
> Wisdom and folly, good and evil labours,
> Incessant of his multitudinous neighbours;
>   He in his turn affecting all of these.

If it is so where men are assembled in the daylight fair, think how it must be in the City of Night; think what "infections of unutterable sadness" must have thickened the atmosphere surrounding that congregation in the City's great cathedral.

XVI

> Our shadowy congregation rested still,
>   As musing on that message we had heard
> And brooding on that "End it when you will";
>   Perchance awaiting yet some other word;
> When keen as lightning through a muffled sky
> Sprang forth a shrill and lamentable cry: —
>
> The man speaks sooth, alas! the man speaks sooth:
>   We have no personal life beyond the grave;
> There is no God; Fate knows nor wrath nor ruth:
>   Can I find here the comfort which I crave?

"*Subitamente questo suono uscìo / d'una dell'arche* . . . ."[43] One of the congregation has chosen to brood aloud; and here the poet prepares the dramatic climax of the poem.

The preacher's speech of the fourteenth canto was, of course, the inevitable outcome of all that had passed before. The separate encounters in the streets of the City, the assemblage of citizens in the cathedral square, the grand roll call, the initiation of the narrator, all pointed to the grand sermon that would formulate their philosophical significance and show the direction of their accumulated moral force. The preacher had cried out passionately for the universal brotherhood of man, and for a new joy to be spread in widest commonality. But it must be, he had insisted, a joy whose grounds are true; for only on the truth — the truth of this sad humanism — will it be possible to build a real world fraternity.

Now, in the sixteenth canto, a voice cries out against this new free-man's worship, against this new humanistic delusion, which is far, far more vain even than the dream of the old Church whose offices it dares to usurp. "Can I find here the comfort which I crave?" the voice had asked. And now it begins its own reply:

> In all eternity I had one chance,
>> One few years' term of gracious human life:
> The splendours of the intellect's advance,
>> The sweetness of the home with babes and wife;
>
> The social pleasures with their genial wit;
>> The fascinations of the world of art,
> The glories of the world of nature, lit
>> By large imagination's glowing heart;
>
> The rapture of mere being, full of health;
>> The careless childhood and the ardent youth,
> The strenuous manhood winning various wealth,
>> The reverend age serene with life's long truth:
>
> All the sublime prerogatives of Man;
>> The storied memories of times of old,
> The patient tracking of the world's great plan
>> Through sequences and changes myriadfold.
>
> This chance was never offered me before;
>> For me the infinite Past is blank and dumb:
> This chance recurreth never, nevermore;
>> Black, blank for me the infinite To-come.

Not an unusual sentiment by any means. "To be and do all this," Hazlitt had exclaimed, "to be and do all this, and then in a moment to be nothing, to have it all taken from us by some juggler's trick or phantasmagoria!"[44] The vehement voice continues:

> And this sole chance was frustrate from my birth,
>> A mockery, a delusion; and my breath
> Of noble human life upon this earth
>> So racks me that I sigh for senseless death.
>
> My wine of life is poison mixed with gall,
>> My noonday passes in a nightmare dream,

> I worse than lose the years which are my all;
>> What can console me for the loss supreme?
>
> Speak not of comfort where no comfort is,
>> Speak not at all: can words make foul things fair?
> Our life's a cheat, our death a black abyss:
>> Hush and be mute envisaging despair. —

The shrill rapid charge of this vehement voice (which plays throughout upon Shakespearean echoes: Jaques' talk on the ages of man,
Richard II's "of comfort no man speak / Let's talk of graves, of
worms, and epitaphs," and The Tempest's "hush and be mute")[45]
draws only silence at first, "for words must shrink from these most
wordless woes." But at last the pulpit speaker, "with humid eyes and
thoughtful drooping head," answered simply:

> My Brother, my poor Brothers, it is thus;
> This life itself holds nothing good for us,
>> But it ends soon and nevermore can be;
> And we knew nothing of it ere our birth,
> And shall know nothing when consigned to earth:
>> I ponder these thoughts and they comfort me.

Just as the magnificent partisan Farinata in the *Inferno* can rise from
his burning sepulcher to say *"Ciò mi tormenta più che questo letto,"*[46]
when he learns that his party's cause is lost, so this mighty preacher,
having witnessed the utter failure of his efforts to console the men
of his congregation, can stand abashed before them in his dark pulpit, grieving, weeping, not for his own sake but for theirs. *"Gli occhi
alla terra, e le ciglia,"* as Dante says, *"rase d'ogni baldanza, e dicea ne'
sospiri . . . ."*[47]

XVII

The seventeenth canto, coming after the dramatic excitement of
the preceding cantos, is like a glimpse of the starlit heavens after a
storm. Indeed it pictures just such a vision:

> How the moon triumphs through the endless nights!
>> How the stars throb and glitter as they wheel
> Their thick processions of supernal lights
>> Around the blue vault obdurate as steel!
> And men regard with passionate awe and yearning
> The mighty marching and the golden burning,
>> And think the heavens respond to what they feel.

Relief of some sort was artistically necessary; but the poet has
not disrupted the movement of his poem to provide it. In the present

canto the convergence of the poem's two lines of development —
noted earlier — enters its third and final phase. In the second phase,
which began with the eleventh canto and culminated in the moral
and philosophical disclosures of the great cathedral scene, the burden of orderly poetic development shifted gradually from the odd-
numbered to the even-numbered cantos: poetic emphasis was transferred from the private experience of the narrator to the general
current of events of which his private experience was but a part. In
the cathartic excitement of the cathedral scene after his initiation as
a citizen, the poet had surrendered all purely personal concern. The
impersonal calm of the present canto represents, accordingly, the
calm of that fleeting moment when serious men allow themselves to
be carried away by the current of the times. The narrator emerged
from the dark interior of the cathedral, like Dante out of hell, cleansed
of his egoism, anxious to see the stars once more. Now, in the seventeenth canto, he recalls that pleasurable anxiety, and for a moment
even rejoices anew at the sight of the moving stars. Yet he is soon
enough reminded that his heaven of stars is not Dante's, but
Leopardi's:

> With such a living light these dead eyes shine,
>   These eyes of sightless heaven, that as we gaze
> We read a pity, tremulous, divine,
>   Or cold majestic scorn in their pure rays:
> Fond man! they are not haughty, are not tender;
> There is no heart or mind in all their splendour,
>   They thread mere puppets all their marvellous maze.
> If we could near them with the flight unflown,
>   We should but find them worlds as sad as this,
> Or suns all self-consuming like our own
>   Enringed by planet worlds as much amiss:
> They wax and wane through fusion and confusion;
> The spheres eternal are a grand illusion,
>   The empyréan is a void abyss.

Having prepared the way for a new and broader perspective, the
Leopardian interlude fades into dark silence.

XVIII

That the poetic perspective has changed does not appear on the
literal level in the opening stanzas of the eighteenth canto. Here, as
in all earlier even-numbered cantos, the narrator engages the reader's
imagination with a dramatic incident recalled from the past.

The tragic developments in the cathedral had thoroughly persuaded the pilgrim that the loose brotherhood of citizens, of which he was a member, could never be embodied purposefully in a humanitarian church militant. Therefore, he resigned himself to spiritual isolation and resumed his lonely wanderings. Walking once in the suburbs of the City, he reached a spot "whence three close lanes led down." Deliberately he took the left-hand lane. But before he had paced a hundred steps, he grew aware of "something crawling in the lane below," crawling like some wounded beast to its den where it would die. Thus it seemed. But "coming level with it" (*per andar par di lui*,"[48] Dante says):

I discerned
That it had been a man; for at my tread
It stopped in its sore travail and half-turned,
Leaning upon its right, and raised its head,
And with the left hand twitched back as in ire
Long grey unreverend locks befouled with mire.

Nervously, as one who guards some prize from thieves, the creature hissed and screeched and threatened, then meekly begged for pity. His prize, he pleaded, was his alone, and would be no prize at all for any other man. And such agony and toil it had cost him! So many years of seeking and yearning! Back along this lane, he explained, two lanes diverge, each marked with blood-drops all the way. One crimson trail is indeed the very prize he has been seeking in vain all these years:

But I am in the very way at last
To find the long-lost broken golden thread
Which reunites my present with my past,
If you but go your own way . . . .

The pilgrim replied that he would at once retire, as soon as he learned "whereunto leadeth this lost thread of gold." Hearing this, the wretched creature immediately drew away contemptuously:

And so you knew it not! he hissed with scorn;
I feared you, imbecile! It leads me back
From this accursed night without a morn,
And through the deserts which have else no track,
And through vast wastes of horror-haunted time,
To Eden's innocence in Eden's clime:
And I become a nursling soft and pure,
An infant cradled on its mother's knee,
Without a past, love-cherished and secure;
Which if it saw this loathsome present Me,
Would plunge its face into the pillowing breast,
And scream abhorrence hard to lull to rest.

In the transparency of the literal meaning the allegorical is plain: mankind erring in the age of Zeus remembers the glorious age of Kronos, when men were born of the earth full-grown, and passed in life's time to infancy and new innocence in the bosom of the world. And this wretched crawling image of the cultural conscience of the modern world half hopes that, by retracing his life's track, he may somehow re-attain the moral innocence and happy freedom which had been his in a by-gone age, before the initial corruption of *amour propre*, before shades of the prison-house began to close about the growing child, before the all-embracing heavenly canopy that sheltered purity and innocence was rent through by Cant and No-religion. Despising the present, this wretched conscience would roll the bloody golden thread of experience into a ball, that he might crawl back into the peace and oblivion of the natal seed, and there await a new and better turn of life. But turning away from this grotesque inversion of the Blakeian image, the narrator reflects on the vanity of that poor wretch's plan

> to seek oblivion through the far-off gate
> Of birth, when that of death is close at hand!
> For this is law, if law there be in Fate:
> What never has been, yet may have its when;
> The thing which has been, never is again.

XIX

To turn back from present ills is impossible. But is it necessary therefore to advance along this foul course which circles ever downward into the hellish pit of insufferable weariness? No, it is not necessary:

> The mighty river flowing dark and deep,
> > With ebb and flood from the remote sea-tides
> Vague-sounding through the City's sleepless sleep,
> Is named the River of Suicides;
> For night by night some lorn wretch overweary,
> And shuddering from the future yet more dreary
> > Within its cold secure oblivion hides.

One man plunges from the bridge, another wades in slowly until the waters furl above him, another sets out in a little boat, drifting out to the desert sea, "to starve or sink from out the desert world." Though many silent men look on, no one attempts to prevent the suicides; for each citizen there cannot help but think how soon he too "may seek refuge in the self-same wave." Why, the onlookers wonder, why do we stay as actors and spectators "when this poor tragic farce has palled us long?" Let us take heart, and spoil the sorry game chance plays with us. Let us follow Zeno, Cleanthes, Cato, and the many other noble pagans who have taught us that, even in a Godless world, mankind need not submit to life. If we would not fulfill life's span, lo, we are ever free, as our preacher has told us, to end it when we will . . . .

> Yet it is but for one night after all:
>   What matters one brief night of dreary pain?
> When after it the weary eyelids fall
>   Upon the weary eyes and wasted brain;
> And all sad scenes and thoughts and feeling vanish
> In that sweet sleep no power can ever banish,
>   That one best sleep which never wakes again.

Viewed together as counterparts of a single vision, this scene and the scene of the preceding canto reveal the ethical, or practical motive underlying the cultural drama enacted in the City of Night: earnest citizens, even kings of modern thought, only long for the past, or shrink altogether from the trials of life into moral death, or simply wait, in silence, to see the future come. Surely it is a representation worthy of St. Augustine's account of the vanity of the Stoic notion of the happy life.[49]

XX

In the twentieth canto the poet turns from the practical motive to the historical significance of his drama. The new vision is apocalyptic: the poet sees in flashes the grand pattern of history to which life in the City of Night conforms. In its setting the spectacle recalls Dante's pageant of Church history in the thirty-second canto of *Purgatorio*. Just as Dante there sees the pitiful transformation of Christ's Universal Church, as it meets the forces of worldliness, so the poet here witnesses the pitiful transformation of Godless humanity as it confronts the dark mystery of life. The vision here rises to the level of the Augustinian philosophy of secular history. In the darkness before the great cathedral's western front:

> Two figures faced each other, large, austere;
> A couchant sphinx in shadow to the breast,
>   An angel standing in the moonlight clear;
> So mighty by magnificence of form,
> They were not dwarfed beneath that mass enorm.

The angel's hands held the cross-hilt of a naked sword, prompt to smite. His "vigilant intense regard" was fixed upon the placid couchant creature, whose "front was set at level gaze" in solemn impassivity. As the pilgrim-narrator "pondered these opposèd shapes," his eyelids sank for a moment — so he tells us — in unnatural stupor. Then, suddenly, he was awakened by a sharp and clashing noise:

> The angel's wings had fallen, stone on stone,
>   And lay there shattered; hence the sudden sound:
> A warrior leaning on his sword alone
>   Now watched the sphinx with that regard profound;
> The sphinx unchanged looked forthright, as aware
> Of nothing in that vast abyss of air.

An heroic image had replaced the divine. The pilgrim again sank into an unnatural, painful sleep; and again a clashing noise aroused him:

> The warrior's sword lay broken at his feet;
>   An unarmed man with raised hands impotent
> Now stood before the sphinx, which ever kept
> Such mien as if with open eyes it slept.

The merely human had succeeded the heroic. Again, says the pilgrim, "my eyelids sank in spite of wonder," until a louder crash shattered their weariness:

> The man had fallen forward, stone on stone,
>   And lay there shattered, with his trunkless head
> Between the monster's large quiescent paws,
> Beneath its grand front changeless as life's laws.

> The moon had circled westward full and bright
>   And made the temple-front a mystic dream,
> And bathed the whole enclosure with its light,
>   The sworded angel's wrecks, the sphinx supreme:
> I pondered long that cold majestic face
> Whose vision seemed of infinite void space.

The divine, the heroic, the human, pass in turn; the terrible cycle is complete. Thus, in the City's penultimate canto, long before Croce and the modern reawakening of interest in Vico's "corsi e ricorsi,"[50] this pathetic conception of cultural history, already ancient in St. Augustine's time, was given what is surely one of its most impressive poetic representations.

XXI

In the concluding canto the poet-narrator passes beyond the practical and historical into the mystical reality of his phantasmagoric vision. We noted in the introductory chapter the external symmetry of the arrangement of the numbered cantos according to length and stanzaic form; and now it is possible to observe that there is also a degree of internal symmetry. The eight stanzas of the second canto represent the plight of a shadowy figure doomed to trace out the perpetually recurring series of a fraction made up of three terms: dead Faith, dead Love, dead Hope. The eight stanzas of the twentieth canto represent the same experience universalized as the pattern of all human history: ages of angelic faith, succeeded by ages of heroic aspiration that end in eras of a disarmed humanity whose hope, no longer grounded in angelic faith and heroic love, is soon reduced to a heap of ruins. The twelve stanzas of the final canto similarly reconsider the subject matter of the first. The poet, however, has come a long way since that preliminary panoramic impression. After twenty cantos of moral and spiritual catharsis he has been cleansed of all attachments to life and light and is ready (*puro e disposto*, as Dante says at the close of his own long spiritual purgation)[51] to sink into a final ecstatic experience of spiritual darkness.

In the opening lines of the Inferno, Dante suggests that he himself came very close to such an experience while straying in the "*selva oscura*." He does not dwell on the moment, because — as he says — he is anxious to relate the good that befell him immediately thereafter.[52] For a brief moment only was he utterly in the dark; and then, to his great relief, he saw for the first time the light of divine grace dimly reflected on the crest of that bleak hill which hangs over the wasteland of Godlessness.

But was there nothing to be seen on that bleak and bare crest before the rays of saving grace invested it with light? Dante says that his experience of that moment was so dreadful that the mere remembrance of it is as terrifying as the thought of imminent death. He himself — perhaps because of the effects of Lethe and Eunoë — did not choose to describe the ecstasy of that dark moment. But here is a new Dante, erring in the same wasteland, and looking up to the same crest, though no doubt from a superior vantage point. His vision is now as clear, in an antithetical sense, as Dante's was when St. Bernard directed it towards the figure of Mary enthroned in heaven; and he too beholds a woman enthroned:

> Anear the centre of that northern crest
> > Stands out a level upland bleak and bare,
> From which the city east and south and west
> > Sinks gently in long waves, and thronèd there

An Image sits, stupendous, superhuman,
The bronze colossus of a wingèd Woman,
    Upon a graded granite base foursquare.

Low-seated she leans forward massively,
    With cheek on clenched left hand, the forearm's might
Erect, its elbow on her rounded knee;
    Across a clasped book in her lap the right
Upholds a pair of compasses; she gazes
With full set eyes, but wandering in thick mazes
    Of sombre thought beholds no outward sight.

The poet knows that, though his words may not be adequate to represent her as she really is, other and greater masters have labored before him in other mediums to familiarize mankind with her aspect. She too has had her jongleur:

Words cannot picture her; but all men know
    That solemn sketch the pure sad artist wrought
Three centuries and threescore years ago,
    With phantasies of his peculiar thought:
The instruments of carpentry and science
Scattered about her feet, in strange alliance
    With the keen wolf-hound sleeping undistraught;

Scales, hour-glass, bell, and magic-square above;
    The grave and solid infant perched beside,
With open winglets that might bear a dove,
    Intent upon its tablets, heavy-eyed;
Her folden wings as of a mighty eagle,
But all too impotent to lift the regal
    Robustness of her earth-born strength and pride.

That pure sad artist who knew perfectly well how to paint a madonna and child of heaven-born strength has here inverted that grand and holy image. The poet of the City of inverted images has therefore only to describe what he sees:

And with those wings, and that light wreath which seems
    To mock her grand head and that knotted frown
Of forehead charged with baleful thoughts and dreams,
    The household bunch of keys, the housewife's gown
Voluminous, indented, and yet rigid
As if a shell of burnished metal frigid,
    The feet thick shod to tread all weakness down;

The comet hanging o'er the waste dark seas,
    The massy rainbow curved in front of it,
Beyond the village with the masts and trees;
    The snaky imp, dog-headed, from the Pit,
Bearing upon its batlike leathern pinions

Her name unfolded in the sun's dominions,
   The "MELENCOLIA" that transcends all wit.

"In suggestiveness," wrote Walter Pater, commenting on the mysteries of Leonardo's *Gioconda*, "only the Melancholia of Dürer is comparable to it." For Pater — burning with a hard gem-like flame — the "crude symbolism," as he called it, of the German master's work disturbed the effect of the whole; but for the poet of dreadful night — blazing with spiritual intensity — there are no difficulties in the symbolism. The mysteries of the *Melencolia* are profounder but not more difficult for the initiated to read than those of Mona Lisa's smile:

Thus has the artist copied her, and thus
   Surrounded to expound her form sublime,
Her fate heroic and calamitous;
   Fronting the dreadful mysteries of Time,
Unvanquished in defeat and desolation,
Undaunted in the hopeless conflagration
   Of the day setting on her baffled prime.

Baffled and beaten back she works on still,
   Weary and sick of soul she works the more,
Sustained by her indomitable will:
   The hands shall fashion and the brain shall pore
And all her sorrow shall be turned to labour,
Till death the friend-foe piercing with his sabre
   That mighty heart of hearts ends bitter war.

It is the strenuous Goddess of the Northern Worlds — the Goddess of the Carlyles and Goethes. One can almost imagine one hears the voice of the author of *Faust* crying, "Save that man!" as he rallies a host of Teutonic angels:

"Wer immer streben sich bemuht,
Den können wir erlösen."[53]

But this poet's vision of ultimate things is surer than Goethe's. He knows that there can be no "salvation" in mere yearning for higher things, nor any holy joy in boundless striving. For though his large heart is given wholly to this Goddess of heroic endeavor, his intellect is not deceived. As he gazes, his comprehension is gradually deepened and strengthened, even as Dante's vision is clarified and brought to perfection as he stares with fixed gaze upon the source of light and love. The narrator describes the effect:

But as if blacker night could dawn on night,
   With tenfold gloom on moonless night unstarred,
A sense more tragic than defeat and blight
   More desperate than strife with hope debarred,

> More fatal than the adamatine Never
> Encompassing her passionate endeavor,
> > Dawns glooming in her tenebrous regard.

Is the poet perhaps on the verge of reading too much significance into Dürer's *Melencolia*? The figure suggested itself to Dürer
in the opening decades of the sixteenth century, on the eve of the
grand awakening of modern physical and technological science. But
we, living in the middle of the twentieth century, are perhaps in a
better position than any other generation of men since Francis
Bacon's time to understand her melancholy. Are we not apt to imagine as we look upon this representation of the spirit of scientific
labor that the man who pictured her thus must have foreseen, as in
a glass darkly, some wonderful flash of ultimate scientific achievement such as many of our contemporaries expect or fear to see face
to face at any moment? Men used to wonder, in the bright days not
long ago, how the threat of the old hymn — "*solvet seclum in favilla*" —
could conceivably be realized. Now science knows; and with that
knowledge she is fast losing the hopeful confidence gained for her
by Galileo and that great *bucinator* of scientific progress, Sir Francis
Bacon. Each passing day her regard darkens with a tragic sense of
blight and desperation:

> The sense that every struggle brings defeat
> > Because Fate holds no prize to crown success;
> That all the oracles are dumb or cheat
> > Because they have o secret to express;
> That none can pierce the vast black veil uncertain
> Because there is no light beyond the curtain;
> > That all is vanity and nothingness.

The language echoes Milton's Nativity "Hymn" and Macbeth's last
soliloquy, but the poetic vision remains Dantesque. Blacker night
dawns on black night here as surely as brighter glory must ever succeed bright glory in Dante's final vision of the High Divinity.

In the concluding stanzas, after the ecstasy of negation, there is a
lull, a death-mask of resignation that hardly seems a mask:

> Titanic from her high throne in the north,
> > That City's sombre Patroness and Queen,
> In bronze sublimity she gazes forth
> > Over her Capital of teen and threne,
> Over the river with its isles and bridges,
> The marsh and moorland, to the stern rock-ridges,
> > Confronting them with a coëval mien.
>
> The moving moon and stars from east to west

Circle before her in the sea of air;
Shadows and gleams glide round her solemn rest.
Her subjects often gaze up to her there;
The strong to drink new strength of iron endurance,
The weak new terrors; all, renewed assurance
And confirmation of the old despair.

———————

So Thomson ends his revision of the earthly approaches to the hell of Dante's poetic universe. In its representation he was able to draw, as we have shown, on a considerable religious, moral, literary, and philosophic culture. But the result is by no means a mere epitome of the poet's education. Poetic alchemy has polished the cultural substance smooth as a mirror, so that — to repeat what was said in the introductory chapter — the finished work of art reflects less what the author thought and felt in writing it than what the reader thinks and feels and brings to bear in reading it. If written words can stir him, he will certainly be struck by the poetic force of Thomson's lines. He will not fail to "see" imaginatively that the poem represents the effects of a great loss of some kind. If he comes to it with a purely biographical interest, he will think that he sees evidences of poverty, insomnia, and alcoholism in it; and he may be moved to pity, or contempt, at the thought that the death of a young girl should have caused the poet all that grief. If he comes to it with a mind full of concern for nineteenth-century social and religious problems, he will feel confident that he can trace evidences in it of the new geological, biological, and social sciences that call all things in doubt. If he takes Professor Gerald's advice and reads it "as *Ecclesiastes* or Aeschylus should be read . . . for purification through pity and fear," he will certainly get more out of it. Whatever his intellectual or moral disposition, he will find that the poem manages to expand in meaning as his interests expand.

According to Thomson's intention, however, there is a minimal requirement; the very least one should bring to bear in attempting to read the poem intelligently is a fair acquaintance with the poetic world of Dante. For it is the effects of the loss or exhaustion of all the good things of that world — not a personal but an historical loss — that is represented in *The City of Dreadful Night*.

NOTES

1. *Poems, Essays, and Fragments*, p. 266.

2. Irwin Edman, editor, *The Philosophy of Schopenhauer* (New York, 1928), P. 332.

3. *Ibid.*, p. 331.

4. *City*, XI.

5. James Thomson, MS. Notebook, first and revised versions of most sections of the *City*, in the British Museum (P9227 Add 38532), London, p. 22.

6. Thomson's introductory "Proem," explaining "why and for whom" the *City* was written, echoes many phrases of *Job*, 10.

7. Hutchinson, editor, Shelley's *Poetical Works*, p. 504, 11. 58-59.

8. The canto beginning "Lo, thus, as prostrate . . ." is numbered XV in the MS., both in the original draft and in a revision, but, on p. 38, in a later hand are the words: "The above for Proem?"

9. Nancy Lenkeith, *Dante and the Legend of Rome* (London, 1952), p. 173. Miss Lenkeith's account accords strictly, in most details, with the view expounded by Professor Dino Bigongiari in his lectures on Dante at Columbia University.

10. *Inferno*, IV, 11. 67-161.

11. Thomson, MS., pp. 21-22.

12. *Ibid.*, p. 38, right side.

13. *Ibid.*, p. 38, left side.

14. *Paradiso*, XVII, 11. 139-141.

15. R. A. Foakes, *The Romantic Assertion*, pp. 169-82.

16. For a brief discussion of the Augustinian ideas of *amor sui* and *amor Dei* see introduction to St. Augustine's *Enchiridion* (Chicago, 1961), edited by Henry Paolucci, pp. xii-sviii.

17. For an explication of the Augustinian argument see "The Testament of Vanzetti," *National Review*, X (1961), pp. 16-17.

18. *City*, X and XIV.

19. The phrase is used by St. Augustine in Book XIV, Chapter 28, *The City of God*.

20. Leopardi, *Opere*, I, 82. Literally translated: "And then of so much maneuvering, of all the motions of every heavenly, every earthly thing, ceaselessly whirling always to return whence they started: what use, what fruit, I am unable to guess."

21. *Ibid.*, p. 920. Thomson translated the lines in his version of the *Operette Morali*, for they introduce the "Dialogue between Ruysch and his Mummies." His very literal version reads (*Essays, Dialogues, and Thoughts*, pp. 204-205):

> In the world alone eternal, unto whom revolveth
> Every thing created,
> In thee, Death, reposes
> Our naked nature;

Joyous no, but secure
From the ancient suffering . . . .
For to be blest
Fate denies to mortals and denies to the dead.

22. T. S. Eliot, *Selected Essays* (New York, 1932), p. 205.

23. Cleanth Brooks, "Irony as a Principle of Structure,"in *Literary Opinion in America*, edited by Morton D. Zabel (Revised edition, New York, 1951), P. 729.

24. In the analysis that begins here, quotations from Thomson's *City* follow the text as found in *Poetical Works* I, 122-72.

25. *Romans*, 10. 14.

26. Shakespeare's *Titus Andronicus*, Act III, Scene 1, 11. 12-13.

27. Edmund Blunden, editor, *The City of Dreadful Night*, p. 11.

28. *City*, XIX.

29. *Inferno*, I, 1. 5.

30. *Purgatorio*, VI, 1. 72.

31. *Inferno*, I, 1. 136.

32. *Paradiso*, XXVII, 11. 25-26.

33. St. Augustine, *The City of God*, Book XII, Chaptger 14: "The wicked walk in a circuit." Sgt. Augustine refers to the cylical theories of history. In the twentieth canto, which is the counterpart of the second in the symmetrical structure of the poem, Thomson will represent the cyclical theory of history iself, symbolically.

34. P. E. More, *Shelborne Essays*, V, 174.

35. R. A. Foakes, *The Romantic Assertion*, p. 171.

36. *Ibid.*, p. 175.

37. *Inferno*, I, 1. 10.

38. Calvin Thomas, editor, *Goethes Faust*, I (Boston, 1892), 113 (line 2436).

39. Milton, *Paradise Lost*, IX, 11. 916-954.

40. *Purgatorio*, VI, 1. 77.

41. Milton, *Complete Poetry and Selected Prose*, p. 459.

42. Lucretius, *De Rerum Natura*, I, 11. 74-75.

43. *Inferno*, X, 11. 28-29.

44. William Hazlitt, *Essays*, edited by C. M. Maclean (New York, 1950), p. 288.

45. *Richard II*, Act. III, Scene II, 11. 144-145. *The Tempest*, Act IV, Scene I, 1. 125.

46. *Inferno*, X, 1. 78.

47. *Inferno*, VIII, 11. 118-119.

48. *Inferno*, XV, 1. 44.

49. St. Augustine, *The City of God,* Book XIX, Chapter 4.

50. Thomas Goddard Bergin, *The New Science of Giambattista Vico* (Ithaca, 1948).

51. *Purgatoria*, XXXIII, 1. 145.

52. *Inferno*, I, 11. 8-9.

53. Calvin Thomas, editor, *Goethes Faust*, II, 330 (11. 11935-11936).

BIBLIOGRAPHY

"Academy Portraits: James Thomson," *The Academy*, LV (1898), 383-84.

Alighieri, Dante, *Tutte le Opere di Dante Alighieri* (Firenze, 1926).

Arnold, Matthew, *St. Paul and Protestantism* (New York, 1924).

Augustinus, Aurelius, Saint, *The City of God*, edited by Sir Ernest Barker, 2 vols. (New York, 1945).

_____, *Enchiridion*, edited by Henry Paolucci (Chicago, 1961).

Baugh, Albert C., editor, *A Literary History of England* (New York, 1948).

Beethoven, Ludwig van, *Sonatas for the Piano*, edited by Hans von Bülow, 2 vols. (New York, 1923).

Billson, James, "Some Melville Letters," *The Nation and the Athenaeum*, XXIX (1921), 712-13.

Black, G. A., "James Thomson: His Translations of Heine," *Modern Language Review*, XXXI (1936), 48-50.

Blodgett, Harold, *Walt Whitman in England* (Ithaca, 1934).

Bonner, Hypatia Bradlaugh, *Charles Bradlaugh* (London, 1908).

Brooks, Cleanth, "Irony as a Principle of Structure," *Literary Opinion in America*, edited by Morton D. Zabel, revised edition (New York, 1951).

Carlyle, Thomas, *The Works of Thomas Carlyle*, XXVIII (London, 1899).

Cazamian, Louis, *Etudes de psychologie littéraire* (Paris, 1913).

_____, *L'Evolution Psychologique et la littérature en Angleterre, 1860-1924* (Paris, 1920).

Chapman, Edward Mortimer, *English Literature in Account with Religion* (Boston, 1910).

Chauvet, Paul, *Sept Essais de littérature Anglaise* (Paris, 1931).

Cotton, Lyman A., "Leopardi and *The City of Dreadful Night*," *Studies in Philology*, XLII (1945), 675-78.

Croce, Benedetto, *The Poetry of Dante* (New York, 1922).

Cross, T. P., C. T. Goode, editors, *Heath Readings in the Literature of England* (Boston, 1927).

Davidson, John, *The Man Forbid and Other Essays* (Boston, 1910).

De Sanctis, Francesco, *Antologia Critica sugli Scrittori D'Italia*, a cura di Luigi Russo, 4 vols. (Firenze, 1931).

Dobell, Bertram, *The Laureate of Pessimism* (London, 1910).

Doorn, Willem Van, *The Theory and Practice of English Narrative Verse since 1833* (Amsterdam, 1932).

Eliot, T. S., *Essays Ancient and Modern* (London, 1936).

_____, *Selected Essays* (New York, 1932).

Elton, Oliver, *A Survey of English Literature, 1830-1880*, II (London, 1920).

Evans, Benjamin I., *English Poetry of the Later Nineteenth Century* (London, 1933).

Fairchild, Hoxie N., *Religious Trends in English Poetry, Vol. IV: 1830-1880* (New York, 1957).

Faverty, Frederic E., editor, *The Victorian Poets* (Cambridge, 1956).

Foakes, R. A., *The Romantic Assertion* (New Haven, 1958).

Foote, G. W., "James Thomson. I. The Man. II. The Poet," *Progress*, III-IV (1884), 250-53, 369-70.

Gentile, Giovanni, *Manzoni e Leopardi* (Firenze, 1937).

Goethe, Johann Wolfgang von, *Goethes Faust*, edited by Calvin Thomas, 2 vols. (Boston 1892).

Grierson, Sir Herbert J. C., J. C. Smith, *A Critical History of English Poetry* (New York, 1946).

Hanford, James H., "The City of Dreadful Night," *The Encyclopedia Americana*, VI, 717-18.

Hardenberg, Friedrich, freiherr von, *Novalis Schriften*, edited by J. Minor, 4 vols. (Jena, 1923).

Harris, Frank, *Contemporary Portraits*, II (New York, 1919).

Hazlitt, William, *Essays*, edited by C. M. Maclean (New York, 1950).

Hearn, Lafcadio, *A History of English Literature* (Tokyo, 1941).

Heath-Stubbs, John, *The Darkling Plain* (London, 1950).

Heine, Heinrich, *Heinrich Heines sämtliche Werke*, edited by Ernst Elster, 7 vols. (Leipzig, 1890).

_____, *The Prose Writings of Heinrich Heine*, edited by Havelock Ellis (London, 1887).

Hiebel, Frederick, *Novalis* (Chapel Hill, 1954).

Hoffman, Harold, "An Angel in *The City of Dreadful Night*," *The Sewanee Review*, XXXII (1924), 317-35.

Hough, Graham, "James Thomson (B.V.)," *Modern Language Notes*, LXVI (1951), 283.

James, William, *The Will to Believe and Other Essays* (New York, 1917).

Jones, W. Lewis, "Matthew Arnold, Arthur Hugh Clough, James Thomson," *Cambridge History of English Literature*, XIII, 85-109.

Lalou René, *Panorama de la littérature anglaise contemporaine* (Paris, 1924).

Lenkeith, Nancy, *Dante and the Legend of Rome* (London, 1952).

Leopardi, Giacomo, *Essays, Dialogues, and Thoughts of Giacomo Leopardi*, translated by James Thomson (London, 1905).

_____, *Tutte le Opere di Giacomo Leopardi*, 4 vols. (Milan, 1945).

Lieder, P. R., R. M. Lovett, R. K. Root, editors, *British Poetry and Prose*, third edition (Boston, 1950).

Lucretius Carus, Titus, *De Rerum Natura*, with an English translation by W. H. D. Rouse (Cambridge, 1947).

Manly, John Matthews, *English Poetry (1177-1892)* (New York, 1907).

Marks, Jeannette, *Genius and Disaster* (New York, 1926).

Mason, Francis Claiborne, A *Study in Shelley Criticism* (Mercersberg, Pennsylvania, 1937).

Meeker, J. Edward, *The Life and Poetry of James Thomson (B.V.)* (New Haven, 1917).

Meredith, George, *Letters*, edited by W. W. Meredith (New York, 1912).

Milton, John, *Complete Poems and Major Prose*, edited by Merrit Y. Hughes (New York, 1957).

More, Paul Elmer, *Shelbourne Essays*, V (New York, 1900).

Neugebauer, Paul, *Schopenhauer in England* (Berlin, 1932).

Plato, *The Works of Plato*, edited by Irwin Edman (New York, 1928).

Rébora, Piero, "Traduttori e Critici Inglesi di Leopardi," *Nuova Antologia di Lettura, Scienze ed Arti* (1920), 269-74.

Ross, William Stewart, *Roses and Rue* (London, 1890).

Saintsbury, George, "The City of Dreadful Night," *The Academy*, XVII (1880), 432-33.

_____, *A History of Criticism and Literary Taste*, 3 vols. (London, 1922).

Salt, Henry S., *The Life of James Thomson ("B.V.")* (London, 1889).

_____, *The Life of James Thomson ("B.V.")*, revised edition (London, 1914).

Sassoon, Siegfried, *Meredith* (New York, 1948).

Schopenhauer, Arthur, *The Philosophy of Schopenhauer,* edited by Irwin Edman (New York, 1928).

_____, *Studies in Pessimism*, selected and edited by T. Bailey Saunders (London, 1890).

Schopenhauer, Arthur, *Die Welt als Wille und Verstellung*, edited by Julius

Frauenstädt, 2 vols. (Leipzig, 1887).

Shakespeare, William, *The Complete Works of William Shakespeare*, edited by W.J. Craig (London, 1944).

Shelley, Percy Bysshe, *The Complete Poetical Works of Percy Bysshe Shelley*, edited by Thomas Hutchinson (New York, 1933).

Tate, Allen, *On the Limits of Poetry* (New York, 1948).

"The Testament of Vanzetti," *National Review*, X (1961), 15-17.

Thomson, James, "Arthur Schopenhauer," *The Secularist*, I (1876), 120-21, 141-42, 173-74.

_____, *Biographical and Critical Studies* (London, 1896).

_____, *The City of Dreadful Night* (London, 1880).

_____, *The City of Dreadful Night*, with an introduction by E. Cavazza (Portland, 1892).

_____, *The City of Dreadful Night*, with an introduction by Edmund Blunden (London, 1932).

_____, *Essays and Phantasies* (London, 1881).

_____, "Heine," *The Secularist*, I (1876), 22-25, 52-55, 67-69, 101-104.

_____, "Henri Beyle (otherwise De Stendhal)," *The Secularist*, XXV (1895), 107.

_____, "Marcus Aurelius Antoninus," *The National Reformer*, XVI (1870), 258-59, 274.

_____, "Mr. Matthew Arnold on the Church of England," *The Secularist*, I (1876), 237-39.

_____, MS. Notebook, dated 1870-1874, P9227 Add 38532, in The British Museum, London.

_____, "Notes on the Structure of Shelley's *Prometheus Unbound*," *The Athenaeum* (1881), 370-71, 400-401, 464-65, 597-98, 666-67.

_____, *Poems, Essays, and Fragments*, edited by John M. Robertson (London, 1903).

_____, *Poems of James Thomson*, with an introduction by Gordon Hall Gerould (New York, 1927).

_____, *The Poetical Works of James Thomson*, 2 vols. (London, 1895).

_____, *Satires and Profanities*, edited by G. W. Foote (London, 1884).

_____, *Selections from Original Contributions by James Thomson to Cope's Tobacco Plant*, edited by Walter Lewin (Liverpool, 1889).

_____, "Spenser, by Dean Church," *Cope's Tobacco Plant*, II (1880), 432-33.

_____, "La Tentation de Saint Antoine par Gustave Flaubert," *The Secularist*, II (1876), 214-15, 291-92.

_____, "Trois Contes, par Gustave Flaubert," *The Secular Review and Secularist*, (1877), 70, 103.

_____, *Vane's Story, Weddah and Om-el-Bonain and Other Poems* (London, 1881).

_____, *A Voice from the Nile*, edited by Bertram Dobell (London, 1884).

Trilling, Lionel, *Matthew Arnold* (New York, 1939).

Untermeyer, Louis, *Modern British Poetry* (New York, 1936).

Vico, Giambattista, *The New Science of Giambattista Vico*, translated by Thomas Goddard Bergin (Ithaca, 1948).

Walker, Hugh, *The Literature of the Victorian Era* (Cambridge, 1910).

Walker, Imogene B., *James Thomson (B.V.)* (Ithaca, 1950).

Walter, Jakob, *William Blakes Nachleben in der englischen Literatur* (Schaffhausen, 1927).

Watts-Dutton, Theodore, *The City of Dreadful Night and Other Poems*," *The Athenaeum* (1880), 560-62.

Weissel, Josefine, *James Thomson, der Jüngere* (Wien, 1906).

Weygandt, Cornelius, *The Time of Tennyson* (New York, 1936).

Willey, Basil, *More Nineteenth Century Studies* (New York, 1956).

_____, *Nineteenth Century Studies* (London, 1949).

Woods, George B., editor, *The Literature of England* (Chicago, 1941).

Wormley, Stanton L., *Heine in England* (Chapel Hill, 1943).

Zacchetti, Corrado, *Shelley e Dante* (Napoli, 1922).

At the time of his death, on January 1, 1999, Henry Paolucci had been retired for eight years from St. John's University and held the title of Professor Emeritus of Government and Politics. He had also continued to serve, until his death, as Vice-Chairman of the Conservative Party of New York State.

He graduated from The City College of New York in 1942 with a BS degree and promptly joined the United States Army Air Force as a navigator. He flew many missions over Africa and Italy and, toward the end of the war in Europe, was placed in charge of 10,000 German prisoners of war. In that capacity he remained in Italy for over a year. Immediately after his discharge, he resumed his education and received a Master's Degree and a Ph.D. from Columbia University. In 1948 he was chosen Eleanora Duse Traveling Fellow in Columbia University and spent a year studying in Florence, Italy. In 1951, he returned to Italy as a Fulbright Scholar at the University of Rome.

His wide range of intellectual interests was reflected in the variety of subjects he taught, including Greek and Roman history at Iona College, Brooklyn College, and The City College; a graduate course in Dante and Medieval Culture at Columbia; and, since 1968, graduate and undergraduate courses in U.S. foreign policy, political theory, St. Augustine, Aristotle, Machiavelli, Hegel, astronomy and modern science.

A frequent contributor to the Op Ed pages of the *New York Times* and magazines like *National Review* and *Il Borghese* (Rome), Professor Paolucci wrote numerous articles for the Columbus quincentenary and helped prepare three volumes of *Review of National Literatures* from materials drawn from the massive eight-volume work of Justin Winsor, the great historian of early America. A lover of music, he also was an accomplished composer. Some of his haunting melodies were used in the videoplay *Cipango!* and others were collected for a longer play, *In the Green Room.*

On his own initiative, he became proficient in Greek, Arabic, and Jewish texts and read with tremendous appreciation the works of Benedetto Croce, Giovanni Gentile, Kant, Pierre Duhem, and others in those areas that interested him. His translations include Cesare Beccaria's *On Crimes and Punishments,* in 1957 Machiavelli's *Mandragola* — the first translation in over 25 years, with an introduction that places the work in political perspective (still in

197

print), and sections of Hegel's *Philosophy of Fine Art* in *Hegel and the Arts*. He edited *The Achievement of Galileo* (translating a number of important pieces for inclusion in the work), Maitland's *Justice and Police*, as well as a collection of *The Political Writings of St. Augustine* and, first of its kind, selections on drama drawn from Hegel's entire opus into a single volume, *Hegel on Tragedy*. His books on political affairs and US foreign policy include the classic *War, Peace and the Presidency* (1968), *A Brief History of Political Thought and Statecraft* (1979), *Kissinger's War* (1980), *Zionism, the Superpowers, and the P.L.O.* (1964) and *Iran, Israel, and the United States* (1991).

In 1964, he was asked by William F. Buckley to accept the New York State Conservative Party nomination for the U.S. Senate, running against Kenneth Keating and Robert F. Kennedy. His stimulating campaign drew considerable interest, and he was written up in the *New York Times* as the "Scholarly Candidate." In 1995, the Party honored him with its prestigious Kiernan O'Doherty Award.

Founder and President of The Walter Bagehot Research Council on National Sovereignty (a not-for-profit educations foundation), Professor Paolucci organized for many years annual meetings of the Bagehot Council at the American Political Science Association, through which he encouraged younger scholars to find a place in the academic community. In 1969 he launched *State of the Nation* – a political newsletter devoted primarily to critical analyses of American foreign policy – and worked relentlessly, through 1980, as its chief editor and major contributor. The monthly series provides important documentation of some of the most dramatic events and major "players" of a difficult period in American history, viewed from a keen long-range historical perspective. At this distance in time, those assessments, unlike most of the journalistic reporting of the time, take on a clarity that seems almost prophetic. Selections from them will soon appear in a single volume.

Like Walter Bagehot himself, Henry Paolucci was also a literary man. After Dante, and perhaps in a more personal way, James Thomson was his favorite poet. He was also familiar with the works of Giacomo Leopardi, the major English and European writers of the Romantic age, Greek and Latin philosophers and the writings of the Church Fathers – as well as the work of Harnack, Caspar, and other great scholars of Church history. At the time of his death he was still active as Chief Researcher and Feature Writer for the international series *Review of National Literatures and World Report*, the annual publication of Council on National Literatures.

WORDSW

ELIAM JAMES•GEORGE MEREI

ANCTIS•THOMAS CARLYLE•HAZLITT•BERTRAND

HOPENHAUER•GIOVANNI GENTILE•HEINRICH HEI

NAU•ALBRECHT DÜRER•CHARLES BRADLAUGH•THE

EMY•THE NATIONAL REFORMER•NATIONAL REVIE

IN•LEOPARDI•VIRGIL•LONGINUS•ZENO•STOICS•PE

USTINE•CATO•ECCLESIASTES•BURNS•LUCRETIUS•K

ASCAL•SHELLEY•LUTHER•SHAKESPEARE•NOVALIS•

FREUD•DE QUINCEY•DANTE•WORDSWORTH•BEE

ERIDGE•WILLIAM JAMES•GEORGE MEREDITH•VICO

THOMAS CARLYLE•HAZLITT•BERTRAND RUSSELL•P

ER•GIOVANNI GENTILE•HEINRICH HEINE•ATHENA

CHT DÜRER•CHARLES BRADLAUGH•THE SECULARI

ATIONAL REFORMER•NATIONAL REVIEW•DARWIN

DI•VIRGIL•LONGINUS•ZENO•STOICS•PELAGIUS•CL

O•ECCLESIASTES•BURNS•LUCRETIUS

LEY•LUTHER•SH